CiTY·SMaRT™

Sacramento

Pat Cosgrove

**AVALON
TRAVEL**
publishing

CiTY·SMaRT: Sacramento
1st edition

Pat Cosgrove

Published by
Avalon Travel Publishing
5855 Beaudry St.
Emeryville, CA 94608, USA

Printing History
First edition— October 2000
5 4 3 2 1

Please send all comments,
corrections, additions, amend-
ments, and critiques to:

CiTY·SMaRT™
AVALON TRAVEL PUBLISHING
5855 BEAUDRY ST.
EMERYVILLE, CA 94608, USA
e-mail: info@travelmatters.com
www.travelmatters.com

ISBN: 1-56261-533-5
ISSN: 1530-8383

Editors: Ellen Cavalli, Leslie Miller
Copyeditor: Jean-Vi Lenthe
Index: Ellen Cavalli
Graphics Coordinator: Erika Howsare
Production: Melissa Tandysh, Ellen Cavalli
Cartography: Allen Leech, Mike Morgenfeld
Map Editors: Mike Balsbaugh, Mike Ferguson

Front cover photo: © Leo de Wys, Inc.—California State Capitol
Back cover photo: © John Elk III—*Delta King* Hotel

Distributed in the United States and Canada by Publishers Group West

Printed in the United States by Publishers Press

CONTENTS

MAP CONTENTS

Restaurants, hotels, museums, and other facilities marked by the
& symbol are wheelchair accessible.

See Sacramento the CiTY·SMaRT™ Way

The Guide for Sacramento Natives, New Residents, and Visitors

In *City•Smart: Sacramento,* local author Pat Cosgrove tells it like it is. Residents will learn things they never knew about their city, new residents will get an insider's view of their new hometown, and visitors will be guided to the very best Sacramento has to offer—whether they're on a weekend getaway or staying a week or more.

Opinionated Recommendations Save You Time and Money

From shopping to nightlife to museums, the authors are opinionated about what they like and dislike. You'll learn the great and the not-so-great things about Sacramento's sights, restaurants, and accommodations. So you can decide what's worth your time and what's not; which hotel is worth the splurge and which is the best choice for budget travelers.

Easy-to-Use Format Makes Planning Your Trip a Cinch

City•Smart: Sacramento is user-friendly—you'll quickly find exactly what you're looking for. Chapters are organized by travelers' interests and needs, from Where to Stay and Where to Eat to Sights and Attractions, Kids' Stuff, Sports and Recreation, and even Day Trips from Sacramento.

Includes Maps and Quick Location-Finding Features

Every listing in this book is accompanied by a geographic zone designation (see the following pages for zone details) that helps you immediately find each location. Staying in historic Old Sacramento and wondering about nearby sights and restaurants? Look for the Central label in the listings and you'll know that that statue or café is not far away. Or maybe you're looking for the Discovery Museum. Along with its address, you'll see a Northeast label, so you'll know just where to find it.

All That and Fun to Read, Too!

Every City•Smart chapter includes fun-to-read (and fun-to-use) tips to help you get more out of Sacramento, city trivia (did you know that the original state constitution was written in both English and Spanish?), and illuminating sidebars (for suggestions on good extended-stay apartment rentals, see page 51). And well-known local residents provide their personal "Top Ten" lists, guiding readers to the city's best sights, restaurants, art galleries, and more.

SACRAMENTO ZONES

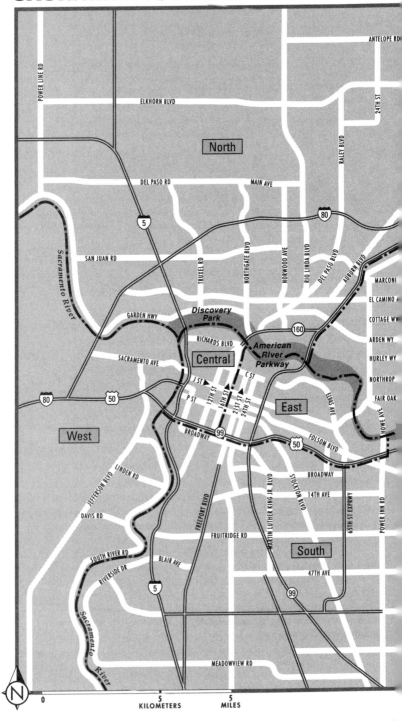

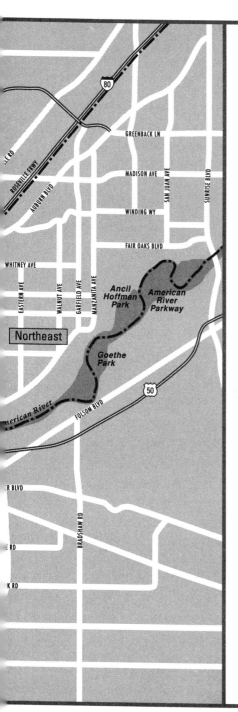

SACRAMENTO ZONES

Central (C)
The governmental and commercial downtown plus the Old Sacramento Historical District. Bounded on the north by the American River, on the west by the Sacramento River, on the south by Business Interstate 80/Highway 50 (Capital City Freeway), and on the east by 16th Street.

East (E)
Midtown and East Sacramento, the eastern portions of the grid. Bounded on the north by the American River, on the south by Business Interstate 80/Highway 50 until this freeway splits (then north of Highway 50 up to the American River), on the west by 16th Street, and on the east by Howe Avenue.

North (N)
Bounded on the south by the American River and on the west by the Sacramento River (including Sacramento International Airport), extending east to Tahoe-bound Business Interstate 80.

Northeast (NE)
Extending from Business Interstate 80 eastward, north from the American River including Folsom, and south from the American River as far as Highway 50.

South (S)
Bounded on the west by the Sacramento River and on the north by Business Interstate 80/Highway 50, then sweeping eastward on the south side of the American River to, and including, Rancho Cordova.

West (W)
Yolo County west of the Sacramento River including Davis.

1

WELCOME TO SACRAMENTO

The state of California is too vast to be easily summarized. There are, in fact, many Californias, and the most significant divide is not the cultural battle line of NorCal versus SoCal—San Francisco in contrast to Los Angeles—but the geologic division between coast and central valleys. In this scheme Sacramento is firmly inland and central in every sense, the point of convergence for arrows of state history, geography, and peoples. It was literally through Sacramento, at the time of the Gold Rush, that an American California was created, so suddenly that we alone in this nation were never a territory before becoming a state.

To the newcomer who is "going California" or to the vacationer exploring an unknown destination, Sacramento will not be the mythologized West Coast of breaking surf and swaying palm trees and glitz. Instead it will reward the active visitor searching for a down-to-earth center of fun that hasn't been synthesized by marketeers. Situated on two recreational rivers and midway between the San Francisco Bay and the alpine beauty of Lake Tahoe, with wine country on three sides, Sacramento is the home of California's first theater (1849) and first public art museum (1873)—a modern working city steeped in history.

Getting to Know Sacramento

Sacramento is large enough to supply all the urban amenities, yet it retains the feeling of a Midwestern town. From the time of its founding to the present, newcomers have remarked on the city's ability to evoke a feeling for the places they left back east. Neighborhoods are ethnically diverse and architecturally distinct, from the mansions of the "Fab Forties" neighborhood to the planned community layout of the Pocket; from tidy Craftsman and Victorian homes in Midtown to small tract homes that multiplied haphazardly during the post-WWII boom of the aerospace industry. And even as the skyline burgeons, preservation efforts gain strength.

All Sacramento neighborhoods are, by California standards, surprisingly affordable—that rare instance of a good (and still improving) economy coupled with lagging (though rising) home prices. And no matter which neighborhood you choose, whether to live in or just to visit, it will be green. Sacramento is the self-billed City of Trees and boasts more of them per capita than any city on earth except Paris.

As the capital of California, Sacramento is a political animal, a western-scale version of the Beltway. Culturally, Sacramento is less confident. Residents are quick to point out what the city is near rather than what it features within its own perimeters. A typical encounter with a newcomer includes a diffident "Do you like it here?" to solicit the expected comment about provinciality. If the answer is positive, it will be met with mild surprise and then a small nod, as if to say, "We already know how nice it is." Sacramento is urban and livable and functions on a human scale. It is perhaps the only city in California that can still make this claim.

Sacramento History

More than in most cities, the people of Sacramento and the surrounding region live out the consequences of geography—and the history created by that geography—every day. Since the time of its riverbanks' first human inhabitants, Sacramentans have been deeply connected to the land.

The city rests at the southern end of the great Sacramento Valley at the confluence of the American and Sacramento Rivers. Here the rivers join waters gathered from extensive watersheds that stretch north to Mount Shasta and east to the Sierra Nevada. The Sacramento River continues alone south and west through the California Delta, then joins with the San Joaquin River and flows into San Francisco Bay. Geographically, the bay is an enormous estuary of the Sacramento River.

Though it will not be obvious in this city now stepping smartly into the twenty-first century, Sacramento's prehistoric location near the edge of a continent shaped its destiny. In a collision of tectonic plates, the Pacific Ocean seabed jammed into and folded under the North American plate. This grinding left rubble at the surface where the plates met—the magnificent Sierra Nevada. But more importantly, the heat and pressure of this plate-grinding created volcanoes that eventually forced molten rock and mineral solutions to the surface, including one prized above all others: quartz laced with gold. And gold created Sacramento.

In the nearly two centuries of exploitation by those who displaced the area's native population (people who had hunted and gathered here as long ago as 8,000 B.C.), Sacramento's history falls into four major epochs: the Gold Rush era; the uniting of the continent by wagon train, railroad, mail, and telegraph; the harnessing of hydroelectric power, which helped create a world market for Sacramento Valley's agriculture; and the establishment of military air bases, leading to the local aerospace industry, which in turn laid the foundation for the current growth of high-tech industry. And of course throughout each of these periods Sacramento has been the political nerve center of California, which by itself would have the world's seventh largest economy.

The Nisenan, a southern branch of a larger group of Native Americans known as the Maidu, could never have anticipated the naked avarice of the nineteenth century, the lawless taking of land, beast, plant, and mineral. But even before Mexican military leaders rode horses over their tribal grounds or paddled up their rivers, the Nisenan got a painful preview: trappers from the east made forays into Sacramento Valley and brought malaria with them. This contagion laid waste to thousands of years of continuous culture and made the highly territorial Nisenan too weak to resist the most singular personality of Sacramento's history: Johann Augustus Sutter.

Sutter was born in Germany. At 16, he returned with his parents to their native Switzerland and became an ineffectual store clerk and a military reservist. The rest of his life revolved in wobbly orbit on an axis between these two poles—the storekeeper and the soldier. He married his wife the day before she gave birth to their first child, and when his business failed eight years later he bankrupted the family and sailed for New York, leaving behind his wife, his children, his creditors, and a police warrant.

Sutter crossed the continent and reached the end of the Santa Fe Trail and then the Oregon Trail in 1838, but this was only the halfway point in what turned out to be a 20,000-mile journey. From Oregon he set out for California, planning to establish a colony. Circumstances, however, forced him to detour to the Sandwich Islands, as Hawaii was then known. Sutter had a knack for ingratiating himself to authorities and strutted sufficiently well in

Sacramento State Capitol

Robert Holmes

SACRAMENTO TIME LINE

8000 B.C.	Nomadic hunters enter Sacramento Valley in pursuit of mastodon, bison, camels, and horses.
900– 1830s A.D.	Wintuns, Maidus, and Miwoks share the valley floor in tribal settlements.
1769	Spain takes possession of California.
1808	Lieutenant Gabriel Moraga explores the valley by horseback and gives the river its name.
1822	Mexico gains independence from Spain and takes control of Alta California.
1825	Jedediah Strong Smith pursues animals for their pelts into the valley from the east.
1833	Mosquitoes carry malaria from European trappers to Native Americans, killing 90 percent of the local population.
1839	Captain Johann (John) Augustus Sutter arrives at the banks of the American River and founds Nueva Helvetia.
1841	The Bartleson-Bidwell Party blazes what will become the California Trail and reaches the New Helvetia fort on foot. Sutter uses New Helvetia as security to purchase the Fort Ross and Bodega Bay colonies from the Russians.
1846	The United States gains control of California and raises the American flag over New Helvetia.
1847	New Helvetia reaches its peak production level. The grain harvest forestalls foreclosure efforts by the Russians.
1848	James Marshall discovers gold during construction of Sutter's sawmill in Coloma. Sam Brannan announces the gold discovery to the public in Yerba Buena.
1849	Surveyors Captain William Warner and Lieutenant William Tecumseh Sherman complete the mapping of Sacramento's street grid.
1850	The population increases 4,000 percent over two years. Sutter's holdings are destroyed by theft, pillaging, and the murder of workers. Sacramento is incorporated as a city.
1850s	The city is destroyed several times by flood, fire, and cholera.
1854	Sacramento is designated as California's capital.
1860	The Pony Express is inaugurated.
1861	The first transcontinental telegram is sent from Sacramento. The Pony Express declares bankruptcy.
1863	The first spike in the transcontinental railroad is driven at Sacramento's Embarcadero. Central Pacific buys an iron works and begins manufacturing all the parts needed for the railroad system.

Sacramento allocates $200,000 to elevate the street level. Two hundred buildings are raised on jackscrews.	1863
E. B. Crocker returns to Sacramento from Europe with the largest privately held art collection in the United States.	1870
The Folsom Powerhouse hydroelectric plant sends 11,000 volts to Sacramento, the longest transmission of electricity at that time. Light-rail is electrified.	1895
Sacramento becomes the center of relief efforts for the San Francisco earthquake.	1906
Completion of the Yolo Causeway creates the first year-round connection with San Francisco by vehicle.	1916
Liberty Iron Works begins production of the Curtiss "Jenny" fighter plane.	1917
Mather Field opens to train army pilots.	1918
The Library and Courts Building and State Office Building #1 become the first state government office spaces outside of the Capitol building itself.	1929
The Tower Bridge opens.	1935
The Japanese are forcibly evacuated from the city.	1942
The Town and Country Center, the first suburban shopping center in California, opens.	1945
The Russian launch of *Sputnik* creates an influx of government money for aerospace research.	1957
The State Highway Commission announces its route for Interstate 5, which is altered to preserve Old Sacramento's waterfront.	1961
The Port of Sacramento opens to oceangoing vessels.	1963
Construction of the American River Parkway begins.	1965
Old Sacramento State Historic Park is created.	1966
Silicon Valley companies migrate to Sacramento.	1970s
The NBA's Kings arrive from Kansas City.	1985
RT Metro light-rail lines open.	1987
The state's EPA office is built. The Central Library is renovated. The East End state office project is approved. The flagship Shriners Hospital for Children relocates from San Francisco to the University of California at Davis's Medical Center in Sacramento.	1990s
Sacramento hosts the U.S. Olympic Track and Field trials (2000), the USA Track and Field Junior Olympics (2001), and the NCAA Track and Field Championships (2003).	2000s

Did We Almost Become Russian?

New Helvetia grew in fits and starts, financed largely on credit. Sutter's ambitions were always grand, and when withdrawing Russians offered him their Bodega Bay and Fort Ross colonies along the Pacific coast in 1841, he agreed to purchase them on credit as well, and put up his own colony on the American River as collateral. Sutter was apparently unaware that the Russians technically had no legal claim to these holdings as they had never purchased the land from Mexico. They had already failed in their efforts to find other buyers when Sutter made the deal. One can only speculate what might have happened if the Russians had still occupied those colonies when a gold nugget turned up at a sawmill owned by Captain Sutter.

his purchased military uniform to solicit numerous letters of introduction. He turned down King Kamehameha III's offer to head an island army, instead accepting the king's gift of sturdy Kanakas—Hawaiian sailors who willingly went with "Captain" Sutter to work on the mainland for three years.

When Sutter finally arrived in California, after a stopover at a Russian colony in Alaska, he put in at Yerba Buena (which had not yet become San Francisco), a village of perhaps a dozen buildings. He was sent instead by a Mexican officer to Monterey, the capital of Mexico's Alta California. There he brandished his letters of introduction before Governor Alvarado, who invited Sutter to help himself to whatever land he desired and return in a year, when he would be awarded a deed to his colony and become a Mexican citizen.

During that year Sutter built his colony as a fort named Nueva Helvetia (New Switzerland) on the American River. He had the assistance of the Hawaiian Kanakas and the few Native Americans willing (or forced) to remain in an area they had cultivated for themselves before the 1833 malaria epidemic. This colony was the first permanent outpost in Sacramento Valley and was the end point for what would later be known as the California Trail, on which increasing numbers of American pioneers arrived from the East. While Sutter dodged creditors his entire life, he also freely gave to anyone arriving in his empire. (Supplies were sent from here to the survivors of the Donner Party disaster.) He was reluctant to pursue his Mexican-assigned mission to try to keep the Americans out, until the U.S. war with Mexico resolved all questions of loyalty. When the conflict ended, the Army renamed New Helvetia "Fort Sacramento" and designated a miffed Sutter second in command to one of their own officers.

In 1847 Sam Brannan brought a party of more than 200 Mormons to New Helvetia, effectively doubling its population. By this time the fort had become a thriving village of workshops. With cooperative weather and the resolution of armed conflicts behind him, Captain Sutter had a spectacular wheat harvest, enabling him to begin paying off his loans. He was on the verge of realizing the vision he'd held since first hearing campfire stories about California along the Santa Fe Trail. But his sawmill foreman, James Marshall, had just noticed something both enticing and disturbing: something that glittered in the tailrace at their mill in nearby Coloma.

The discovery of gold, not just at the mill but also in the placer (gravelly deposits, pronounced "plasser") of creekbed after creekbed, undid Captain Sutter. Rapacious fortune seekers stripped his compound of every resource as they scrambled after the precious metal. Sam Brannan instead became the paradigm of Sacramento's founding: a man who knew how to take ruthless advantage of a commercial situation and exploit every man about him. When Brannan ran through the streets of Yerba Buena to shout that gold had been discovered, he had already bought up all the supplies the miners would need. He thus became California's first millionaire—not by mining gold, but by mining the miners.

In the greatest Gold Rush ever, the mad hordes may have arrived at the piers of San Francisco, but it was at the Embarcadero on the bank of the Sacramento River that the world's goods were disgorged to equip the madness. By now, Sutter's son, John Augustus Jr. had arrived with the rest of Sutter's family from Switzerland. John Jr. helped sort out his father's remaining debts and paid them off by designing and then selling lots in what would become the city. Central Sacramento was now established at the Embarcadero along the Sacramento River and not at a site chosen by the Captain several miles south, which he called, unsurprisingly, Sutterville. A grid was laid out that remains to this day. Numbered and lettered streets in geometric neatness ran alongside the river that connected this isolated outpost to San Francisco Bay. The new town was named for the river that carried its economic lifeblood, and in 1850 the state enacted legislation to incorporate the City of Sacramento.

By then most of the workers who had made New Helvetia into an authentic inland empire had abandoned the fields, shops, and livestock to go into the hills in search of gold. What is now known as Sutter's Fort lay in ruins, thievery and murder having overwhelmed the few remaining loyal employees. Sutter himself retreated to a farm he'd built to the north, until

TRIVIA

At the time of its founding, the New Helvetia's ethnic majority was Hawaiian (eight Kanakas). There were also a German, an Irishman, a Belgian, the Swiss Sutter, and a Native American.

Aerial view of Sacramento

an angry guest burned it to the ground. Sutter and his wife left California forever to resettle back east and search fruitlessly for a government pension to reward his service and material sacrifice in the settling of the State of California. He and his old mill foreman both died penniless.

That Sacramento survived the sheer avarice of the Gold Rush years is remarkable. That it also survived a quick succession of equal disasters borders on the miraculous. In little over a decade, Sacramento was flooded under four feet of water (January 1850), burned to the ground (April 1850), devastated by a cholera epidemic (October to December, 1850), flooded through a broken levee (March 1852), burned again with a loss of over 90 percent of the city (November 1852), flooded when the Sacramento came over the levee (Christmas 1852), burned with a loss of twelve city blocks and a greater dollar loss than in 1852 (July 1854), flooded (December 1861), and flooded again (January 1862). There were more than a few newspaper editorials from other towns suggesting that Sacramento should simply cease to exist and spare everyone further grief. A typical response? Within 30 days of the 1852 fire, 761 buildings had been replaced; 65 of them were built with brick.

In 1852 the Sacramento Valley Railroad was incorporated to run California's first rail line from Sacramento to Folsom, roughly 20 miles up the American River. The SVRR hired a young engineer named Theodore Judah, who had other ideas as well, including a very big one: to build a transcontinental railroad. Locals dubbed him "Crazy Judah," but he did his own surveying and much of his own fundraising to prove that it was feasible to cross the Sierra by rail.

Unable to interest San Francisco financiers, Judah at last recruited what became known as the Big Four: a dry-goods merchant named Charles Crocker, a grocer named Leland Stanford, and hardware merchants C. P. Huntington and Mark Hopkins. The Big Four formed Central Pacific Railroad and named Judah their chief engineer. They were motivated as much by the prospect of monopolizing the traffic in goods between California and the Nevada silver mines as by the notion of uniting a continent. In July of 1862 Abraham Lincoln signed the Pacific Railroad Act, and federal aid poured into the project—money well spent, in Union eyes, if it would keep California and its gold on the North's side in the Civil War.

Ground was broken in Sacramento in January of 1863, and the race was on to build quickly from the west and claim maximum ownership of the transcontinental line and its adjacent land by pushing the meeting point with Union Pacific Railroad as far east as possible. Soon the material needs of railroad building transformed the city. Central Pacific bought the Sacramento Iron Works in 1863 to manufacture their own rolling stock and rails—everything needed to make a train. Sacramento thus became the first center of heavy industry in California.

In the same month that ground was broken for the transcontinental rail line, Sacramentans took their chronic flood problems in hand. Levees were not foolproof, and since they lacked the elaborate dam and weir systems that would eventually be built, the people of Sacramento were not yet able to lower the river. Instead, they raised the city. Bucket by bucket, dirt was scraped up and carried into the streets, where merchants were required to build brick walls in front of their stores to hold the dirt. It took 10 years of arduous work, chaotic traffic, and many drunken falls down unlit ladders to the old ground level before the city was smoothed over

The Quintessential Californian

California has always given the American immigrant's story a twist. While one usually goes to America to become a better version of oneself, one goes to California to become a better version of someone else. In this way Johann (alias John) Sutter was a quintessential Californian. During his original journey across the country (1834–38), Sutter had ridden the Santa Fe Trail twice and the Oregon Trail once; kept company with Native Americans, soldiers and trappers, drinkers and gamblers; picked up a bit of Spanish; and graduated from his true status as reservist lieutenant in the Bern (Switzerland) infantry to being a captain and a veteran of the King of France's Swiss Guards who had fought in a revolution. He became a model of self-reinvention and a master self-publicist. Who better to found modern California?

and could be paved at a uniform level. But Sacramento was never completely flooded again.

Since statehood had been greatly accelerated by the Gold Rush, Sacramento, the key supplier for the madness, was naturally considered for the capital when California became the 31st state in 1850. Sacramento was centrally located and the commercial hub of the state. But, as already seen, by 1854 the city had been wiped out not once but several times by flood, fire, and disease. The capital was passed back and forth between Monterey, San Jose, Vallejo, Sacramento, Vallejo again, and Benecia until 1860, when construction finally began on the Capitol building in Sacramento.

Sacramento was the western terminus for a remarkable series of continent-crossing enterprises. In addition to the wagon trains and railroad, the Pony Express began and ended its storied run here. Ironically, the company did its business in the same building that housed the California State Telegraph Company. For all its legendary glory, the Pony Express existed for a scant 18 months, and as the Pony Express rider was finishing the return leg of the first roundtrip between Sacramento and St. Joseph, Missouri, Sacramentans already knew he'd left St. Joseph on time—they'd gotten a telegram from Placerville telling them so. Sacramento sent its first transcontinental telegram (a message to President Lincoln to assure him of California's Union loyalty) on October 18, 1861. Eight days later the Pony Express declared bankruptcy.

The next great era for the city began with electrification. While Sacramento Valley grew rapidly as a produce supplier through large-scale farming techniques and the invention of refrigerated boxcars that could carry the produce to Chicago and beyond, Sacramento continued to expand its urban grid eastward. By 1861, light-rail was in place to make this possible, allowing commuters to reach downtown from ever greater distances. Wheeled trolleys were first pulled by horses, but by 1880 the horse-drawn cars were on rails. What was needed was a reliable supply of cheap current to revolutionize urban traffic.

On July 13, 1895, Sacramento got its jolt: 11,000 volts coursed into the city from a hydroelectric plant, the new Folsom Powerhouse. The 22-mile transmission (to a powerhouse substation still in use at Sixth and H Streets) was the farthest that electric power had ever been sent. The city could now expand to whatever distance light-rail carried its commuters.

In 1882 the Capitol Packing Company opened the first successful fruit cannery, and mechanical improvements in the process enabled the industry to

TRIVIA

Beginning 100 million years ago, between the Sierra Nevada and the Coast Range, a vast inland sea formed that no human ever saw. The Sacramento Valley floor gradually filled in with sediment to a depth of over 40,000 feet in some places—eight times deeper than the Grand Canyon.

Sacramento's Real Gold

The easily available gold was panned out of the placer within a few short years, and John Sutter's most enduring legacy was to demonstrate the agricultural potential of Sacramento Valley. By the time gold-digging supplies no longer provided enough business to sustain a sizable city, Sacramento had become the shipping center for farming done on a vast scale. One of the products was a tough kind of wheat that matured into kernels so hard and durable in Sacramento Valley's intense heat that it could survive the five-month voyage—by rail, steamboat, and then sailing ship—to England.

blossom. After the Panama Canal opened in 1914, Sacramento canned goods were shipped not only across the nation but to Europe as well. Sacramento Valley now fed the world. (To this day the nicknames "Sackatomatoes," "Sacratomato," and "the Big Tomato" persist, and dodging tomatoes with your car as they tumble out of open-bed semi-trailers along I-5 and I-80 is an odd, but common, diversion in summer and fall.)

Early in the twentieth century the Yolo Causeway was completed, connecting Sacramento to San Francisco by vehicle year-round. During the Great War (WWI), area farmers stepped up production to feed the armed forces. More significant for the city's future, the Globe Iron Works became the Liberty Iron Works and began producing its first line of fighter plane, the Curtiss JN-4 (known as the "Jenny"). Mather Field opened shortly thereafter to train army pilots.

After World War II the unincorporated areas around the McClellan and Mather air bases added more than 36,000 homes to the region. In 1945, California's first suburban shopping center, the Town and Country Center, opened. Urban flight was on, and the decay of the central city accelerated. By most reckoning, at mid-century downtown's West End had become the biggest Skid Row west of Chicago. In response, the Sacramento Redevelopment Agency was formed. Beginning with a redeveloped Capitol Mall, the '50s and '60s saw a determined effort not only to raze hopeless decay, but to preserve a historical legacy unequalled in the West.

A proposal by the State Highway Commission to bulldoze the waterfront in order to continue I-5 from Mexico to Canada touched off a firestorm of protest. An alternative proposal saved several blocks of the original waterfront Embarcadero. The highway was pushed inland toward the newer downtown, and buildings that could be saved were literally picked up and moved out of the highway's path to what became Old Sacramento. In 1961 Newton Cope renovated the decrepit Firehouse No. 3 into a place where his friends could go slumming. The Firehouse Restaurant was such a huge success that the entire "Old Sac" district became a desirable address for retail. By 1966 the National Trust for Historic Places had registered Old Sacramento as a landmark.

But not everything valuable could be saved. The Alhambra Theater, a magnificent Hollywood palace, was razed in 1973 after a preservation bond was defeated. In response, the Sacramento Preservation Board formed to preserve and revitalize downtown. In 1974 a new convention center opened, and in 1976 the restoration of the Capitol began.

In 1957 the Soviet Union's launch of *Sputnik* changed the world. But perhaps nowhere did it change more than in Sacramento. Government contracts to Aerojet and McDonnell-Douglas brought aerospace research cash into the region. Then, in 1963, the world came again to the Sacramento River's banks as the Port of Sacramento opened, accessed by a new deepwater canal. Four years later the Sacramento Metropolitan Airport opened, and work had begun to build the American River Parkway, one of America's great urban preserves.

In the '70s a trend began that continues to this day: Silicon Valley companies started building new high-tech offices and facilities in the Sacramento region so they could take advantage of inexpensive land, low-cost housing, and an educated workforce. And even though the '80s saw sizable cutbacks in government spending, the private workforce was steadily increasing.

As growth continued, the new and unshakable issue became the "Los Angelization" of the region. How and where to build housing and office space still bedevils fragmented planning boards, who are hamstrung by their lack of both a regional plan and the authority to coordinate the area's needs.

No Melting Pot

The World War II years saw the total destruction of the Japanese community. When President Roosevelt signed Executive Order 9066 in 1942, nearly 4,000 citizens were forcibly evacuated to the Camp Walerga assembly center. Most were transferred from there to the Tule Lake Relocation Center near the Oregon border. Many never returned. Conversely, the labor shortage caused by the war created job opportunities for African Americans who had never before been welcome. Employers actively recruited these new employees—to the workplace, but not to housing. African Americans employed at the air bases oftentimes resorted to living in the discarded 8-by-10-foot shipping crates that airplane parts arrived in.

(Water districts, in contrast, are learning how to share.) In 1985 a very different kind of growth indicated the city's move into the major leagues—literally: A Sacramento developer purchased Kansas City's National Basketball Association franchise and transformed the team into the Sacramento Kings.

Time loops forward and back. In 1981 the Sacramento Transit Development Agency formed to design and build light-rail for the region. In March of 1987 the RT Metro opened, and in 1999 ground was broken for a new major rail line heading south from downtown.

Sacramento does not await the future; it is actively creating it day by day. The region's communities are preparing for what everyone agrees will be immense growth, from a population of 1.8 million to 3 million by 2020. Whatever forms that growth may take, Sacramento history started when the land folded under itself and gold streamed forth.

Pleasure boats dock near Tower Bridge in Old Sacramento.

© Tom Myers 1996

People of Sacramento

Sacramento is, and has always been, incredibly diverse, peopled by immigrants from the world over, though the various ethnic and racial groups have not always been well treated. The oldest inhabitants were a branch of the Maidu known as the Nisenan who lived contentedly east of the Sacramento River. They enjoyed a rich and varied diet and a well-stocked medicine cabinet, all gathered from the land and water around them.

When the Swiss "Captain" John Sutter arrived in California, he brought with him a willing crew of Hawaiians. A year later he went to Monterey and returned with an African American barrel maker. And during the Gold Rush frenzy, the world literally came to Sutter's door, with South Americans arriving to mine gold even before the pioneers from the eastern United States. Chinese miners were right behind them. The story has never changed: Russians, Japanese, Hmong, Portuguese, Mexicans, Croats, and many others have arrived in successive waves. The Sacramento City Unified School District sums the present mix nicely: 26.3 percent white, 23.5 percent Hispanic, 22 percent African American, and 26.8 percent Asian. The larger community, the greater Sacramento area, is 69.1 percent white, 6.8 percent African American, 14 percent Hispanic, and 10 percent Native American and Asian.

This historical blending of peoples has not eliminated intolerance, but the newcomer may be encouraged by the relative lack of racial tension in

Sacramento compared to other cities of similar size. This is a family-oriented town. It's middle-class in character and friendly and open toward strangers—yet another legacy of its pioneers.

The Weather

"Gee, sure gets hot up there."

This was a frequent reaction to one recent newcomer, who had announced he was about to leave southern California for Sacramento. Without question, summers here are intense. Portions of July, August, and September are guaranteed to be beastly, each month capable of including a full week with highs in the 100s. The tradeoff is that this is country that abounds with water recreation, and while the surf won't be up, the whitewater will be.

Generally, Sacramento is hot in the summer, quite cool (but not freezing) in the winter, with a long and balmy spring and fall. In the City of Trees, there is a surprising blaze of fall color and leaf drop to comfort those who can't live without four seasons.

The standard Californian gardening reference, *Sunset Western Garden Book,* describes Sacramento's climate zone as "inland . . . with some ocean influence." This ocean influence, afforded by a fortuitous gap in the Coast Range, is crucial to both the agricultural richness and the overall climate here. San Francisco Bay is the gate to more than golden sunsets. This opening between the Pacific Ocean and Sacramento Valley allows

Sacramento's Monthly Averages

	Avg. High Temp. (°F)	Avg. Low Temp. (°F)	Avg. Rainfall (in.)
January	54	40	3.6
February	71	44	3.0
March	75	45	2.6
April	72	48	1.5
May	80	53	0.6
June	87	57	0.2
July	93	60	trace
August	92	60	trace
September	88	58	0.3
October	78	43	0.8
November	64	45	2.0
December	55	40	3.5

Who Are the Real Californians?

In 1879 a new state constitution barred the hiring of Chinese work-ers, and seven years later Sacramento hosted an Anti-Chinese Con-vention. The Japanese were grudgingly welcomed to replace the aging Chinese farmworkers, whose own countrymen could no longer be hired. Once the transcontinental railroad was completed, the Chinese workers who had built it were not welcome anywhere ex-cept in the Sacramento Delta. Here they built levees by hand to re-claim the boggy marshes from the river and make possible yet another commercial triumph—new farmland from which Sacra-mento shipped produce throughout the world. But it was land its workers could not own.

what is called the Delta Breeze to penetrate and moderate the region's weather. Otherwise, the four seasons would be more pronounced, with produce-killing freezes in the winter and even more scorching heat in the summer. This moderation creates a Mediterranean climate, and as a re-sult, virtually anything that grows will do well here.

The summers, in particular, are much more tolerable than they would be otherwise. Though the mercury might bang the top of the thermometer, the Delta Breeze penetrates the heat at night. Hot daytime air rises and the re-sultant low pressure acts like a vacuum, pulling cool moist air from outside the Bay through the gap. A 100-degree-Fahrenheit day will very likely have a nighttime low in the 60s. The city itself, in particular the west side, receives the greatest cooling effect; the rest of the county less so. In winter, mois-ture from the ground reacts with the cool air at the bottom of Sacramento Valley to form tule fog, which can blind drivers on the area's freeways.

Visitors will almost never encounter rain from late spring to early fall. Then, typically, rain will be common from November through April, dividing the year between warm and dry, cool and wet.

Dressing in Sacramento

Just be relaxed: everyone else is. While downtown, during weekdays, will have the expected scurrying of well-attired business and political people, a casual atmosphere dominates everywhere else. With very rare excep-tions, dress codes are unheard of, and even in the fanciest restaurants, you're as likely to be seated next to a tank top and tie-dyed T-shirt as to a tie and suit.

In summer, the sun is intense and the air dry; dress to let air get to your skin while you protect it with sunscreen. From late fall to spring, lightweight jackets are all the insulation from cold you'll need, and umbrellas will get a heavy, if brief, workout.

When to Visit

Sacramento offers year-round activity. Depending on your interests, different opportunities follow the seasons. Boating, rafting, and swimming are great ways to celebrate the heat. Cooler weather will offer a subdued list of local outdoor action, but the tradeoff will be a variety of day trips best made in the fall (Wine Country), spring (Gold Country), or winter (Tahoe skiing), combined with downtown dining, theater, museums, and shopping. There are festivals in town for each season, with the warmth of spring and summer offering the most activities in Old Sacramento and the greatest variety of ethnic food festivals across the city.

The fortunes of pro sports franchises are written in sand, but at the turn of the century it's a great experience to sit with a Sacramento Kings crowd during the NBA season. The San Francisco Giants and Oakland A's are each less than two hours away during baseball season, as are the San Francisco 49ers and the Oakland Raiders through the NFL season. Hiking and biking can also be year-round activities, depending on your preferred seasonal ambience.

Calendar of Events

JANUARY
Martin Luther King Community Celebration, Sacramento Convention Center
Home and Landscape Expo, Cal Expo
Great American Train Show, Old Sacramento
Rare Book and Ephemera Show, Sacramento Convention Center
International Sportsmen's Expo, Cal Expo

FEBRUARY
Austrian Winterfest, St. Ignatius Catholic Church
Museum Day, throughout the city
Chinese New Year Celebration, Isleton, the Delta
Country Folk Art Show, Cal Expo
Mardi Gras, Old Sacramento
Sacramento Sports, Boat, and RV Show, Cal Expo
Sacramento Home and Garden Show, Cal Expo

MARCH
Sacramento Camellia Show, Sacramento Convention Center
Sacramento Valley Boat Show, Cal Expo
Ishi Day, California State Indian Museum

Pacific Rim Street Festival

Annual Golden Tea Party, Sacramento Memorial Auditorium
St. Patrick's Day Weekend, Old Sacramento
Sacramento Golf Show, Sacramento Convention Center
Sacramento Gourmet Festival and Gift Fair, Cal Expo

APRIL
Bockbierfest, Turn Verein Hall
Spring Collectors' Faire, Old Sacramento
LPGA Longs Drugs Challenge, Twelve Bridges Golf Club, Lincoln
Festival of the Arts, California State University, Sacramento
Sutter Street Antique Market, Folsom
Pioneer Traders' and Crafts Faire, Sutter's Fort
Festival de la Familia, Old Sacramento and Downtown Plaza
Harvest Festival, Cal Expo
Highland Scottish Games, Yolo County Fairgrounds, Woodland
Crocker Golf Classic, Serrano Country Club, El Dorado Hills
River City Day, California State University, Sacramento

MAY
Annual Evaluation Day, Crocker Art Museum
Elk Grove Western Festival, Elk Grove Regional Park
Cinco de Mayo celebrations, Southside Park
Sutter Street Arts and Crafts Fair, Folsom
Waterfront Art Festival, Old Sacramento
Sacramento County Fair, Cal Expo
Strawberry Festival, Veterans Field, Galt
Spring Italian Music Festival, Festival Cultural Park, Auburn Road
Pacific Rim Street Festival, Old Sacramento
Tuesday Evening Music in the Zoo (May–July)

California State Fair

Sacramento Jazz Jubilee, Old Sacramento and other venues
Pacific Coast Rowing Championship, CSUS Aquatics Center, Lake Natoma
Gathering of Honored Elders, California State Indian Museum
California State Capitol Memorial Day Parade
Shakespeare Lite!, Fridays through July, St. Rose of Lima Park

JUNE
Water Festival, Granite Bay on Folsom Lake
Art Auction, Crocker Art Museum
Western States Horse Expo, Cal Expo
Pony Express ReRun, Old Sacramento
Meadowview Jazz Festival, Meadowview Park
Sacramento Heritage Festival, Camp Pollock, Northgate
Croatian Extravaganza, Croatian Cultural Center
Crawdad Festival, Isleton, the Delta
Filipino Food Faire, Jose P. Rizal Community Center
Sacramento Shakespeare Festival, William Land Park
Railfair, Old Sacramento
Jewish Food Faire and Craft Sale, Congregation Beth Shalom
Capital Cuisine—A Bite of the City, Crocker Park
Fair Oaks Renaissance Tudor Fayre, Fair Oaks Park
Volleyball Festival, Cal Expo and other venues in Sacramento and Davis

JULY
Folsom Championship Rodeo, Dan Russell Arena, Folsom
Fourth of July Extravaganza, Cal Expo
Eppie's Great Race, Goethe Park
Strauss Festival, Strauss Island, Elk Grove Regional Park

Raley's Mini Gold Rush (July–August), Old Sacramento
SacFest!, Cesar Chavez Park
Ice Cream Safari, Sacramento Zoo

AUGUST

Japanese Cultural Bazaar, Sacramento Buddhist Church
Breakfast with the Beasties, Free Admission Day, Sacramento Zoo
Festa Italiana, Festival Cultural Park, Auburn Road
California State Fair (late August through Labor Day), Cal Expo
Wine and Food Festival, Nimbus Winery

SEPTEMBER

Greek Food Festival, Sacramento Convention Center
Second Great Gold Rush Festival, Old Sacramento
Chalk It Up to Sacramento!, John C. Fremont Park
Old Sacramento Heritage Days
Sacramento Festival of Cinema
Best of Broadway, Bert Chappell Theatre, Hiram Johnson High School
Autumn Collectors' Faire, Old Sacramento
Dance in the Wild, Sacramento Zoo
Jazz on the Waterfront, Old Sacramento
Peddlers' Faire Antiques and Collectibles Sale, Folsom
Galt Old Car Show, Harvey Park, Galt
Sacramento Reads, Downtown Plaza
The Great River Otter Amphibious Race, Old Sacramento

OCTOBER

Oktoberfest, Turn Verein Hall
Harvest Festival, Cal Expo
Wild Affair, Sacramento Zoo
Art on the River, Old Sacramento Waterfront
Acorn Day, California State Indian Museum
Salmon Festival, Nimbus Hatchery, Lake Natoma

Who Built the Transcontinental Railroad?

In 1865 the first Chinese tracklayers were hired, and by the time the last spike was driven in Promontory, Utah, in 1869, the Chinese had done the brunt of the dangerous, backbreaking work, putting tons of rails and engines over and through the mountains. As many as 15,000 Chinese worked to build the line; a thousand or more died doing it.

Serbian Food Festival, Serbian Hall
ZooBoo Halloween Maze of Fun, Sacramento Zoo
PGA Raley's Senior Gold Rush Classic Golf Tournament, Serrano Country
  Club, El Dorado Hills
Crocker Art Museum Antique Show and Sale, Scottish Rite Masonic Center
Zoo Zoom, 5K and 10K races, children's races, Sacramento Zoo
Harvest Haunt and Goosebump Express, California State Railroad
  Museum, Old Sacramento
Winterfest (October–February)

NOVEMBER
Sacramento Celebration of Lights, Cal Expo
ThankZoo, free admission day to Sacramento Zoo
Toy Train Holiday, California State Railroad Museum, Old Sacramento
Native American Arts and Crafts Holiday Fair, California State Indian
  Museum
Santa Parade, State Capitol Park
Santa's Train, Old Sacramento
Holiday Arts and Crafts Sale, Crocker Art Museum
Country Folk Art Show, Cal Expo
Heritage Holidays (through December), Old Sacramento

DECEMBER
Annual Baroque Ball, Crocker Art Museum
Christmas in the Village, Fair Oaks
Christmas Memories Celebration, Governor's Mansion
Annual Holiday Tea, Crocker Art Museum
California International Marathon, Folsom to Sacramento
Christmas Craft Faire, Sutter Street, Folsom
Crocker Celebrates the Season, Crocker Art Museum
The Nutcracker, Sacramento Community Center Theater

Business and Economy

In Sacramento, business and politics have intertwined like elements of an
arabesque design ever since John Sutter arrived with his dream of a private empire, only to have the New Helvetia trading post ripped from his
hands. Even a century and a half ago, Sacramento was a nexus for a
world economy, as well as a center of governance for one of the nation's
dominant states. Government has been the steadier, ever-growing force,
as businesses endured the wild ups and downs of the free market. Only
very recently has the service sector surpassed state, county, and city government as the larger employer.
   While much of the character of Sacramento is due to its deep roots as a
well-preserved, nineteenth-century river town, Sacramento's future is
bright. One example in the expanding local job market is a recent surge of
telephone call centers locating in the area. A ready and willing labor pool

and seismic stability are major factors. (This last issue, odd as it may seem to non-Californians, is also the reason the gigantic Wells Fargo Bank recently moved its computer records from the Bay Area to Sacramento. The capital of the Golden State will remain standing long after San Diego has slid past Seattle on its way toward Alaska.)

In the '50s, military and aerospace concerns dominated the area. Recently, Mather Air Force Base closed (although it's still active as a commercial cargo airport and office park) and McClellan is in the process of shutting down. This is compensated for by the rise in computer-related interests in the area. Silicon Valley has become almost unlivable for anyone but the rich; Hewlett-Packard, Apple, and Intel have led a host of high-tech businesses in discovering the Sacramento region as an alternative location, where their employees as well as the company can prosper. This, of course, is by California standards, but comparatively cheap (and available) land and low-cost housing make it easy for these companies to convince their Bay Area employees to move a hundred miles inland.

There is a price to be paid for this. Most of the job and housing growth is literally headed for the hills, up the Interstate 80 and U.S. 50 corridors toward Tahoe. Tax incentives offered to these new companies have made it undesirable for foothills communities to provide housing for anyone but the well-to-do, fracturing the region further into have and have-not areas of increasingly less economic and ethnic diversity as you get away from the city. Contentious issues such as suburban sprawl, growth versus no-growth

How Sacramento Became the Capital

As the capital drifted from city to city, an offer of land for the capitol building was made by Vallejo, and it was much more generous than anything Sacramento had offered. But enterprising Sacramentans had guile on their side. In 1854, after two years in the confines of Benecia City Hall, the legislators were restless and unhappy with the limited accommodations available in either Benecia or Vallejo for their extended stays. When the legislature reconvened in Benecia in January, more than 300 Sacramentans journeyed to town ahead of them and booked all of Benecia's available hotel rooms. Sacramento, which had just achieved another of its recoveries from disaster, looked suddenly quite wonderful, with its variety of new hotels, restaurants, saloons, theaters, and churches. Grumpy, tired lawmakers chose Sacramento as the permanent capital.

development fights, and lengthening commute times for increasingly far-flung suburbanites are not yet being resolved by regional planning.

The metropolitan area is expected to double in population over the next 20 years from 1.8 million to over 3 million. Where will this growth take place? Downtown Sacramento is remaking itself. Preservation is becoming more respectable and young government workers and entrepreneurs are moving into old neighborhoods and restoring the Victorians. There are still wide-open, even rural areas within city limits, especially in the north. But Sacramento will have to successfully manage its in-fill projects in the older suburban areas to make the city as a whole work. The city is committed to revitalizing some of its older commercial corridors, such as Florin Road, Franklin and Stockton Boulevards, and Broadway.

But to a certain degree, there is still a donut hole effect, with rings of growth spreading outward as parts of the inner city languish. Without the guidance of a regional plan, the rising housing demand encourages outlying subdivision development and a competition for the big boxes of discount retail. One community's gain in tax base is another community's loss. But there is a bright spot of cooperation. The Water Forum recently designed a water use plan for the entire foothill area that provides for the new century's growing commercial and residential needs while also enabling farmers and wildlife to thrive.

Cost of Living
The State of California has both a state income tax and a sales tax (the latter being roughly 7.5–7.75 percent). Food is exempt. A recent statewide average for property taxes was 1.25 percent, which varies from community to community. Mello-Roos taxes for funding local parks and other amenities may apply, but almost exclusively to new housing subdivisions. Your realtor must disclose these. Resale homes in older neighborhoods are unlikely to be affected. If you plan to commute, state gasoline taxes are higher than in most other states, as smog controls and an extensive highway system are financed in part at the pump.

Below is an overview of average costs of common goods and services in Sacramento.

Five-mile taxi ride:	$10
Hotel double room:	$100
Dinner for two:	$30
Movie admission:	$8
Daily newspaper:	50¢

Housing

Everything is available. Everything. From Victorians to modern riverside and lakeside mansions, old subdivision tracts to new self-contained, planned communities. Every age, style, and price range is represented in one part of the metropolitan area or another, often mixed door-to-door. This is part of the intrigue in driving around downtown—the character of a neighborhood will sometimes change mid-block. Generally, the farther it is from downtown, the more homogenized the housing will be, in a common city/suburb pattern. The city has always been able to spread across flat, open land, but there is a heightened awareness that this should not continue. How growth, congestion, and sprawl are dealt with will determine the character of every community as rapid change takes place.

Though there is a shortage of new homes, new housing developments are approved constantly. The North Natomas area near the airport, for example, has now unleashed a pent-up frenzy of new-home building after finally resolving its years-long fight over flood-control zoning regulations.

While home prices may not impress visitors from areas of the South or the Midwest, compared to coastal California, Sacramento is a bargain town. Homes in the area sell for half—or less than half—of what they would fetch in the Bay Area or in Los Angeles. Equity-bearing residents of the Bay Area are arriving by the thousands, willing to commute if need be, to have twice the house they could otherwise afford. Rentals reflect this relative affordability as well. Downtown studios can be found for under $400 per month; two-bedroom apartments in Greenhaven are in the $500-to-$600 range; three-bedroom homes in Fair Oaks cost under $1,000. But, while rates have recently jumped, almost every combination of cost and size is available.

Schools

The Sacramento City Unified School District recently made headlines in the *Los Angeles Times* in what was called a Cinderella story. In the mid-'90s, the district was mired in bad politics, dropping performance ratings, and an endless blame game at the administrative level. The school board was largely voted out of office and a remarkable turnaround took place. Test scores are now uniformly on the rise across the district. Voters have approved hundreds of millions in federally matched dollars to repair and upgrade the physical plants and build a new high school. Wall Street has improved SCUSD's bond rating to A1, which should convert to AA when the new bond is figured into the formula. Private schools are abundant, but the public system is back on its feet, and an unexpected rise in enrollment indicates a return of private school students to public schools.

The region also hums with community-college activity, with area adults enrolling for personal enrichment alongside students preparing themselves for transfer to four-year programs. There are two major universities: California State University, Sacramento ("Sac State"), and the University of California, Davis. The McGeorge School of Law is here (affiliated with the University of the Pacific in nearby Stockton), as are business colleges and extension campuses of major universities from across the state.

2

GETTING AROUND

The city has roughly 400,000 inhabitants. Not a big place. But considering that the four-county metropolitan area has about 1.8 million people, it's quickly clear that Sacramento's transportation concerns are regional in scope—especially since, as everyone expects, the region will double in population in the next 20 to 30 years.

On an area map, Sacramento has a very simple shape. The few major highways that intersect here make a spidery H shape, with Interstate 5 and Highway 99 running north-south, and Interstate 80 and U.S. 50 running east-west. The central city is, and has been from the time of its inception, a lettered and numbered grid that can be intuitively used by the complete stranger. Numbered streets go north-south, starting at the Sacramento River. Lettered streets go east-west, starting at the American. (The only exceptions are the use of Front Street for First, and Capitol for M Street.) The block numbers help the scheme by starting where the alphabetized or numbered streets start and going up by 100 at each block. If you know, for instance, that you want to find 818 K Street, depending on your starting point you head toward the beginning or end of the alphabet for the east-west K Street, then go to the block between Eighth and Ninth Streets. An address on the 1200 block of a numbered street will be near L Street, the 12th letter of the alphabet.

The fact that there is such a usable grid reflects the one-word, all-encompassing description of Sacramento: flat. While Californians from almost anywhere else in the state will feel bump deprivation, the flatness explains in part why Midwesterners feel so comfortable here. The defining topographical feature is water, not land. The two rivers, the Sacramento flowing slowly north-to-south, and the somewhat more excitable American moving from east-to-west, define boundaries and determine where—and whether—people can live. Residents on the downtown (south) side of the American might not have to cross a bridge for weeks at a time. Those who live across the river deal with bridge bottlenecks constantly.

By sheer distances, Sacramento is very easy to navigate. Almost any neighborhood can be reached from any other neighborhood in 20 minutes or less. "Sheer distance" is deceptive, however, because timing is everything. Traffic fairly zips about town in the middle of the day, but at rush hour every major artery into or out of town clogs severely.

Sacramento Layout

Beyond the commonsensical grid, things get more complicated. Once out of downtown, the driver will have no other predictable scheme of roadwork, as the central city and its older, close-in suburbs quickly give way to a suburban sprawl that would be familiar to any California resident. The flatness, combined with the lush growth of tall trees everywhere, eliminate visual landmarks that might give one his or her bearings. (Even the rivers are largely hidden behind levees, until you cross one over a bridge.) Remarkably, a look at a nineteenth-century map would at first glance be completely familiar to a modern Sacramentan, as the major highways and surface streets largely duplicate original wagon trails. The obvious solution for the driver outside of the grid is to plan a route in advance and carry a good map.

Commuters from the northeast come into town on Interstate 80, from the east along the river on U.S. 50, from the south on either Interstate 5 or Highway 99, and from the north on the converged Interstate 5/Highway 99. The only bypass is where Interstate 80 swings north of downtown, while the Business 80 goes more or less straight and converges with U.S. 50 to form the Capital City Freeway through town. The most explosive growth is occurring north in the Natomas area (since they finally resolved their flood-control zoning problems) and south beyond the city limits in Elk Grove and Laguna. It doesn't take a genius to realize that many more houses are going up, but no new highways will be built and commutes will only get worse. West of the river, civilization seems to suddenly stop. It appears natural that the Davis-Sacramento corridor would fill in completely, yet there is an emptiness save for rice fields to the north or south of Interstate 80. The reality is that this is slough ("slew") country, and

Your one-stop transit shop: call the Smart Traveler Information Line for comprehensive information about transit routes, fares, and schedules, plus rail, highway, and bike information (800/266-6883, English and Spanish).

when the Sacramento and American Rivers become otherwise unmanageable at severe flood levels, the water is drawn off through a system of weirs into these flood basins. They are the city's safety valve.

Public Transportation

The Sacramento Regional Transit District (RT) reinvented itself out of the old Sacramento Transit Authority in 1973. They've been expanding bus service ever since. RT now operates more than 70 bus routes, covering a 418-square-mile service area, and uses more than 200 buses that operate 365 days a year from five in the morning to midnight. Pickups should occur every 15 to 60 minutes, depending on the route, at over 3,500 bus stops throughout Sacramento County. Residents can—and do—use RT to get to work and school every day, but the visitor will have to be aggressive about finding the proper route in a large, mazelike system. Two easy exceptions are the hotel and downtown DASH shuttles operated by RT. The hotel run will take you from the cluster of hotels near Arden Fair Mall and bring you downtown to the Convention Center Tuesday through Saturday for free. From there you can transfer for just 50¢ to the downtown DASH, which loops back and forth from Sutter's Fort to Old Sacramento, going west on L Street and east on J Street along either side of the K Street Mall.

Fortunately, city, county, and state government officials cooperated when it came time to develop light-rail. In 1987 the 18.3-mile system opened, linking the northeastern and Rancho Cordova areas with downtown Sacramento. It's a sort of sideways V-shaped system whose arms parallel the Interstate 80 and U.S. 50 corridors in and out of town. What now totals over 20 miles of light-rail operates, as buses do, 365 days a year, from 4:30 a.m. to 1 a.m., with service every 15 minutes during the day and every 30 minutes in the evening. The system includes 31 light-rail stops or stations, nine bus and light-rail transfer centers, and 10 free park-and-ride lots. By 2003 RT hopes to have almost doubled its light-rail by extending more than 18 miles of new track east to the city of Folsom and south to Meadowview Road in south Sacramento. It is also planning a half-mile downtown Sacramento extension to the Amtrak Depot, where light-rail will connect with Amtrak's intercity and Capitol Corridor service, as well as local and commuter buses.

RT light-rail in Downtown Sacramento

While light-rail routes are quite simple (and serve primarily the suburban commuters north and east), the bus routes are not as obvious or intuitive, so a good RT map is needed to sort things out. Regular fare is $1.50. Seniors, youth, and riders with disabilities pay 75¢, but a photo ID must be used. Those over 80 ride free, again with a photo ID. All-day or unlimited-ride monthly passes are also available. It's possible to ride in the central city for just 50¢, if you do so without a transfer. Remember that if you want a transfer to another bus or to light-rail, you must ask as you board the bus. From light-rail to bus, the rail ticket is a valid transfer.

Taxis

There are dozens of taxi companies listed in the phone book, and many will offer the expected amenities—24-hour service, radio dispatch, flat rates out of town, vans, airport specials, and credit-card payment. But don't look for a fleet cruising the streets. It's best to call for your specific needs and have the cab dispatched directly to you. Yellow Cab (916/444-2222) boasts of having the largest fleet in town, but there are many choices.

Regional Transit (RT) offers several resources to help you get where you're going. For bus, rail, and ID photo information, call 916/321-BUSS (Many grocery stores sell inexpensive bus-route maps, as well.) Pass and ticket orders: 916/321-2849. TTY equipment: 916/483-4327. Also visit www.sacrt.com for routes, schedules, and fares.

RT mails free pocket timetables, trip planners, ticket mail-order forms, and other information upon request. Write to Regional Transit, P.O. Box 2110, Sacramento, CA 95812-2110.

RT's entire bus and light-rail system is accessible to the disabled community. (The one exception is the light-rail station at 12th and I Streets—it's accessible southbound only, not toward Mather Field.) Also, RT provides a door-to-door transportation service for area residents who are unable to use fixed-route service, as it must under the Americans with Disabilities Act. RT provides this service through a contract with Paratransit Inc., whose ridership has more than doubled since 1993. Call 916/429-2009 or 916/429-2568 (TTY).

Driving in Sacramento

The grid comprising Downtown, Midtown, and East Sacramento has an old-fashioned urban feel, with all the attendant pleasures and annoyances. The grid is extremely easy to use, as far as orienting yourself. Driving, however, can be exasperating, as there are many one-way streets, with no clear rhyme or reason to the one-way scheme. Often the driver has to nose into traffic to see which way cars are pointed before finding the arrow sign. In the more residential neighborhoods, "calming devices" (barriers plopped into the middle of intersections) are used to discourage commuters from using neighborhood streets as fast tracks in and out of town. They also have the effect of making Midtown business, in particular, slower than need be. Just be patient, be grateful that you can never get lost in the grid, and enjoy the urban forest that soars above your head.

Always drive with quarters. The common wisdom holds that there is little

Traffic Trends

In the 1999 annual report by the Texas Transportation Institute, Sacramento was ranked as the 21st-worst urban area for traffic congestion in the nation (out of 68 studied). By contrast, Los Angeles was number one and San Francisco was number three. The optimist says, "Things are bad, but we're no L.A." The pessimist, however, notices that, according to the report, the time spent taking a peak-time trip takes 380 percent longer than it did 15 years ago, compared to a nationwide increase of 107 percent. Widened highways have tried to keep up with population increases, but they can't match sprawl, which leaves no option but to drive.

The Sacramento Metropolitan Air Quality Management District (916/874-4800) provides bikeway maps by mail, or you can pick them up at RT centers. The main RT office also has information about bikes-on-board rules, bike carriers on buses, and bike lockers. The main RT office is at 818 K Street, and the RT service center is at 1400 29th and N Streets.

Also call Rideshare for information about bikeway maps, bicycle partner matching, and bicycle safety tips at 916/451-7433.

street parking downtown, yet meters can usually be found (except at lunchtime) if you're willing to cruise a block or two. The meters take quarters only and are limited to an hour in many cases. Revisit the meter, as the parking patrols seem omnipresent. If you use one of the many parking structures downtown, keep your ticket with you because it's always worth asking any place you do business if they validate parking. The structures are reasonably priced: You can usually do several hours of business or shopping for a few dollars. In Midtown, try getting off the east-west lettered streets to see if there is free parallel or angled parking on the numbered cross streets.

To get in and out of town, the freeways are easy to use and very efficient. But during morning or evening rush hour they can grind to a crawl. If you're stuck south of the city, try getting off the freeway and using surface streets. Freeport Boulevard, which runs between Interstate 5 and Highway 99, will always be moving, though with traffic lights. If Interstate 80 north of town is a parking lot, try using east-west surface streets to shift over to under-utilized Highway 160, which comes into downtown across the American River.

Biking in Sacramento

The Jedediah Smith/American River Bike Trail has been the showpiece for this bike-loving region for years, and well it should be. Almost 32 miles of paved pathway stretch from Old Sacramento to Beals Point at the Folsom Lake State Recreation Area, passing through a nature preserve. But until recently biking in the city itself was a frustrating experience, particularly for commuters trying to get into the city. This is changing, as ground was broken in the summer of 1999 to restore a safe link between the American River Trail and downtown as far as 20th and C Streets. This new trail, which includes a tunnel beneath the Union Pacific tracks, makes it possible for riders all along the American River and points north to get into the city without dodging cars and trains. Moreover, recent approval was given for the Walt Ueda Parkway, which will create a paved path from the far north end of the county all the way south to the American River Trail, opening up commute possibilities for the whole North Zone.

Once the rider is in the city, things become more problematic. The streets must be shared with cars, always a risky proposition. Many streets are

American River Bike Trail, Discovery Park

designated as bike routes, often—but not always—with lane markers, though traffic is still present. In many neighborhoods there are off-road pathways for recreational use, but they're not practical for commuters, as they do not continue into the business district. There are some ambitious plans on the drawing boards, in particular for the Pocket neighborhood south of downtown, which has an intermittent bike path along the river that should eventually link northward all the way into Old Sacramento, and from there to the American River Trail. It will also be extended south, following the river from Garcia Bend Park to the Meadowview neighborhood of South Sacramento.

Air Travel

The Sacramento International Airport (916/874-0700, www.sacairports.org) boasts a brand-new terminal and ever-increasing connections with other major airports. It's convenient (about 15 minutes northwest of downtown on Interstate 5), easy to use, and reachable from downtown for about a $25 cab ride or a $10 shuttle-van fare. The first-time visitor who arrives on the runway during daylight gets a quick visual summary of Sacramento's place in the world: A modern city skyline skims the horizon, while the plane descends over plowed fields, mostly rice. Vital metropolis, farm town. The River City is both.

The airport is international in name only. There are currently no direct connections to overseas destinations because the airport lacks funds to construct Federal Inspection Services, which include customs and immigration stations. But international flight is the goal, and it's expected to be reached in the near future.

Who Was Walt Ueda?

Walt Ueda was regarded as a visionary by his colleagues. The Parkway that will bear his name was one of those visions, though sadly he did not live to see it become reality. Ueda died in 1995 at the age of 56, at a time when he had already advanced from being a county landscape architect to the acting director of Sacramento's Department of Parks and Community Services. He literally shaped the region, helping to design the Ancil Hoffman golf course, the Elk Grove and Gibson Ranch Regional Parks, and the Sacramento softball complex. His complete vision was to eventually link Downtown, Folsom, Del Paso Heights, and Roseville, a 60-mile loop through Sacramento and Placer Counties that will serve as a commute route and recreational jewel.

The Sacramento Executive Airport (916/395-4335), on Freeport Boulevard just south of downtown, is for private, light craft only. It's a very convenient, full-service place to land if you pilot yourself.

Carriers serving Sacramento International Airport (SMF)

Alaska Airlines	800/426-0333
American Airlines	800/433-7300
America West Airlines	800/235-9292
Delta Air Lines	800/221-1212
Delta Connection	800/453-9417
Horizon Air	800/547-9308
Northwest Airlines	800/225-2525
Southwest Airlines	800/435-9792
Trans World Airlines	800/241-6522
United Express	800/241-6522
U.S. Airway Express	800/428-4322

Train Service

The downtown Amtrak Passenger Depot at Fifth and I Streets is a beautiful historic building, as you might expect in a city that was at the center of Western railroad history. The building's future is in limbo until the city decides how to remake the unused rail yards immediately north of downtown, but the depot currently serves the California Zephyr line that runs

Sacramento International Airport

© Sally Myers 1999

from the Bay Area to Chicago, and the Coast Starlight running from Seattle to San Diego. Trains also leave several times a day to head south through San Joaquin Valley to Southern California. For more regional use, the Capitol Corridor is a seven-train-per-day Amtrak roundtrip route from the foothills of Auburn in the north down to Sacramento, Davis, the Richmond BART Station, Berkeley, Oakland, Santa Clara (and the Great America amusement complex), and San Jose. At Emeryville (on the Bay's edge, between Berkeley and Oakland), bus service connects passengers across the Bay Bridge to downtown San Francisco or San Francisco International Airport. Call 800/USA-RAIL or visit www.amtrakcapitols.com for full rail and bus schedules.

There are also seasonal trains with special fares for vacationers, such as Amtrak service to Yosemite and Sierra Nevada ski areas. Call the number above for further details.

Long-Distance Bus Service

The Greyhound bus terminal is at 715 L Street, just around the corner from the K Street Mall and Downtown Plaza. That may change, as there are plans to expand the Downtown Plaza, possibly consuming the block where the terminal is located, though that will take years to develop. For now, contact Greyhound at 800/231-2222 or locally at 916/444-7270. Other stations in the region are:

Sacramento NE	2426 Marconi Ave.	916/482-4993
Rancho Cordova	10369 Folsom Blvd.	916/363-1036
Roseville	201 Pacific	916/783-4101

3

WHERE TO STAY

Variety is the striking feature of Sacramento accommodations. There are traditional downtown hotels, Victorian bed-and-breakfasts, long-stay furnished apartments, chain motels, and even the restored rooms of a paddle wheeler steamboat, all in a concentrated geographic area. A century and a half ago, Sacramento's founder, John Sutter, was generous to a fault, welcoming visitors and sharing his empire with settlers, pioneers, and adventurers from around the world. Their numbers and the avarice of the Gold Rush were eventually Sutter's undoing, but from those early days to the present, travelers have unfailingly remarked on the welcoming nature of this city.

Downtown is a highly livable, urban setting. Almost all rooms are within walking distance (or at most a five-minute drive) of shopping, restaurants, and museums, since the core of Sacramento is on a human scale—this is still a town, not a metropolis. Restoration of fading mansions is taken seriously here, and converting century-old Victorians into modern accommodations has been a successful strategy for offsetting the cost of their rescue.

The heart of the city has surprisingly few large-scale, high-rise hotels, although this is changing, with new buildings already approved or under construction. Near the government and museum center of Sacramento, chain motels are common. The national hotel chains are heavily represented, but, with a few notable exceptions, their locations are in clusters outside the Downtown grid, notably near the Arden Fair Mall shopping district (across the American River, northeast of Downtown) or farther up the river toward either Folsom or Rancho Cordova. These centers are all a very short drive from the Capitol, and the facilities inevitably advertise themselves as being some variation of "minutes from downtown." Corporate

CENTRAL SACRAMENTO

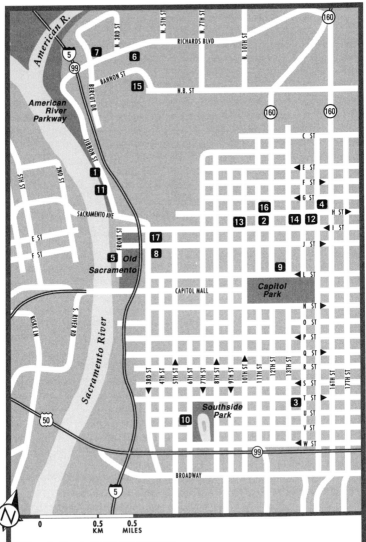

Where to Stay in Central Sacramento

1. Best Western Sandman
2. Best Western Sutter House
3. Capitol Park Inn Bed-and-Breakfast
4. Clarion Hotel
5. *Delta King* Hotel
6. Governors Inn

7. Hawthorn Suites
8. Holiday Inn Capitol Plaza
9. Hyatt Regency Sacramento
10. Inn at Parkside Bed-and-Breakfast
11. La Quinta - Downtown
12. Quality Inn

13. Sacramento International Hostel
14. Sterling Hotel
15. Super-8 Executive Suites - Capitol
16. Travelodge Sacramento - Downtown Capitol
17. Vagabond Inn - Old Town

housing, a long-term option, particularly for the business traveler, is increasingly available, especially in the Natomas area toward the airport, where office-park development is in high gear.

Price-rating symbols:
$ $50 and under
$$ $51 to $75
$$$ $76 to $125
$$$$ $126 and up

CENTRAL

Hotels

CLARION HOTEL
700 16th St.
800/443-0880, 916/444-8000
916/442-8129 (fax)
$$$–$$$$
Close to the capitol and the convention center, the Clarion offers airport transportation, free parking, the Mansion Court restaurant (which supplies room service and caters conferences and receptions), a lounge, cable TV, fitness area, guest laundry, and an indoor pool. Business amenities include modem ports in the rooms, front-desk fax availability, and conference facilities for up to 250. The rates are good for such a central location (an ideal midpoint between the attractions of Downtown and the retail and dining of Midtown), and you can also splurge here in the Tower Suite, which has two beds and a parlor ($200), or in the Governor's Court, which has two bedrooms and a living-room area ($295). The hotel's garden setting provides a bit of peaceful quiet in the midst of the city, and its courtyard is sometimes used for weddings. A light-rail line is nearby. Kids 17 and under stay free. Pets are welcome. Ask about government and corporate discounts. (Central)

DELTA KING HOTEL
1000 Front St.
Old Sacramento
800/825-KING, 916/444-5464
916/444-5314 (fax)
www.deltaking.com
$$$–$$$$
There aren't many hotels around that once visited other towns. Yet, from the late '20s to the late '40s, the *Delta King* and her sister paddle wheeler, the *Delta Queen,* began each day in either San Francisco or Sacramento, traded places by churning up or down the river, and then did it all over again the next day. The steamboat is now permanently moored at the waterfront of Old Sacramento and is not only a completely refurbished hotel, with 43 staterooms and an elegant Captain's Quarters suite, but also features the Pilothouse Restaurant, the Delta Lounge, a meeting and banquet facility for up to 200, the *Delta King* Theatre, and the Suspects Murder Mystery Dinner Theatre. The best rooms are considered to be those in the middle on the river side. Wedding packages are available, as are laundry facilities and a continental breakfast. You can step right up the gangplank into Old Sacramento's shops and restaurants. You're also a short distance from the bike trails of the American River Parkway. Valet parking is offered. ♿ (Central)

HAWTHORN SUITES
321 Bercut Dr.
800/767-1777, 916/441-1200

916/441-6530 (fax)
www.hawthorn.com
$$$–$$$$

The Hawthorn Suites, offering 272 rooms, is located off Interstate 5 just north of Old Sacramento and the Amtrak station. They offer both studio and two-bedroom suites (all with microwave oven, refrigerator, coffeemaker, VCR, video rental, and cable TV), as well as a presidential suite. An exercise room, sport court, hot tub, BBQ area, guest laundry, convenience store, free daily newspaper, and valet service are available. You'll also find airport transportation, free parking, a lounge, restaurant, outdoor swimming pool, car rental, and a full complimentary breakfast. A number of restaurants, offering everything from fast food to fine seafood, are very close by. The business traveler can take advantage of two speakerphones (each with two lines and data ports) and six meeting rooms, the largest of which can handle 150. Kids 17 and under are free. ර් (Central)

HOLIDAY INN CAPITOL PLAZA
300 J St.
800/HOLIDAY, 916/446-0100
916/446-0117 (fax)
$$$–$$$$

From the door of this 364-room high-rise you can step right into all the attractions, shopping, and dining of Old Sacramento. Also adjacent to the old site of Chinatown, the Holiday Inn Capitol Plaza offers 11,000 square feet of meeting space and its own lounge, restaurant, and pool. The Downtown Plaza mall is right around the corner for convenient shopping, and fine restaurants dot the surrounding blocks. There are also a concierge, a health club with

a spa, guest laundry, and swimming pool. Kids 16 and under are free. ර් (Central)

HYATT REGENCY SACRAMENTO
1209 L St.
800/233-1234, 916/443-1234
916/497-0132 (fax)
$$$$

The Hyatt is the dominant high-rise hotel of downtown and filled a large gap in Capitol-area accommodations when it opened several years ago. It meets all the expectations for an urban branch of a worldwide chain and is furnished with touches of luxury. There are 500 rooms and 30,000 square feet of space for business functions, including the Regency Ballroom, which can handle a banquet of thousands. Then there's location: Across the street on one side is the State Capitol Building, while on the other side are the Convention Center and Esquire IMAX Theater. It's also within easy walking distance of downtown shopping (the K Street Mall and the Downtown Plaza) and only a block away from the stately Memorial Auditorium. The more ambitious could walk to Old Sacramento from here as well. On-site dining includes Dawson's and the oddly eclectic Ciao-Yama, which combines Italian and Japanese dishes on its menu. Ciao-Yama serves breakfast, lunch, dinner, and Sunday brunch, offers complimentary valet parking, and is well worth visiting on its own. The hotel's amenities are endless, but include a piano bar, pool, concierge, live entertainment, travel services, health club, beauty salon, and laundry and dry-cleaning services. Many rooms have fax service and—true to the hotel's political nerve-center address—live coverage of legislative sessions and subcommittee hearings. Garage and valet parking are available. ⅄ (Central)

STERLING HOTEL
1300 H St.
800/365-7660, 916/448-1300
916/448-8066 (fax)
$$$$

The height of elegance in Sacramento accommodations, this shining white Victorian is often mistaken for a bed-and-breakfast, but it's a 16-room, full-service hotel with a glass conservatory for receptions, conferences, and business meetings. A few blocks from the capitol, the convention center, Memorial Auditorium, and the legal/courthouse district, the Sterling includes a bar and the Chanterelle restaurant, which offers gourmet French/Californian cuisine and patio dining. All rooms have Jacuzzis and some have balconies, preserved in the style of the ornate architecture. There is a free continental breakfast, and you're close to the 12th and I light-rail station. Kids 12 and under are free. Weekends are costly. ⅄ (Central)

Motels

BEST WESTERN SANDMAN
236 Jibboom St.
800/528-1234, 916/443-6515
916/443-8346 (fax)
$$-$$$

Easily accessible off Interstate 5, this motel is close-in to downtown, with the convenience of free parking. An outdoor pool, a spa, cable TV, and guest laundry make these 116 air-conditioned rooms a convenient and reasonable accommodation. A small family restaurant (Perko's) is just across the parking lot, and a cluster

of restaurants offering a complete range of dining lies just across Interstate 5. You'll have to drive to local attractions, but Old Sacramento lies just south less than five minutes away. There is a complimentary breakfast, and kids 12 and under are free. ⅄ (Central)

BEST WESTERN
SUTTER HOUSE
1100 H St.
800/830-1314, 916/441-1314
916/441-5961 (fax)
www.thesutterhouse.com
$$-$$$

This Best Western features 98 non-smoking rooms. It's at the heart of the capitol area, within easy walking distance of all the attractions here: the capitol and its park, the convention center, the K Street Mall, the Downtown Plaza, and Old Sacramento. Easily characterized as an overgrown bed-and-breakfast, Sutter House amenities include a deluxe continental breakfast, key-card security, a private landscaped courtyard near the pool, fax machines in the rooms, ironing boards and irons, hair dryers, guest laundry, voicemail, HBO, and pay-per-view movies. Grapes, the new restaurant at Sutter House, has drawn rave reviews for reproducing the cuisine of the Napa Valley wine country. Kids

---

TRIVIA

Sam Brannan and John Fowler began building City Hotel, Sacramento's first, in June 1849. It was built, in part, from the remnants of John Sutter's unfinished flour mill.

---

12 and under are free. Rated three diamonds by AAA. ♿ (Central)

GOVERNORS INN
210 Richards Blvd.
800/999-6689, 916/448-7224
916/448-7382 (fax)
$$$
Governors Inn is across the rail yards on the north side of Sacramento, but it's a very short distance from Downtown. It's also very close to Discovery Park and its bicycle paths and jogging trails. Specializing in "convenience for the business traveler," it offers deluxe rooms with desks and work areas, generous meeting facilities for up to 200, continental breakfast, free cable TV with HBO, in-room coffee and tea, a swimming pool, spa, free airport transportation, and a "sherry get-together." Kids 12 and under are free. Rated three diamonds by AAA. ♿ (Central)

LA QUINTA—DOWNTOWN
200 Jibboom St.
800/531-5900, 916/448-8100
916/447-3621 (fax)
$$
Part of a motel row between the Sacramento River and Interstate 5, La Quinta has 165 rooms (some with a river view) and three suites. It also has meeting space, a free continental breakfast, a complimentary shuttle, a swimming pool, an exercise facility, and a laundry room. Downtown is moments away down the highway. A number of restaurants are very close, as is the American River Parkway. Pets are welcome. ♿ (Central)

QUALITY INN
818 15th St.
800/228-5151, 916/444-3980

916/444-2991 (fax)
$$
Only two blocks from the convention center and a block from Memorial Auditorium, the Quality Inn has free parking, cable TV, a pool, and in-room coffee. It's close to the 12th and I Street light-rail line. Kids 12 and under are free. ♿ (Central)

SUPER-8 EXECUTIVE SUITES— CAPITOL
216 Bannon St.
800/800-8000, 800/471-1777
(in California), 916/447-5400
916/447-5153 (fax)
$$–$$$
On the north side, this Super-8 is close to downtown. While Super-8 has sometimes referred to itself as the "McDonald's of motels," it's not without amenities. The rooms have refrigerators, microwave ovens, air conditioners, and cable TVs, and there are a spa and a sauna on-site. Some business services are available, and the continental breakfast is free. The Super-8 Motel at 221 Jibboom Street (916/442-7777) is nearby and slightly less expensive. Kids 12 and under are free. ♿ (Central)

TRAVELODGE SACRAMENTO— DOWNTOWN CAPITOL
1111 H St.
800/578-7878, 916/444-8880
916/447-7540 (fax)
$$$–$$$$
This 71-room Travelodge is housed in two buildings near the capitol. Choose from queen-size, king-size, or two double beds. The motel offers a complimentary breakfast, in-room coffee, *USA Today,* cable TV with HBO, same-day laundry and dry cleaning, direct dialing from the 24-hour switchboard, and free parking. You're close to the 12th and I Street

light-rail station, and only blocks from the convention center, Memorial Auditorium, and the east end of the K Street Mall. Kids 17 and under are free. ♿ (Central)

VAGABOND INN—OLD TOWN
909 Third St.
800/522-1555, 916/446-1481
916/448-0364 (fax)
$$$
Directly across the street from all that Old Sacramento offers and only blocks from the Downtown Plaza, the Vagabond Inn has some business services, free parking, guest laundry, a free airport shuttle, a heated pool, and free continental breakfast. It's also conveniently located next door to a Denny's. Pets are welcome and kids 18 and under are free. This may be the only motel you'll ever stay at with a pagoda-style tile roof. It was built to match the block's Chinatown Mall. ♿ (Central)

Bed-and-Breakfasts

CAPITOL PARK INN
BED-AND-BREAKFAST
1300 T St.
877/753-9982, 916/414-1300

916/414-1304 (fax)
$$$$
Tucked away in a mixed residential/commercial neighborhood near the south edge of Downtown, this is a historic Federalist home built in 1910. Only six blocks from the capitol, the four bedrooms, named for the Big Four of railroad fame, offer king- and queen-size beds and private baths (some with Jacuzzis), modems, TVs, and VCRs. Some rooms also have double-wide showers and gas-log fireplaces. Rates include a full breakfast from a menu, and there are complimentary movies, sherry, and cookies. Original touches still intact are marble inlays and the threshold on the front porch, as well as the twisting doorbell ringer on the front door. The interior is cozy, full of dark wood paneling and pillars, with a beamed ceiling. A fenced-in back-yard contains a brick patio with out-door furniture beneath a towering palm tree. Parking is off-street in the rear of the building, and you're only two blocks from a light-rail station. (Central)

INN AT PARKSIDE
BED-AND-BREAKFAST
2116 Sixth St.

Something Different

Though it is occasionally listed as such, Ricci's Italian Restaurant is not a bed-and-breakfast, and the restaurant downstairs from the four suites doesn't open until 11 a.m. But the apartment-style rooms have full kitchens and separate bedrooms, and they're in the heart of the business district at Seventh and J Streets. Call manager Angelina Murray at 916/442-6741 for further information.

800/995-7275, 916/658-1818
916/658-1809 (fax)
www.innatparkside.com
$$$–$$$$
This beautiful old mansion is roughly 10 blocks from Old Sacramento. Though there is little yard, delicate Japanese maples frame the front of the home, and the house sits directly across from Southside Park, the site of a city pool, jogging trails, a small lake, tennis and basketball courts, and towering redwoods and cedars. Built in 1936 as a residence for an ambassador, its seven rooms provide private baths, Jacuzzis, telephones, TVs, and VCRs, and are all furnished with antiques. The walls and even the ceilings are covered with neoclassical artwork, giving the place an overall Mediterranean feel. Relax in the library or on a deck, or even play records on an antique phonograph. A guest kitchenette is available 24 hours a day. There are also a conference facility and a ballroom with a maple spring-loaded dance floor. Prices vary by room. The Olympus Suite is a favorite for honeymooners and has a bath surrounded by marble, a spa for two, a king-size bed, a wood-burning fireplace in the bedroom, two electric gas log fireplaces, and a glass brick and marble shower for two. The Olympus requires a two-night minimum stay. (Central)

Hostels

SACRAMENTO INTERNATIONAL HOSTEL
900 H St.
916/443-1691
$
Located in one of the city's restored Victorian mansions (built in 1884 by Llewelyn Williams), the International Hostel has already impressed visitors from around the world. A recent *Sacramento Bee* article stated that in 1998, 27 percent of the hostel's guests were from foreign countries, mostly Europe, where hostels are more familiar. Travelers often stop just to see the building itself, admiring its imposing staircases and its gorgeous woodwork and veranda, or they use it (like they do Sacramento in general) as a stopover on the way from San Francisco to the Sierra Nevada, the wine country, or the Mother Lode gold country. There are private rooms ($20 to $40), as well as the dorm-style rooms ($15) common at most hostels. Those who are not members of Hostelling International pay three dollars extra. The hostel is more or less halfway between the capitol and Old Sacramento, and only a block from the Central Library. Shopping and museums are within easy walking distance in either direction. The beautifully decorated common areas can be rented for the day for meetings, retreats, and weddings. The kitchen is a self-serve common area. ♿ (Central)

EAST

Motels

ECONO LODGE
711 16th St.
800/55-ECONO, 916/443-6631
916/442-7251 (fax)
www.econolodge.com
$–$$
This Econo Lodge is at the border of Downtown and Midtown, which is a rather arbitrary division—nothing separates the two zones except a generalized image of a business

district versus a shopping/restaurant district, but both areas have plenty of each activity. The capitol is 10 blocks west, and Sutter's Fort is 10 blocks east. The motel has the consistent quality of a national chain, with such amenities as family suites, HBO/CNN/ESPN, hair dryers and free shampoos, and free continental breakfast. Some rooms have refrigerators and microwaves. The national chain has a discount program for those over 50. Pets are welcome and kids 18 and under are free. ♿ (East)

Bed-and-Breakfasts

AMBER HOUSE
BED-AND-BREAKFAST INN
1315 22nd St.
800/755-6526, 916/444-8085
www.amberhouse.com
$$$–$$$$

Midway between Capitol Park and Sutter's Fort, Amber House is in fact three historic mansions in Craftsman, Mediterranean, and Dutch Colonial Revival styles. It's at the heart of Midtown, Sacramento's eclectic shopping district, where restaurants abound. There are 14 rooms, all named for poets, painters, and musicians, and they each have a private marble-tiled bathroom (most include a Jacuzzi for two), cable TV with VCR, and a modem-ready phone with personal voice-

mail. Bicycles—and even a tandem bike—are available at no charge. As you'd expect, breakfast is a specialty and can be served in your room, in the dining room, or in the garden—you name the time. Cookies and beverages are served in the evening, and tea or coffee with a newspaper will be waiting for you at your door in the morning. Rated "outstanding" by the American Bed-and-Breakfast Association and given four diamonds by AAA. Guests must park on the street. (East)

HARTLEY HOUSE
BED-AND-BREAKFAST
700 22nd St.
800/831-5806, 916/447-7829
www.hartleyhouse.com
$$$–$$$$

Built in 1906, Hartley House has, according to its Web site, been preserved with "original inlaid hardwood floors, stained woodwork, leaded and stained-glass windows, and original brass light fixtures converted from gas. Authentic antique furnishings, period artworks, and collectibles decorate the parlor, dining room, and guest rooms." Designed to attract business travelers, this "office within a guest room" provides a multi-line digital speakerphone, voicemail, modem port, fax and copy services, private bathrooms, robes, fine soaps and shampoos, hair dryers, ironing boards

GREATER SACRAMENTO

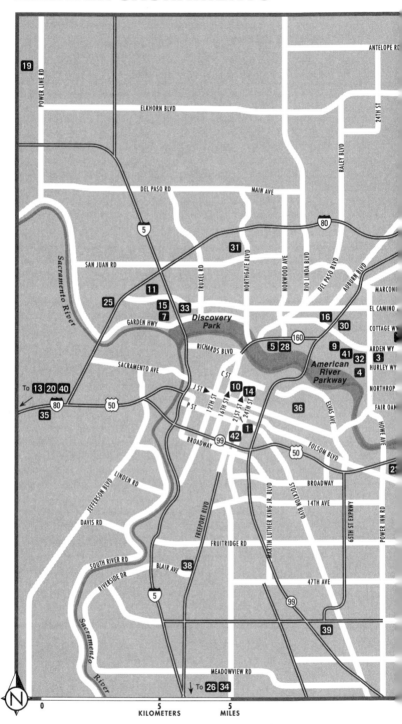

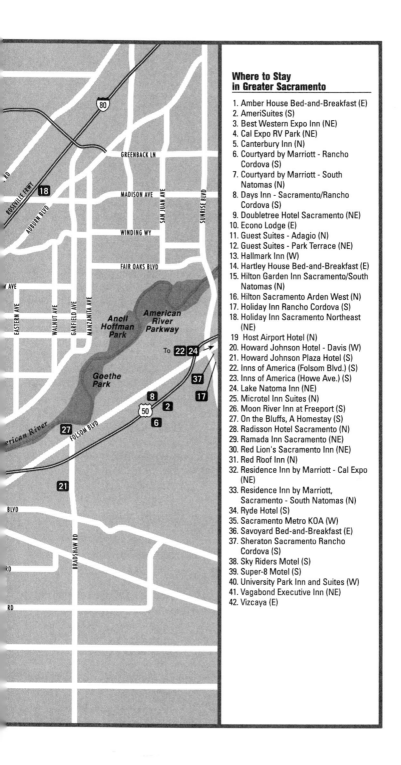

Where to Stay
in Greater Sacramento

1. Amber House Bed-and-Breakfast (E)
2. AmeriSuites (S)
3. Best Western Expo Inn (NE)
4. Cal Expo RV Park (NE)
5. Canterbury Inn (N)
6. Courtyard by Marriott - Rancho Cordova (S)
7. Courtyard by Marriott - South Natomas (N)
8. Days Inn - Sacramento/Rancho Cordova (S)
9. Doubletree Hotel Sacramento (NE)
10. Econo Lodge (E)
11. Guest Suites - Adagio (N)
12. Guest Suites - Park Terrace (NE)
13. Hallmark Inn (W)
14. Hartley House Bed-and-Breakfast (E)
15. Hilton Garden Inn Sacramento/South Natomas (N)
16. Hilton Sacramento Arden West (N)
17. Holiday Inn Rancho Cordova (S)
18. Holiday Inn Sacramento Northeast (NE)
19. Host Airport Hotel (N)
20. Howard Johnson Hotel - Davis (W)
21. Howard Johnson Plaza Hotel (S)
22. Inns of America (Folsom Blvd.) (S)
23. Inns of America (Howe Ave.) (S)
24. Lake Natoma Inn (NE)
25. Microtel Inn Suites (N)
26. Moon River Inn at Freeport (S)
27. On the Bluffs, A Homestay (S)
28. Radisson Hotel Sacramento (N)
29. Ramada Inn Sacramento (NE)
30. Red Lion's Sacramento Inn (NE)
31. Red Roof Inn (N)
32. Residence Inn by Marriott - Cal Expo (NE)
33. Residence Inn by Marriott, Sacramento - South Natomas (N)
34. Ryde Hotel (S)
35. Sacramento Metro KOA (W)
36. Savoyard Bed-and-Breakfast (E)
37. Sheraton Sacramento Rancho Cordova (S)
38. Sky Riders Motel (S)
39. Super-8 Motel (S)
40. University Park Inn and Suites (W)
41. Vagabond Executive Inn (NE)
42. Vizcaya (E)

with irons, fresh flowers, morning newspapers, and early coffee service. Craftsman bungalow and Colonial Revival styles are both reflected in the Hartley House architecture. The beautiful neighborhood surrounding it generally reflects the new wealth of the early-twentieth century, as distinct from the Victorians, Queen Annes, and Italianates of a previous era. A cooked-to-order breakfast is served in the dining room or a garden courtyard. ♿ (East)

SAVOYARD BED-AND-BREAKFAST
3322 H St.
800/SAVOYARD, 916/442-6709
www.savoyard.com
$$$
Billing itself as the "finest accommodations in the best neighborhood," this Italian Renaissance–style home rests across the street from the rose garden in McKinley Park, which has been routinely voted the favorite park in the city by local magazine and Internet popularity polls. The home's front garden is part of a three-block stretch known to locals as "Azalea Row" and includes camellias (the city flower) and a tulip tree. Two of the rooms have private baths, and each room is decorated with antiques and artworks. In addi-

tion, each room comes with a telephone, a clock-radio, and a TV. Bicycles are available at no charge, and you can quickly pedal to the bike trails of the American River Parkway. Just so you know, the home's name refers to light-opera devotees who enjoyed a late dinner at the Savoy Hotel after a Gilbert and Sullivan performance at the Savoy Theatre. Hence, they were "Savoyards," as is the owner. (East)

VIZCAYA
2019 21st St.
800/456-2019, 916/455-5243
$$$$
This Colonial Revival home is in the Poverty Ridge neighborhood, so named during one of nineteenth-century Sacramento's floods because it was the high-ground refuge for waterlogged area residents. That time is, of course, long past, and now this beautifully restored home, roughly eight blocks from the heart of Midtown shopping and dining, offers nine rooms, three with fireplaces and five with Jacuzzis. There is also a large reception and meeting area, a favorite for conferences and political events. A full breakfast is included in the room rate. Kids 12 and under are free. ♿ (East)

T I P

Looking for Abigail's Bed-and-Breakfast at 2120 G Street? It's been taken over by the folks at Hartley House, who answer the old number (916/441-5007). This Colonial Revival home has five rooms, all with private baths, and a hot tub in the garden. It's within walking distance of Sutter's Fort and the State Indian Museum, and lies just north of the shopping and restaurant richness of Midtown.

NORTH

Hotels

CANTERBURY INN
1900 Canterbury Rd.
916/927-3492, 916/641-8594 (fax)
$$
The Canterbury Inn has a long list of amenities, including HBO, free parking, conference room, airport shuttle (for a fee), restaurant, lounge, guest laundry, swimming pool, and spa. You have access to a nearby fitness center (across the street at the Radisson) and bike trails. A very short drive can take you either to the Del Paso Boulevard neighborhood, an emerging arts district full of galleries, or to the Arden Fair Mall, Sacramento's highest-density shopping area. You're also near a light-rail station. Directly across the American River are Downtown and Old Sacramento. Pets are welcome and kids 15 and under are free. ✥ (North)

COURTYARD BY MARRIOTT—SOUTH NATOMAS
2101 River Plaza Dr.
916/922-1120, 916/922-1872 (fax)
www.courtyard.com
$$–$$$
The spacious 151 rooms and 12 suites of Marriott's Courtyard each have a separate sitting area and a large work desk with a lamp. Other amenities include a lounge, a restaurant, a swimming pool, whirlpool and exercise room, and a complimentary airport shuttle, plus a safe-deposit box, fax and copying facilities, and a printer. Two conference rooms provide 1,300 square feet of space. Room service, a coffee shop, valet and self-service laundry, hair dryer, ironing board, in-room coffee, cable/satellite TV, data ports, voicemail, and complimentary newspaper (Monday through Friday) are also available. Only minutes south of the airport and Arco Arena, the Marriott is also near the river (for easy access to Downtown and Old Sacramento) and in the neighborhood of great riverside dining along the Garden Highway and Bercut Drive. Only guide dogs are permitted, and parking is free. Rated three diamonds by AAA and three stars by Mobil. ✥ (North)

GUEST SUITES—ADAGIO
2804 Grasslands Dr.
800/227-4903, 916/925-4247
guesuite@ix.netcom.com
www.guestsuites.com
$$–$$$
One of several Guest Suites in the region (the others are Bishops Court in the Northeast zone and Park Terrace in the South zone), the Adagio includes 55 one- and two-bedroom suites with full-size kitchens—furnished apartments, in effect. Spouses and children stay free, with daily maid service, cable TV, and free HBO and local calls. There is also a swimming pool, and each room has a washer and dryer. Tennis and basketball courts and private garages make extended stays easy. Rooms can be reserved on a daily, weekly, or monthly basis, but there is a minimum stay of four nights. An airport shuttle is available and parking is free. ✥ (North)

HILTON GARDEN INN SACRAMENTO/SOUTH NATOMAS
2540 Venture Oaks Way
916/568-5400, 916/568-5072 (fax)
$$
This new hotel has 154 rooms, each with a coffeemaker, microwave

oven, and refrigerator. Business services include meeting facilities for up to 90, a complimentary 24-hour business center, plus two two-line phones in each room (with voicemail and data ports) and a free *USA Today.* Airport transportation is available, as are a heated outdoor swimming pool, exercise center, whirlpool, and restaurant. Add $10 to the low rate for breakfast. Room service is available until 10 p.m., and there's a 24-hour pantry full of beverages, snacks, and convenience items for sale. ♿ (North)

HILTON SACRAMENTO ARDEN WEST
2200 Harvard St.
800/445-8667, 916/922-4700
916/649-1311 (fax)
$$$–$$$$
This large, 331-room facility has newly renovated, deluxe rooms. The two "executive floors" have upgraded amenities (robes, newspapers, hairdryers, mini-bars) plus balconies, Jacuzzis, and continental breakfasts. There are electronic locks, ironing boards, nonsmoking rooms, video games, data ports, and premium-channel and pay-per-view TV. The hotel also has a children's facility, laundry, kitchenettes, and conference rooms. You'll also find an outdoor pool and Jacuzzi, a fitness center and sauna, resort sports, the Cameo lobby lounge, and the Harvard Street Bar and Grill. Parking is free. Arden Fair Mall, with its theaters, restaurants, and huge array of stores, is an easy walk just on the other side of Business 80, but you can use a hotel shuttle. ♿ (North)

HOST AIRPORT HOTEL
6945 Airport Blvd.
800/903-HOST, 916/922-8071
916/929-8636 (fax)
www.hostairporthotel.com
$$$
At the Host Airport Hotel you're only steps away from the baggage claim at Terminal B and 10 minutes from Downtown. Convenience is favored over amenities, though there is a continental breakfast, an exercise/weight room, and, of course, all the usual attractions of an airport terminal (restaurants, gift shops, and an ATM). Ninety rooms afford soundproofing against the roar of jets, and the hotel offers banquet facilities and meeting rooms for up to 200 people. A spa and gazebo amidst grassy landscaping are tucked out of view from the airport terminals and offer a surprisingly restful retreat. You can arrange discounted rates if you book 20 or 30 days in advance, although you pay ahead and the payments are nonrefundable. For a fee, the hotel will arrange to store your car. Complimentary luggage assistance is available in the terminal. Kids 12 and under stay for free. ♿ (North)

RADISSON HOTEL SACRAMENTO
500 Leisure Lane
800/333-3333, 916/922-2020
916/649-9463 (fax)
www.radisson.com/sacramentoca
$$$–$$$$
The Radisson considers itself a "full-service resort," and many of the 307 rooms overlook a private artificial lake from either a patio or a balcony. The conference facilities (including the Grand Ballroom) can handle up to 2,000 people, and there is an outdoor theater with name performers. There is also a "wedding terrace." The grounds have spacious gardens, and locals

often take advantage of the facilities and beautiful setting for banquets, weddings, and graduations. Amenities include a fitness center, paddleboats for the lake, and free parking. It's all just a short hop from Downtown, Midtown, or Arden Fair Mall. Kids 15 and under stay for free. ♿ (North)

RESIDENCE INN BY MARRIOTT, SACRAMENTO—SOUTH NATOMAS
2410 West El Camino Ave.
800/331-3131, 916/649-1300
916/649-1395 (fax)
$$$–$$$$

This hotel has 126 one- and two-bedroom suites with fully equipped kitchens, plus an exercise room, meeting room, outdoor pool, and spa. A complimentary breakfast is offered, as is a "hospitality hour." Dinner can be delivered from local restaurants, and there are complimentary newspapers in the lobby, safe-deposit boxes, and a full business center. Rooms include a work desk and lamp, voicemail, data ports, cable/satellite TV, in-room movies, VCR, a full kitchen with refrigerator and coffeemaker, and an ironing board. Some suites have fireplaces, and pets are welcome, for a fee. ♿ (North)

Motels

MICROTEL INN SUITES
2654 El Centro Rd.
888/771-7171, 916/920-4451
916/561-0665 (fax)
$$

Only five years old, this chain emphasizes the newness of its facilities and tries to offer an affordable, predictable experience. Located in a triangle formed by Interstate 5, the Garden Highway, and Business 80, the Microtel Inn has quick access to sites in every direction. You can walk to a Burger King or drive a few minutes to fine riverfront dining. The inn offers a free continental breakfast, nonsmoking rooms, TV with free HBO/CNN/ESPN, free local calls on direct-dial phones with data ports, a fax service, and group rates for corporate, government, and military travelers. You can upgrade to a suite (some have microwaves and refrigerators) for just $10. In short, Microtel has more nice touches than most bargain chains. ♿ (North)

RED ROOF INN
3796 Northgate Blvd.
916/927-7117
$$

These 136 affordable rooms may be a bit removed from the attractions of the central city (although an easy highway trip away that takes only minutes), but they're close to Arco Arena, the airport, and the "big box" Natomas Park retail center, in an area that's growing at a fantastic rate. The Red Roof Inn has a complimentary breakfast, swimming pool and spa, and airport shuttle. Car rentals and a fitness center are nearby. ♿ (North)

NORTHEAST

Hotels

DOUBLETREE HOTEL SACRAMENTO
2001 Point West Way
800/222-TREE, 916/929-8855
916/924-0719 (fax)
www.doubletreehotels.com
$$$–$$$$

Is there anyone who truly does not welcome the marketing gimmick of complimentary chocolate chip cookies offered upon arrival? This is a large, full-service, 448-room facility, including suites. It has a fitness center, indoor swimming pool, spa, two restaurants (Cityside Café for light dining or the more elegant Maxi's Dining Room), a sports bar (R.J. Grins, with dancing and karaoke), in-room movies, and free parking. There are laundry facilities, a concierge, fax services, hair dryers, robes, and a conference center for 1,500. The Doubletree is across the street from Arden Fair Mall and a quick highway trip from Downtown. Pets are welcome and kids 16 and under stay for free. ᴴ (Northeast)

GUEST SUITES—PARK TERRACE
2264 Cottage Way, Ste. 1
800/227-4903, 916/925-4247
916/641-2533 (fax)
www.guestsuites.com
$$–$$$
As mentioned earlier, this is one of several Guest Suites in the region. At Park Terrace you'll find one- and two-bedroom suites with full-size kitchens—furnished apartments, in effect. Spouses and children stay free, with daily maid service, cable TV, and free HBO and local calls. There is also a swimming pool, and

each room has a washer and dryer. Tennis and basketball courts and private garages make extended stays easy. Rooms can be reserved on a daily, weekly, or monthly basis, but there's a minimum four-night stay. Everything is just a few blocks from Arden Fair Mall and Cal Expo, and a quick trip on the highway from Downtown. ᴴ (Northeast)

HOLIDAY INN SACRAMENTO NORTHEAST
5321 Date Ave.
800/388-9284, 916/338-5800
916/334-2868 (fax)
$$–$$$
This Holiday Inn is a large, 230-room, full-service hotel, and offers 14,000 square feet of meeting space. The inn has a lounge (live entertainment at Shakey Jake's), restaurant (Bravo Grill), fitness center, outdoor swimming pool, and spa. The rooms have on-demand movies and Nintendo, voicemail and data ports, laundry facilities, and video checkout. Depending on availability, there is a free airport shuttle after 6:30 a.m. ᴴ (Northeast)

LAKE NATOMA INN
702 Gold Lake Dr.
Folsom
800/637-7200, 916/351-1500
916/351-1511 (fax)

www.lakenatomainn.com
$$$–$$$$
In a beautiful lakeside setting, the Lake Natoma Inn offers full resort facilities. The outdoor pool and spa, nine-hole putting green, volleyball court, half-court basketball court, fitness center, and indoor spa will keep you moving. The inn will organize activities for you, including spa services (there are massages and body treatments at Elite), canoeing, kayaking, biking, volleyball, boating, wine tasting, waterskiing, whitewater rafting, and other tours. Business needs are accommodated with private meeting rooms and on-site catering. There are also laundry facilities, a beauty salon, free parking, and the on-site Lakeside Bar and Grill, which offers breakfast, lunch, dinner, and room service. Folsom is about 20 miles up the river from downtown Sacramento. It's a great jumping-off point for wine-country and gold-country touring and has its own shopping and historical districts. The inn is a block from historic Sutter Street near the Folsom Lake State Recreation Area. ⅙ (Northeast)

RAMADA INN SACRAMENTO
2600 Auburn Blvd.
916/487-7600
916/481-7112 (fax)
$$–$$$
You're a little farther out here, but right next to Haggin Oaks Golf Course, one of the city's finest. This Ramada Inn has a restaurant (the Mesa Grill and Bar), room service, lounge, and complimentary airport shuttle from seven in the morning until seven at night. Other amenities include a swimming pool, laundry, health club/spa, business services, complimentary continental break-

fast, and meeting facilities. Pets are welcome and kids 17 and under are free. ⅙ (Northeast)

RED LION'S SACRAMENTO INN
1401 Arden Way
800/RED-LION, 916/922-8041
916/922-0386 (fax)
$$–$$$$
One of the city's largest facilities, this 376-room Red Lion Inn is next door to Arden Fair Mall and down the street from Cal Expo. There are three swimming pools (one indoors), free parking, a concierge, miniature golf, a fitness club, in-room coffee, plenty of meeting space, phones with data ports, hair dryers, irons and ironing boards, and live entertainment. The live-music dance venues—Rage (for the young) and In Cahoots (for those who've gone country)—are right across the street. The inn's bar has a dance floor and karaoke, and the Cafe Garden restaurant is known for its brunches. Pets are welcome and kids 16 and under are free. ⅙ (Northeast)

RESIDENCE INN BY MARRIOTT—CAL EXPO
1530 Howe Ave.
800/331-3131, 916/920-9111
916/921-5664 (fax)
$$$–$$$$
The 176 rooms of this Residence Inn offer a variety of choices: oversized studios, two-bedroom suites, and a bi-level penthouse. Many of the suites have fireplaces and all have full kitchens with refrigerators. A complimentary breakfast and "evening hospitality" are included. There are also a meeting room of 425 square feet, an outdoor pool with whirlpool, valet and self-serve laundry, free newspapers in the lobby, and a safe-deposit box at the desk.

Room amenities include voicemail, data ports, cable/satellite TV, ironing boards, and coffeemakers. Cribs are available. Just outside the State Fairgrounds at Cal Expo, the inn is only a few blocks from Arden Fair Mall and has easy street access to the Sac State campus, East Sacramento, and Midtown. Pets are welcome, for a fee. &(Northeast)

Motels

BEST WESTERN EXPO INN
1413 Howe Ave.
916/922-9833, 916/922-3384 (fax)
$$–$$$
This 127-room Best Western offers large rooms with kitchenettes and two-room suites with guest sitting areas. Adjacent to Cal Expo in a neighborhood awash in retail activity, the inn has a conference center, guest laundry facilities, free continental breakfast, a heated swimming pool, and a spa and fitness center. Arden Fair Mall is close by, and there's quick access to downtown Sacramento. Pets are welcome. & (Northeast)

VAGABOND EXECUTIVE INN
2030 Arden Way
800/793-2030, 916/929-5600
916/929-2419 (fax)
$$–$$$
These 190 rooms have microwave ovens, refrigerators, and complimentary breakfasts in a garden setting with a swimming pool and meeting facilities. & (Northeast)

Campgrounds

CAL EXPO RV PARK
1600 Exposition Blvd. (entrance at Ethan and Hurley Way)
916/263-3187, 916/263-3163 (fax)

www.rvparks.com
$
This RV park is on the grounds of Cal Expo, the secure site of the annual State Fair and Waterworld USA. There is easy access from here to downtown, and you're only blocks away from Arden Fair Mall (the heart of Sacramento's mall shopping). The park is adjacent to the American River Parkway, with boat ramps and fishing available. Amenities include laundry facilities, a store, a snack bar, a restaurant, a meeting room, propane sales, phone hookups, and a dump station. There are 106 sites with full hookups (maximum site size is 55 feet) and 46 pull-through sites. The park offers 30-amp power, with 50 amps available for a two-dollar-per-day charge. RV storage is available. Rates are $20 per day, $105 per week, and $360 per month. The park is a member of the California Travel Parks Association. & (Northeast)

SOUTH

Hotels

AMERISUITES
10744 Gold Center Dr.
Rancho Cordova
800/833-1516, 916/635-4799
916/635-6627 (fax)
$$$
Amerisuites is a budget-minded, all-suites hotel with 128 rooms. Living and bedroom areas are separate, and there's a kitchenette. You'll also find an on-site business center, a swimming pool, laundry facilities, a health club/spa, conference rooms, and free parking. Breakfast is complimentary. Pets are welcome. & (South)

Corporate Housing

Extended-stay apartment rentals are a relatively recent option, meant particularly for the business and government traveler or for families who are relocating. Features and amenities vary site by site, and you will need to contact each facility directly for particulars, but in general they are furnished apartments with flexible, short-term leases. Some will require minimum stays (although some will have overnight options), and some offer discounts depending on the length of lease you require. Some of the region's best:

CALIFORNIA SUITES
9940 Business Park Dr.,
Ste. 135
Sacramento
800/367-9501, 916/363-9700
916/368-3550 (fax)
(South)

EXECUSTAY BY MARRIOTT
4407 Roseville Rd., Ste. 110
North Highlands
916/338-7690
916/338-7695 (fax)
(North)

EXECUTIVE LIVING
1761 Heritage Ln.
Sacramento
800/466-1993, 916/921-9494
(Northeast)

HOMESTEAD VILLAGE
GUEST STUDIO
2810 Gateway Oaks Dr.
Sacramento
916/564-7500,
916/564-7515 (fax)
(North)

OAKWOOD CORPORATE
HOUSING
Multiple locations
800/483-1335, 916/631-3777
916/631-3773 (fax)

OLIVE GROVE
Executive Suites
6143 Auburn Blvd.
Citrus Heights
916/807-1835
916/726-5091 (fax)
(Northeast)

RESIDENCE INN—
RANCHO CORDOVA
2779 Prospect Park Dr.
Rancho Cordova
916/851-1550 (phone/fax)
(South)

STONESFAIR MANAGEMENT
7434 Auburn Oaks Court
Citrus Heights
916/722-2200
916/722-8964 (fax)
(Northeast)

COURTYARD BY MARRIOTT—RANCHO CORDOVA
10683 White Rock Rd.
Rancho Cordova
800/321-2211, 916/638-3800
916/638-6776 (fax)
www.courtyard.com
$$–$$$$
This Marriott features 144 rooms and 12 suites, plus three meeting rooms with up to 1,500 square feet of space. Stay fit in the outdoor heated pool, spa, and exercise room, or on nearby jogging trails. The Courtyard Café is open for breakfast, and there's also a lounge. Dinner can be delivered from local restaurants. Like all of Marriott's Courtyards, rooms include a work desk with lamp, voicemail and data ports, cable/satellite TV, movies, a free daily newspaper, free coffee, and an ironing board. Cribs are also available. Valet and self-serve laundry; fax, copy, and printing facilities; and a safe-deposit box are also available. Parking is free. Rated three diamonds by AAA and three stars by Mobil. & (South)

HOWARD JOHNSON PLAZA HOTEL
3343 Bradshaw Rd.
Rancho Cordova
800/446-4656, 916/366-1266
916/366-1266 ext. 100 (fax)
www.hojo.com
$$
Located along the Highway 50 corridor, this HoJo has a three-story atrium with fireplaces, a conference center, six meeting rooms, banquet facilities for 200, bridal suites, a heated indoor/outdoor pool, a dry-heat sauna, a hot tub, an exercise room, Judy's Family Restaurant, and a sports lounge. Amenities include laundry and valet services, non-smoking rooms, coffeemakers, daily newspapers, and limited room service. Call for group rates. RV and truck parking are available. Pets are welcome. & (South)

HOLIDAY INN RANCHO CORDOVA
11131 Folsom Blvd.
Rancho Cordova
916/638-1111, 916/635-3297 (fax)
www.holiday-inn.com/ranchocordova
$$$
All the amenities associated with this national chain are here. Conference and banquet facilities, with four meeting rooms, can seat up to 150. The 130 rooms include an "Executive Level" and are newly renovated (as of September 1999). Guests receive a complimentary continental breakfast and have access to a restaurant, lounge, fitness center, outdoor pool, and spa. Parking is free, the better to drive to the area's shopping and factory outlet stores. & (South)

RYDE HOTEL
14340 Hwy. 160
Ryde

TRIVIA

The Orleans Hotel, destroyed in the 1852 fire, had been prefabricated in New Orleans and was brought to Sacramento by ship. After the fire it was rebuilt in a mere 20 days and became the most prominent hotel of the era and the biggest (according to some) in the entire state of California.

On the Horizon

There is more hotel space on the way. Embassy Suites has broken ground for a 249-suite, eight-story, river-view hotel right at the waterfront where Capitol Mall meets the Tower Bridge. The land was donated by the State Transportation Department, and the projected opening date is in late 2000. A 500-room Sheraton Grand Hotel is also under construction near the Convention Center.

888/717-RYDE, 916/776-1318
916/776-1195 (fax)
www.rydehotel.com
$$–$$$$

The Ryde Hotel, with its black-lacquered, art-deco opulence, was built during Prohibition and served as a riverboat way station, a bordello, or a speakeasy—take your pick. Bootleg whiskey and jazz flowed above a trapdoor that, as legend has it, opened down into a tunnel to the river's edge. The Ryde has seen them all—celebrities, politicians, mobsters, and the levee builders who made the Delta possible. New owners and a recent renovation have made history and modernity work together, with the stated goal of combining the best of a bed-and-breakfast with a country-club ambience. To this end, the Ryde has a short nine-hole, par-three golf course winding through the adjacent pear orchards, a swimming pool, and a private boat dock free to hotel or restaurant guests (reservations required). The rooms, including some suites, include iron bed frames and flapper-era beaded shades. Rates are very reasonable for a European-style room that shares a bath; more

expensive options include a golf-course suite, a river-view room with a Jacuzzi, and the honeymoon suite. For about $35 you can order the "Romantic Getaway Package," which includes champagne, chocolates, flower petals on your pillow, a scented candle, and bubble bath.

This is Delta country. To get there from Sacramento take Interstate 5 south for about 20 minutes to the Twin Cities Road exit. At the stop sign turn right and follow the signs to Walnut Grove. Go through the town of Locke to Walnut Grove. Turn right over the bridge, then turn left onto Highway 160 and follow this for three miles to Ryde. Rising out of the flat Delta, the peach-colored hotel with its black-and-white-striped awnings cannot be missed. (South)

SHERATON SACRAMENTO RANCHO CORDOVA
11211 Point East Dr.
Rancho Cordova
800/851-2400, 916/638-1100
916/638-5803 (fax)
$$$–$$$$

Everything at this Sheraton is big. It features 262 oversized rooms and suites, an expanded fitness center,

13 rooms of meeting space (totaling 14,000 square feet), a poolside restaurant (Café Del Sol), cocktail lounge, spa, business center, and club floor. Weekend rates available, with or without breakfast. ♿ (South)

Motels

DAYS INN—SACRAMENTO/ RANCHO CORDOVA
10800 Olson Dr.
Rancho Cordova
916/638-2500, 916/638-2672 (fax)
$–$$
Economy and convenience are emphasized here. You're close to U.S. 50 and about halfway between downtown Sacramento and Folsom (with quick access to either). A continental breakfast is served daily, and a swimming pool, HBO, laundry facilities, free parking, and conference rooms are available. Call for group discounts. If you're over 50, check out their September Days Club for special rates on rooms, meals, car rentals, tours, and travel insurance. ♿ (South)

INNS OF AMERICA
25 Howe Ave.
800/826-0778
$$–$$$
A second Inns of America outlet is at 12249 Folsom Boulevard in Rancho Cordova (800/826-0778). Both offer remodeled rooms, a heated swimming pool, cable TV, and a continental breakfast. Nonsmoking rooms are available, as are fax services, modems, and free local calls. Both are also near restaurants, shopping, and either downtown Sacramento or the Folsom area. The Rancho Cordova motel is 15 miles from the capitol and has a meeting room and a suite. The Howe motel is

a block from the light-rail system and five miles from the capitol. Pets are welcome. ♿ (South)

SKY RIDERS MOTEL
6100 Freeport Blvd.
916/421-5700, 916/485-1433 (fax)
$
Affordable and frankly modest on the exterior, the Sky Riders Motel has a unique location among city accommodations. Across the street from the Executive Airport, where small private planes come and go, the motel is also near Sacramento City College and a number of small, interesting restaurants along Freeport Boulevard. The motel has a swimming pool, and each room has a phone and free HBO. (South)

SUPER-8 MOTEL
7216 55th St.
800/800-8000, 916/427-7925
916/424-9011 (fax)
$$
These affordable rooms are along a commercial corridor full of malls and fast food, with quick access to downtown Sacramento via Highway 99. Free HBO and morning coffee are offered. (South)

Bed-and-Breakfasts

MOON RIVER INN AT FREEPORT
8201 Freeport Blvd.
Freeport
916/665-6550
$$$–$$$$
You're at the edge of another world here, as Freeport is close-in to Sacramento but has more in common with the Delta. The Moon River Inn sits roadside, acting as a gateway to the Delta towns to the south. It offers modern amenities including a Jacuzzi and TV in each room, and

First Food, Now a Place to Stay

Randy Paragary, the area's incredibly successful restaurant owner, has entered the hotel business. He's bought a building to be renovated in Midtown near Sutter's Fort and J Street shopping. More important, it's near Sutter General Hospital, as Paragary intends to provide a "different world" for the family members visiting patients there. Modeled on European inns, it will include in-room kitchens, Internet access, and marbled bathrooms. Rates are anticipated to be in the $100-to-$120 range.

has conference space for seminars, retreats, and meetings. (South)

ON THE BLUFFS, A HOMESTAY
9735 Mira del Rio Dr.
916/363-9933 or 916/363-3412
www.usa-411.com/otbluffs.html
$$$
Upriver along the south bank of the American River, this "mini-bed-and-breakfast" overlooks both the river and the American River Parkway with its walking, jogging, and bike trails. There are three guest rooms: one with a feather bed, TV, and private entrance; a second stocked with romantic novels and a canopy bed; and the third, at a slightly greater expense, with a king-size bed, private bath, and views of the pool and river. Relax on the elevated deck as you watch the wildlife along the water, enjoy afternoon refreshments in the living room, or use the nearby trails. It's easy to drive into East Sacramento, Midtown, and Downtown via Folsom Boulevard or to cross the river at northbound Watt Avenue and head for the Arden Fair Mall shopping district. Exit U.S. 50

onto Bradshaw Road north and follow it until it dead-ends, then turn left onto Mira del Rio Drive. On the Bluffs is the first house on the right. (South)

WEST

Hotels

HALLMARK INN
110 F St.
Davis
800/753-0035, 530/753-3600
$$$
The Hallmark Inn features 135 rooms and suites in the heart of a university town. A complimentary breakfast and a "Manager's evening reception" are included. There's also a swimming pool. (West)

HOWARD JOHNSON HOTEL—DAVIS
4100 Chiles Rd.
Davis
800/I-GO-HOJO, 530/792-0800
530/753-0225 (fax)
www.hojo.com

$$$–$$$$

The Howard Johnson Hotel offers a wide range of amenities, including in-room coffeemakers, refrigerators, microwave ovens, cable TV with HBO, free local phone calls, and a free cooked-to-order breakfast. There are also two meeting rooms, a 24-hour front desk, free parking, hair dryers, modems, non-smoking rooms, free newspapers, an outdoor pool, a fitness center, tennis facilities, and laundry and valet services. The hotel was renovated in 1998. There are also suites available. AAA, AARP, group, government, and corporate discounts are given. & (West)

Motels

UNIVERSITY PARK INN AND SUITES
1111 Richards Blvd.
Davis
530/756-0910, 530/758-0978 (fax)
$$–$$$
Right at the exit from Interstate 80 for the University of California, Davis campus, the University Park Inn and Suites is also near the charm of Davis's old downtown. Recently renovated, the rooms and suites come with an outdoor pool, fitness center, the on-site Caffe Italia, a lounge, a wedding terrace, complimentary breakfast, and enough meeting space for 50. Some rooms have a fireplace and patio. & (West)

Campgrounds

SACRAMENTO METRO KOA
3951 Lake Rd.
West Sacramento
800/KOA-2747, 916/371-6771
916/371-0622 (fax)
www.koakampgrounds.com
$
This KOA offers pull-through sites. LP gas, the snack bar, and movies are available for a charge. Fishing and firewood are available at no charge. Thirty-amp service is available. A swimming pool is open from mid-April to mid-October. (West)

© Tom Myers 1999

4

WHERE TO EAT

Sacramento has no business fielding the large number of fine restaurants that it does—it's too small and too provincial, or so the unknowing outsider might assume. But the kaleidoscopic menu choice here is entirely in keeping with the "open door to the world" approach that defines the region. The central concept that touches almost every eating establishment, intentionally or not, is California cuisine. This exists in protean form, having one meaning in an Italian setting and quite another in a Chinese restaurant. But what's consistent throughout is the emphasis on fresh local ingredients. ("Local," in Sacramento, has taken on a radically different meaning, as a quick perusal of the city's organic farmers' markets will attest: It no longer refers to just tomatoes, almonds, and more tomatoes.)

California cuisine is, to a large extent, a legacy of Alice Waters and her Berkeley restaurant, Chez Panisse, which put California cooking on the world map several decades ago. Mike Dunne, the very fine food writer for the *Sacramento Bee,* has summed up what California cuisine entails: "Cook simply, with the best ingredients, preferably fresh, local, and seasonal, grown organically and harvested when perfectly ripe." This approach has evolved into menus that defy categories, and cuisines which must, in the current trend, be called "fusion" because they combine world traditions with California freshness. And that is the essence of Sacramento dining. In keeping with the town-versus-metropolis comfort level of Sacramento, almost any dining experience will be cozy and intimate, often in restaurants that appear to be small, indifferent storefronts until, after a few visits, someone just might remember your name.

In the following pages, you'll find a wide—but not comprehensive—sampler of the variety Sacramento has to offer.

The follow price-rating symbols reflect the average cost of an entrée.

Price-rating symbols:
$ less than $10
$$ $11–15
$$$ $16 and over

RESTAURANTS BY CUISINE TYPE

Breakfasts/Cafés
Café Bernardo (E), p. 66
Capitol Garage Coffee Company (C), p. 59
Corner Stone (E), p. 68
Eddie's Land Park Grill (S), p. 81
Freeport Bakery (S), p. 82
Jamba Juice (E), p. 69

Breweries/Pubs
Fox and Goose (C), p. 62
River City Brewing Company (C), p. 64
Streets of London Pub (E), p. 72
Sudwerk Brewery and Grill (NE, W), p. 85

California/American Cuisine
Bandera (NE), p. 75
Chanterelle (Sterling Hotel) (C), p. 59
Enotria Café and Wine Bar (N), p. 74
Esquire Grill (C), p. 61
Fourth Street Grille (C), p. 62
Grapes (C), p. 63
Mace's (NE), p. 79
Moxie (E), p. 71
Paragary's Bar and Oven (E), p. 71
Rio City Café (C), p. 64
Twenty Eight (E), p. 73

Chinese
Bamboo (E), p. 66
Chinois City Wok (NE), p. 75
Frank Fat's (C), p. 62
Jumbo Seafood (S), p. 83
Royal Hong King Lum (C), p. 65

Dessert
Gunther's Ice Cream (S), p. 82
Leatherby's Creamery (NE), p. 79
Rick's Dessert Diner (E), p. 72
Vic's (S), p. 84

Diners
Jack's Urban Eats (E), p. 69
Joe Marty's El Chico (S), p. 82
Lucky Café (E), p. 71
13th Street Café (C), p. 65

French/Continental
Alexander's Meritage (NE), p. 74
Amadeus (NE), p. 75
La Bohéme (NE), p. 78
Slocum House (NE), p. 80
Waterboy (E), p. 73

Italian
Biba (E), p. 66
Español (E), p. 69
Il Fornaio (C), p. 63
Old Spaghetti Factory (E), p. 71
Virga's (C), p. 66

Japanese
Edokko (S), p. 81
Fuji (S), p. 82
Mikuni (NE), p. 79
New Edokko (S), p. 81
Samurai Sushi (S), p. 84
Taka's (E), p. 72

Mexican/Spanish/Caribbean
Célestin's Caribbean Restaurant (E), p. 68
Centro Cocina Mexicana (E), p. 68
Ernesto's Mexican Food (E), p. 68
Habanero Cava Latina (E), p. 69
Tapa the World (E), p. 72

Seafood/Steaks
Dawson's (Hyatt Regency) (C), p. 61
Delta King Pilothouse (C), p. 61
The Firehouse (C), p. 61
Morton's of Chicago (C), p. 63
Scott's Seafood (NE), p. 80

CENTRAL

AMARIN THAI
900 12th St.
916/447-9063
$$

Wide selection and the exotica of spices not often encountered in other cuisines make the Amarin—and Thai food generally—worth repeated visits. Here you'll be enveloped in a faraway atmosphere, with Thai music and art to accompany the aromas. Seafood in curry sauces, marinated and barbecued chicken served with sweet and sour sauce, stir-fried noodles with choice of meat or shrimp, and a large vegetarian selection make for a nearly endless variety of experience. Be sure to try either the Thai Spring Rolls or the Amarin Rolls, which are rice paper wrapped around mint, rice noodles, and fresh lettuce, served with plum sauce. If you have a favorite ingredient not listed in a dish, the chef will accommodate your request. Lunch, dinner daily. ♿ (Central)

CAPITOL GARAGE COFFEE COMPANY
1427 L St.
916/444-3633
$

Known to some as the "Capitol Garage Café and Cabaret," live music turns this little coffee shop into a hopping nightspot. In the mornings, though, it's a quiet place, where you can get a gigantic cup of coffee and a breakfast burrito that will keep you going for hours. They also have espresso drinks, pastries, desserts, grilled sandwiches, salads, soups, wine, and beer on tap. It's a great place to wander into after buying a used book at Beers Books next door before you go through Capitol Park and the capitol itself, which are both a block away. Breakfast, lunch, and dinner served daily. ♿ (Central)

CHANTERELLE (STERLING HOTEL)
1300 H St.
916/442-0451
$$$

Chanterelle is everything you expect a four-star restaurant to be. It features California regional tastes, with offerings such as Dungeness crab cakes and grilled Jamaican marinated pork tenderloin, served with asparagus and wild mushroom risotto. As for desserts, a Godiva Truffle Torte says volumes. The romantic setting, in a small Victorian hotel, features a stonework patio and a beautiful garden. A flat-fee brunch is served on Sunday in the ballroom ($16.95), and you're encouraged to load your plate with too

CENTRAL SACRAMENTO

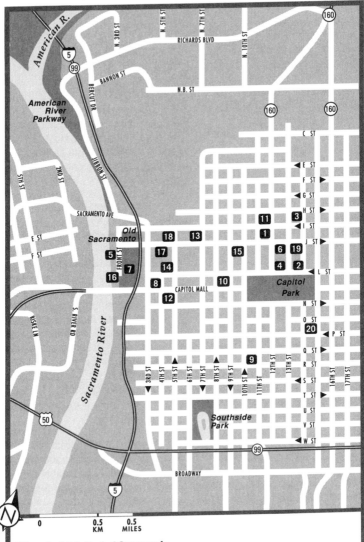

Where to Eat in Central Sacramento

1. Amarin Thai
2. Capitol Garage Coffee Company
3. Chanterelle (Sterling Hotel)
4. Dawson's (Hyatt Regency)
5. *Delta King* Pilothouse
6. Esquire Grill
7. The Firehouse
8. Fourth Street Grille
9. Fox and Goose
10. Frank Fat's
11. Grapes
12. Il Fornaio
13. India Restaurant
14. Morton's of Chicago
15. Ras Teferi
16. Rio City Café
17. River City Brewing Company
18. Royal Hong King Lum
19. 13th Street Café
20. Virga's

much food drawn from too many choices. An on-hand chef will cook made-to-order omelettes, if you get that far after loading your plate(s) with chicken cordon bleu, cracked crab, salad, fruit, pasta, sausage, eggs Benedict, Belgian waffles, antipasti, bread pudding, and desserts. Open for lunch Mon–Fri, dinner nightly, Sun brunch. & (Central)

DAWSON'S (HYATT REGENCY)
1209 L St.
916/443-1234
$$$
Dawson's is in an elegant setting within the Hyatt and was voted one of the city's best business lunch establishments in a recent *Sacramento* magazine poll. The open kitchen turns out charcoal-grilled steaks, chops, and seafood. There's also an oyster bar (not to be confused with the piano bar). Three hours of complimentary valet parking. Lunch Mon–Fri, dinner Mon–Sat. & (Central)

DELTA KING PILOTHOUSE
1000 Front St. at K St.
Old Sacramento Waterfront
916/441-4440
$$$
As described in the hotel chapter, the setting at the *Delta King* Pilothouse is just the best. It's aboard an authentic, restored paddle wheeler permanently moored at the Old Sac waterfront. Whether it's Sunday brunch or dinner, the food is both traditional and first class—with views. They offer fresh seafood, pasta, steaks, and a terrific clam chowder. Specialties include a Caesar salad with grilled chicken, petrale sole sautéed in wine, sweet butter, garlic, and parsley, and fish-

erman's stew. Sun brunch, lunch Mon–Sat, dinner nightly. & (Central)

ESQUIRE GRILL
1215 K St.
916/448-8900
$$
This is the newest restaurant created by Randy Paragary. Paragary has steadily built a small empire of quality dining spots in town, not by franchising his original idea, but by spinning variations on California cuisine to meet almost any taste and budget. Originally trained as a lawyer, he seems to be as much urban planner as restaurateur, and he was long urged by city officials to bring his magic touch to this end of the K Street Mall. The Esquire Grill's location at the foot of the Esquire Plaza high-rise guarantees a clientele of tourists, shoppers, businesspeople, conventioneers, and Imax Theater patrons. The Esquire, a classic American grill, offers shrimp and crab *louies,* prime rib, grilled steaks, and freshly roasted seafood such as halibut. Salads, sandwiches, and burgers are served, too, so you have a wide choice in price and taste. The Esquire's high-quality food, beautiful interior design, and fine wine, as well as Paragary's track record, ensure a quality experience. Lunch and dinner daily. & (Central)

THE FIREHOUSE
1112 Second St.
Old Sacramento
916/442-4772, 916/442-6617 (fax)
$$$
Even if dining quality was of no concern, the Firehouse would be worth a visit. It's easy to imagine the crew of Company No. 3 leaping into the horse-drawn fire engines, charging through the door into the

cobblestone street, and dodging between gas lamps in their efforts to save other Gold Rush–era buildings. The old building had fallen into decrepitude when a prescient businessman renovated it and reopened it as the Firehouse in 1960, with its original brick interior walls intact. Its immediate success spurred other retail efforts in Old Sacramento, which saved the district from demolition; eventually most of the gaps were filled in. The Firehouse features elegant, period-decorated dining rooms full of rescued local artifacts, along with an enchanting garden courtyard that offers a cool, fresh-air retreat. It was at the Firehouse that Governor Ronald Reagan held his post-inauguration parties, and photos and sketches of visiting celebrities cover several walls. However, dining does also figure into the restaurant's fame, and the Firehouse has been rated five stars by the California Restaurant Association for the past three years. It also wins local awards yearly for its service and its steak, seafood, and continental cuisine. Banquet facilities and valet parking are available. Lunch Mon–Fri, dinner Tue–Sat, prime rib served Thu–Sat. & (Central)

FOURTH STREET GRILLE
400 L St.
916/448-2847
$$
Right at the heart of Downtown, where Old Sacramento meets the business district, this small space wraps around one corner of the first floor of an office building. But once you're inside, it feels like home, with loads of dark, glossy woodwork and a big shiny bar. Chatty and bustling, it's a favorite of the business crowd, who come for a menu that empha-

sizes freshness and changes its entrées seasonally. One recent visit yielded not only the best corn chowder one diner had ever tasted, but the best oak-grilled pork chop, served moist under an apple glaze—part of the Grille's "New American" cuisine. It's an upbeat, friendly place and also offers pastas, pizzas, interesting breads, and desserts to die for (or from). Catering is available. Lunch Mon–Fri, dinner Mon–Sat. & (Central)

FOX AND GOOSE
1001 R St.
916/443-8825
$
This is a re-creation of the English public house, otherwise known as a pub. In this reclaimed warehouse building you get crowded, cheerful atmosphere, along with your carbohydrates. Besides being a nightspot with live music Tuesday through Saturday, the pub also serves one of the top breakfasts in the city. British cuisine may be a staple of comedic material when it comes to dinner, but they know breakfast: kippers (Atlantic herring); omelettes stuffed with red onions, spinach, Swiss cheese, and avocado; potatoes with bell peppers and onions; and homemade granola—all served up with a backdrop of English knickknacks coating the walls. Brunch Sat–Sun, breakfast and lunch Mon–Fri, limited informal dinner Mon–Fri. & (Central)

FRANK FAT'S
806 L St.
916/442-7092
$$$
Long considered the classiest of Sacramento's Chinese restaurants, this modest-looking establishment opens into elegance—in both set-

ting and menu. Open since 1939, Frank Fat's has long been a hangout for the political elite, and its success enabled the Fat family to open several other restaurants nearby based on different themes. Here, enjoy Cantonese, Hunan, Szechuan, Peking, and Shanghai cooking. For the less adventurous, they also serve choice cuts of steak. There is a full bar, and appetizers are served between the lunch and dinner hours. Their banana cream pie makes every list of the area's best desserts. Banquet facilities are available. Lunch Mon–Fri, dinner nightly. ♿ (Central)

GRAPES
815 11th St.
916/447-6272
$$$
With the ambience of a winery's tasting room, Grapes seeks to recreate a Napa Valley wine country dining experience without the hassle of driving all the way over there. This largely means taking the basics of California cuisine and applying the cooking methods (and ingredients) of cuisines from areas as varied as France, Italy, Asia, and even the American South, to create new and inventive combinations that change seasonally. Examples of this exotic mix—a trend referred to as "fusion"—include pot-stickers made of artichoke, chicken, and hazelnut, or crab raviolis with an orange soy glaze.

What a *Sacramento Bee* reviewer described as a "young and inviting California wine list" is grouped by wines of similar weight and style rather than type. From candles to corkage fee, this is serious dining. Takeout is available. Parking is available at the restaurant, on the street, and in a public lot nearby. Lunch Mon–Fri, dinner nightly. ♿ (Central)

IL FORNAIO
400 Capitol Mall
916/446-4100
$$
Yes, it's a chain, but it's an exceptional chain. In an elegant setting at the foot of the Wells Fargo building, the emphasis at Il Fornaio is on Northern Italian cuisine like fresh pastas, grilled fish, roasted meats, and traditional desserts. People have been known to come here just for the bread. The bakery also turns out wood-fired pizza. Lunch Mon–Fri, dinner nightly. ♿ (Central)

INDIA RESTAURANT
729 J St.
916/448-9046
$$
For a taste of Indian authenticity just off the K Street Mall, check out the India Restaurant, which offers specialty breads, chutneys, *raita,* beer, and wine. This may be the only place where you can find a taste of India *and* pizza—something to keep in mind if you have less than adventurous kids along. Specialties include *aloo gobhi* (potatoes and cauliflower cooked with herbs and spices), *tika* (chicken cooked scarlet red with spices), and *aloo chole* (sautéed chickpeas). This restaurant was recently voted Best Indian Restaurant in town in a poll of *Sacramento* magazine readers. Lunch Mon–Fri, lunch buffet Sat, dinner nightly. ♿ (Central)

MORTON'S OF CHICAGO
521 L St.
916/442-5091

$$$

Though it is also a chain restaurant (see Il Fornaio above), Morton's of Chicago has a national reputation as a fine steakhouse. You won't find any of that wimpy California stuff here. The huge portions of steaks and chops are expensive, but worth it. They also serve seafood and live Maine lobster. They boast of having a "speakeasy atmosphere" (complete with white tablecloths), but show few if any tommy guns. There's a full bar, and banquet facilities are available. Dinner nightly. ♿ (Central)

RAS TEFERI
1009 9th St.
916/443-8031
$

As you might expect, this is the only Ethiopian restaurant in the city. Ras Teferi offers a delicious and different experience, from the uniquely prepared meat and vegetarian entrées to the Ethiopian beer and wine. More than most cuisines, this one needs some explaining. *Yesiga Tibbs* is chunks of lean beef sautéed with onions, garlic, *berbere* (a spice that combines red peppers, cumin, cardamom, ginger, coriander, and other similar spices), and clarified butter. The chicken version is *Yedoro Tibbs*. With lamb it's called *Yebeg Tibbs* and is sautéed with more or less the same onions, garlic, vegetables, and spicy, clarified butter.

Vegetarian choices include *Mitten Shiro* (ground chickpeas cooked with fresh garlic and herbs), Eggplant *Tibbs* (freshly sliced eggplant, garlic, onions, and bell peppers sautéed with either turmeric or berbere), and *Yemisser*

Wot (lentils prepared in a special blend of Ethiopian spices). Catering is available. Lunch and dinner Mon–Sat. (Central)

RIO CITY CAFÉ
1110 Front St.
Old Sacramento
916/442-8226
$$$

This café has the perfect ambience. Fashioned from a reclaimed, renovated riverfront building, it sports a deck full of outdoor tables that look out on the water, the I Street and Tower Bridges, and that peculiar ziggurat on the west side of the Sacramento River. Plus, it's backed up by the buzz of Downtown and Old Sacramento. This is one of the Old Sac restaurants where locals elbow tourists aside. Sticking with classic steak, ribs, seafood, and pasta choices is probably a good idea for the first-timer, as some of the more experimental New Cuisine embellishments are a bit unpredictable. Lunch and dinner daily, Sun brunch. ♿ (Central)

RIVER CITY BREWING COMPANY
545 Downtown Plaza (at Fourth and K Sts.)
916/447-2739
$$

This brewery restaurant regularly wins prizes for its microbrews. An oak-fired spit roasts up the entrées, and a large selection of California wines complement the European-style brews. River City Brewing Company is located in the Downtown Plaza, with hours and a menu to accommodate shoppers and the business crowd. Lunch and dinner daily, with a "midday menu" from 2:30 to 5:30 p.m. and a "late-night menu" from 10 p.m. to midnight, so

Burgers, or Everyone versus In-N-Out

The hamburger, an item on most people's lists of foods that they cannot (or will not) live without, is a revealing touchstone of a dining scene. Finding a great burger is, for many, a personal triumph in eating what you ought not to eat (at least not too often). How then to account for a franchise winning every "best of" poll? In-N-Out earns the honor honestly—they make a great, if small, burger, on a grilled bun, with lots of stuff on it to ooze down your wrists, as well as fries, soft drinks, and shakes. That's the entire menu. Having originated in Southern California, In-N-Out is the classic drive-in experience (in fact, you'll get your food faster if you drive through, rather than come inside), and as of this writing there are only a handful of the joints in the area, which is sure to change. But vying for second place are a number of great local entries. Try Ford's Real Hamburgers (S), Hamburger Mary's (E), Willie's Burgers and Chiliburgers, or Nationwide Freezer Meats (E), for a one-of-a-kind, bigger-than-your-head burger.

there's never a time not to go. ᕦ (Central)

ROYAL HONG KING LUM
419 J St.
916/443-1584
$$
The facade of the Royal Hong King Lum stirs movie-memory fantasies of what a Chinese restaurant should look like: It's a mysterious, forbidding wall in pink and red.

That aside, the Royal Hong King Lum is also Sacramento's oldest restaurant, dating from 1906, and is one of the few establishments from old Chinatown still in place. It specializes in Mandarin and Cantonese dishes and has a full bar and banquet facili-ties. Lunch is

served Mon–Fri, dinner nightly. (Central)

13TH STREET CAFÉ
1100 14th St.
916/446-1005
$
Forget the 14th Street address and the fact that this café appears to have been duct-taped to the side of the Convention Center. The 13th Street Café, at the corner of 13th and J, is a great source of home-grown success stories, like Java City coffee and espresso, and Merlino's Freeze. They make great sandwiches, salads, burgers, and the house specialty, garlic fries. Some patio seating is available. Lunch only, Mon–Fri. ᕦ (Central)

VIRGA'S
1501 14th St.
916/442-8516
$$

Virga's has been consistently voted one of the best Italian restaurants in town in local polls. Ravioli, lamb, fresh fish, seafood, pastas, and risotto are all featured in a cozy bistro setting. Come hungry and venture through the appetizers, then try the spinach salad with sweet walnuts. Only blocks from the Community Center, this is a perfect before- or after-theater stop. Free hors d'oeuvres during happy hours (Tue–Fri 4–7 p.m.). Anything Goes, their catering service, is considered top-notch. Lunch Tue–Fri, dinner Tue–Sat. & (Central)

EAST

BAMBOO
2431 J St.
916/442-7200
$

Recently voted one of the Best New and Best Chinese restaurants in *Sacramento* magazine, Bamboo's owner/chef David SooHoo and his wife, cookbook author Elaine Corn, re-create "the food of the countryside" in an open kitchen. Their Asian soups, salads, and noodle and rice dishes go well with Asian beer, sake, and fine wines. The chow mein has pan-fried Hong Kong noodles and is generous with the shrimp, chicken, barbecued beef, and greens. Or try the "Laughing Buns"—steamed buns containing green onions and orange-flavored beef. The banana cream pie competes with the same dessert at Frank Fat's for best in the city. Lunch Mon–Fri, dinner Mon–Sat. & (East)

BIBA
2801 Capitol Ave.
916/455-2422
$$$

Biba makes every imaginable list in the city—Best Italian, Most Romantic, Best Expensive (dubiously), and "Willie Brown's Favorite" (a dated distinction, from the stylish San Francisco mayor's days as House Speaker). Elegantly decorated in its historic Tavern Building location, Biba specializes in Northern Italian dishes that owner/chef Biba Caggiano constantly updates. She knows whereof she cooks: Caggiano was the host of her own Learning Channel cable TV show and has authored several cookbooks on her cuisine. Pianist Wed–Sat nights. Lunch Mon–Fri, dinner Mon–Sat. & (East)

CAFÉ BERNARDO
2726 Capitol Ave.
916/443-1180
$$

One of the early spin-offs of the Paragary success story, Café Bernardo has light fare, with choices for all, and tends toward vegetarian and non–red meat dishes that are fresh, quickly served, and reasonably priced.

Those are just some of the reasons to bring the kids here, especially for breakfast, when the cheerfully busy clatter from fellow diners and the open kitchen will keep embarrassing moments to a minimum. The eggs here are great. Try the breakfast burritos. Try the malted Belgian waffle. But try it all early, because by late morning there will be a line. During the rest of the day you can also find pizzas, sandwiches, soup, stir-fries, salads, fresh pies and cakes, and a

EAST SACRAMENTO

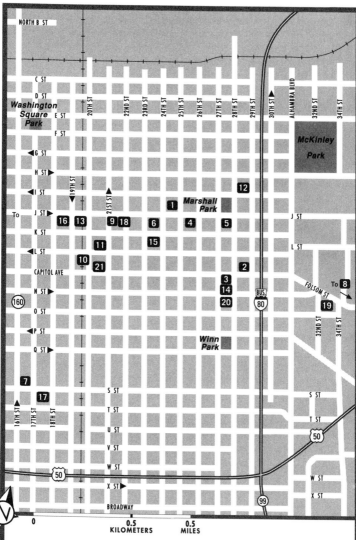

Where to Eat in East Sacramento

1. Bamboo
2. Biba
3. Café Bernardo
4. Célestin's Caribbean Restaurant
5. Centro Cocina Mexicana
6. Corner Stone
7. Ernesto's Mexican Food
8. Español
9. Habanero Cava Latina
10. Jack's Urban Eats
11. Lucky Café
12. Moxie
13. Old Spaghetti Factory
14. Paragary's Bar and Oven
15. Rick's Dessert Diner
16. Streets of London Pub
17. Taka's
18. Tapa the World
19. 33rd Street Bistro
20. Twenty Eight
21. Waterboy

juice bar. Breakfast, lunch, and dinner daily. &. (East)

CÉLESTIN'S CARIBBEAN RESTAURANT
2516 J St.
916/444-2423
$$$

What is Caribbean dining? Gumbos, shrimp Creole, chicken curry, corn cakes, black beans, and bread pudding are typical items, but naming them doesn't tell the whole story. The warmth of the cuisine's aromas, colors, and spices, the relaxed atmosphere, and the cheery setting will transport you to another clime. There's a lot of frying that goes on, like the *fritailles,* an appetizer that makes a great introductory sampler. It's a combination of *grio* (braised pork with tomato, mayonnaise, shallots, chiles, and herbs), lamb fritters, fried plantains, shrimp croquettes, and sweet potatoes. The defining dish is any one of 24 available gumbos, which are spicy, rich stews. The house gumbo's ingredients sell themselves: shrimp, scallops, snapper, chicken, and kielbasa or andouille sausage. Vegetarian gumbo is available as well, and the signature dessert is coconut pie. Lunch Tue–Fri, dinner Tue–Sun. &. (East)

CENTRO COCINA MEXICANA
2730 J St.
916/442-2552
$$

With the success of the other restaurants in the Paragary Group, Centro Cocina Mexicana's Executive Chef, Kurt Spataro, had the luxury of actually touring the kitchens of Mexico. He learned the original methods of preparing Mexican cuisine and now reproduces authentic regional tastes from the Yucatán Peninsula,

Oaxaca, and Veracruz, among others. The Centro has a full bar with specialty house drinks, including more than 50 aged tequilas. Lunch Mon–Fri, dinner daily. &. (East)

CORNER STONE
2330 J St.
916/441-0948
$

This is one of those little neighborhood storefront diners where, when you're feeling down, they pull you in and call you "Hon." You're home. This is not a place you go to be seen, but a place for comfort food. Breakfast is the best, and it's served all day. Start with a vegetable potato platter, where the home fries are mixed in with tomatoes, mushrooms, onions, bell peppers, and cheese. If you can go further, try the Sunrise Omelette with marinated chicken, tomatoes, avocado, and cheddar cheese. Then push it all down with good-as-home pancakes. Don't even think about going to the gym, at least not for a few hours. Arrive early so you won't get marooned in the back room. There are two other area locations. Open 6 a.m.–2:30 p.m. daily. &. (East)

ERNESTO'S MEXICAN FOOD
16th and S Sts.
916/441-5850
$$

Ernesto's has been consistently rated in local polls as the best Mexican food in the city. Some listings add "and Great Margaritas" to the full restaurant title. Outdoor seating gives you that special "dining in Sacramento feeling"—in a city but not overwhelmed by it, with balmy evening breezes most of the year. Their motto is that Mexican cooking "isn't just our livelihood . . . it's our heritage." Breakfast Sunday, lunch and dinner daily. ♿ (East)

ESPAÑOL
5723 Folsom Blvd.
916/457-1936
$$

Español is all about family: it's family-owned with family-style dining, and even the staff, many of whom have been on hand for years, feel like family. Despite the name (a holdover from its origins as a Basque restaurant), it's been serving reasonably priced Italian food for nearly 80 years in a casual and relaxed atmosphere that's great for a kids' night out. A tureen of minestrone is always served at dinner, and there's a full cocktail lounge and wine list. Lunch and dinner Tue–Sun. ♿ (East)

HABANERO CAVA LATINA
2115 J St.
916/492-0333
$$

Whether you call it "New World" or "Latin Rim," at Habanero Cava Latina you're getting out-of-the-ordinary cuisine from Cuba, Puerto Rico, Central and South America, and the Yucatán Peninsula. Here's an example to whet your appetite: *jocon,* a chicken breast simmered in *pipian verde* sauce from Guatemala, served with avocado, tomatoes, rice, and corn tortillas. The decor will take you to another world, with hot colors of the southern regions reflected in the room's fabrics. The restaurant serves beer and wine only, but try the wine margarita. Live Latin jazz enriches the atmosphere Thursday through Saturday nights. Lunch is served Mon–Fri, dinner served nightly. ♿ (East)

JACK'S URBAN EATS
1230 20th St.
916/444-0307
$

Voted Best New Restaurant for 1999 in *Sacramento* magazine, Jack's Urban Eats also gets votes for Best Diner, Best Place to Take the Kids, Best Place to Dine Inexpensively, Best Sandwiches, and Best Salad Bar. Imagine Boston Market, only more and better. Their entrées include oven-roasted turkey, grilled chicken breast, meatloaf, and flank steak. There are also salads and side dishes to help you create your own cafeteria-style meal. Beer and wine are available, as is outdoor seating. Lunch Mon–Fri, dinner nightly. ♿ (East)

JAMBA JUICE
1901 J St.
916/441-3330
www.jambajuice.com
$

Here's a new answer to "What's for dessert?" Jamba Juice, with several locations throughout the area, offers smoothies loaded with natural ingredients for the healthy set, yet you don't have to sacrifice fun or flavor to get a natural boost with no sugar buzz. All smoothies include one free "juice boost" (of vitamins, antioxidants, or protein) and can be made nondairy. They fall into categories like "Power Smoothies" (which will give you a power boost, burn body fat, increase your immune system, give you extra protein, and maybe even give you a higher rate of return on your mutual funds), non-fruit smoothies, and Berry Patch, Tropical, and Citrus Grove Smoothies. The most expensive is $3.95, and for this you get all the nutrients (and

Our Ten Favorite Places to Eat Vegetarian in Sacramento
by Joyce and John Espinosa

Both Joyce and John were born and raised in Sacramento and John works as a realtor with Realty World Sacramento 2000.

1. **Sacramento Natural Foods Co-op**, 1900 Alhambra Blvd., 916/455-2667. For a quick snack or a hearty lunch, the food is always very good and naturally good for you.

2. **Mums**, 2968 Freeport Blvd., 916/444-3015. Great for a romantic dinner for two. Hearty food that changes with the seasons.

3. **Vic's Ice Cream**, 3199 Riverside Blvd., 916/444-0892. Fresh peach and blackberry ice cream are our summertime favorites. For the non-vegetarian, Vic's also makes great grilled hot dog sandwiches.

4. **Fortune House**, 1211 Broadway, 916/443-3128. Several vegetarian items are on the menu, including mustard greens and mushrooms, but almost anything can be ordered without meat. They also make a fabulous walnut shrimp.

5. **Piatti**, 571 Pavilions Ln., 916/649-8885. Pasta primavera, pesto, and a wide variety of other pasta dishes. Great atmosphere, although a little on the noisy side.

6. **Il Fornaio**, 400 Capitol Mall, 916/446-4100. The food is excellent, although we have to admit that we go there primarily for the bread.

7. **The Fruit Stand at Winding Way and Hackberry.** The best in-season produce and the best of the local growers at the best prices.

8. **Trader Joe's**, 2601 Marconi Ave., 916/481-8797. Bargain priced Ghirardelli chocolate—at less than half what you would pay in San Francisco. They also have the best price on soymilk. Lots of gourmet cheese and wine and nifty things to taste at the ends of the aisles. You must try Trader Joe's veggie taco mix; you'll swear you are eating meat.

9. **Wild Oats Market**, 5104 Arden Way, Carmichael, 916/481-1955. This supermarket-size health food store with low prices is always well stocked.

10. **The California State Fair**, late August through Labor Day only. Here's where you can eat a month's worth of calories in one day. Deep-fried veggies, cinnamon rolls, fresh salads, and smoothies. Lots of ethnic choices for the whole family.

The train depot that houses the Old Spaghetti Factory was one of Harry Truman's whistle-stops during the 1948 presidential election campaign.

satisfaction) of a full meal. A recent addition to the menu is "Souprimos"—four flavors of hot vegetable soup blended in a cup. It's low fat, low calorie, high fiber, and all good things veggie. Open at 7 a.m. Mon–Fri, at 8 a.m. weekends, until 7 p.m. daily. ♿ (East)

LUCKY CAFÉ
1111 21st St.
916/442-9620
$

The Lucky Café is an unassuming diner that people drive to from out of town. You don't have to go figure: it's the food, and the great breakfasts are ample evidence. They serve up smoked duck sausage, whiskey and fennel sausage, pork chops with applesauce, waffles, and a homemade corned beef hash, which, the menu tells you, is "the best corned beef hash you will ever taste." Breakfast and lunch daily. ♿ (East)

MOXIE
2028 H St.
916/443-7585
$$

Eating at Moxie is what living in town should be like: you visit a small place that feels like your neighbor's beautiful, private dining room, and yet it's casual. The menu borrows inspiration from many places, with great results and great flexibility. If you don't see what you want on that day's menu, ask for it anyway and you'll probably get "I

can do that" as a response. The jambalaya is first-rate, and lamb, pasta, seafood, beef, and pork dishes are served with strong, distinct flavorings. The sea bass served atop horseradish mashed potatoes is outstanding. Lunch Mon–Fri, dinner Mon–Sat. ♿ (East)

OLD SPAGHETTI FACTORY
1910 J St.
916/443-2862
$

This is a national chain restaurant with a local touch. It's housed in a historic train depot building where you can be seated inside an old trolley car and still hear working trains rumble by. The menu is simple and inexpensive, with an upbeat, crowded atmosphere that makes it an easy place to bring the kids—all fun and no hassles. Besides sandwiches and salads, they serve pasta and chicken dishes. Try the cream sodas, if not the full service bar or the beer and wine. Takeout is available. Lunch and dinner daily. ♿ (East)

PARAGARY'S BAR AND OVEN
1401 28th St.
916/457-5737
$$

The best known (and most duplicated) of the Paragary Group, the Bar and Oven distinguished itself with a wood-fired pizza oven. They use local produce at its seasonal best in the creation of "New Italian

Cuisine," including dishes like hand-cut rosemary noodles with chicken and pancetta. They have a fireplace and a bar inside, and a patio with a waterfall outside that might make you forget you're in the middle of busy Midtown. Lunch Mon–Fri, dinner nightly. & (East)

RICK'S DESSERT DINER
2322 K St.
916/444-0969
$

The operative word for the menu here is decadence: pies, cakes, tarts, tortes, and cheesecakes. Open from 10 a.m. daily until late at night, Rick's makes it possible to live an entire, brief life on nothing but desserts. It looks like a tile-walled diner on the outside, with art deco touches. One serving is probably enough for two people. & (East)

STREETS OF LONDON PUB
1804 J St.
916/498-1388
$

Opened by three Brits (and not one of them named Nigel), this small storefront establishment is designed to duplicate the street-corner pub experience of England. They serve fish and chips, of course, but their shepherd's pie and bangers and mash move this pub far beyond H. Salt, Esq. Try an English-style breakfast or the Sunday roast. It's a bright and friendly atmosphere that features live English soccer on TV during the weekend, as well as live music and Sunday-evening trivia competitions. They also advertise 17 imported beers on tap. Lunch and dinner daily, breakfast Sat and Sun. & (East)

TAKA'S
1730 S St.
916/446-9628
$$

Sacramento magazine claims that here you'll find the finest sushi you've ever had. Since Taka's has adorned their choices with names like Madonna Roll or Rodman Roll, you know you'll get something beyond the ordinary. They also offer the only sushi delivery service in town. Lunch and dinner Mon–Sat. & (East)

TAPA THE WORLD
21442-4353
15 J St.
$$

First, what's a tapa? A century ago, servers in Spanish courtyard restaurants would place a slice of bread atop a wine glass to keep it free of pests. Gradually, chefs began to embellish the bread, creating toppings meant to be gobbled up by the non-pests paying for the wine. Think of it as Spanish-inspired dim sum: small servings of intensely flavored mini-dishes intended to be mixed and matched. Three or four plates make a full meal for two. The grilled vegetable and calamari tapas are especially tasty. If you're unfamiliar with Spanish wines, ask your waitperson for some equivalents to more familiar varietals, such as a cabernet or merlot, and you may be rewarded with a new favorite. Sidewalk tables are a treat on balmy nights, but stay inside if you'd like to hear the nightly live music at 7:30, which often features beautiful guitar pieces. This is a favorite among Second Saturday gallery-goers (see chapter 6, Museums and Galleries for more information) and has also become popular, almost by default, with locals

For our modern, stressed-out, double-income lifestyle, there is now a fitting cuisine: Somebody Else's. Kerried Away (E) and Gourmet To-Go (E) do takeout at the level of fine dining, creating complete entrées that may be hot or only need minimal reheating upon delivery. Corti Brothers supermarket (E) and the Italian Import Company (multiple locations) have ready-made meals as well, as does the Sacramento Natural Foods Co-op (E).

who want a late meal, as few other places are open until midnight. Tapa the World also serves traditional Spanish cuisine, such as paella and lamb dishes. Lunch and dinner daily. & (East)

33RD STREET BISTRO
3301 Folsom Blvd.
916/455-2233
$$

Here's something you don't see every day: Ranier Panini focaccia slathered with mango mayonnaise and stuffed with roasted chicken, smoked mozzarella cheese, and caramelized onions. Or maybe, if you live in the neighborhood, you *do* see it every day, because the 33rd Street Bistro is a local favorite, one of those places you love to live near. The dish described above is part of the weekend brunch offering, along with berry-loaded pancakes and an omelette made with smoked turkey and Sonoma Jack cheese. For lunch or dinner the menu is inspired by the Pacific Northwest, featuring fresh salmon, hardwood-roasted poultry, and fish dishes, with beers and wines from that region. Braille menus are available. Breakfast, lunch, and dinner daily. & (East)

TWENTY EIGHT
2730 N St.

916/456-2800
$$$

Twenty Eight is the most elegant of the Paragary empire of area restaurants. Want a defining dish for contemporary California cuisine? Try sesame-crusted ahi tuna with crispy noodle cake, stir-fried vegetables, and Chinese black bean sauce. Overstuffed, upholstered booths and chandeliers sparkling in mirrors make you feel like you're touring on a luxury dining car from another era, only with elbow room. French and Asian touches accent the trademark Paragary use of fresh produce, and there's a large selection of French and California wines. Lunch Mon–Fri, dinner Mon–Sat. & (East)

WATERBOY
2000 Capitol Ave.
916/498-9891
$$$

The Waterboy offers a rewarding mix of seasonal freshness with Provençal regional taste, while providing the light atmosphere of a bistro for an experience less intimidating than French restaurants can sometimes be. Start with bread from the Grace Baking Company and finish with one of locally renowned dessert chef Edie Stewart's creations, such as a warm calzone filled with fresh pear under marzipan and drizzled with caramel sauce.

The entrées include veal, lamb, and duck, with sides such as porcini mushrooms in risotto and polenta. Guests must park on the street. Lunch Tue–Fri, dinner Tue–Sun. & (East)

NORTH

ENOTRIA CAFÉ AND WINE BAR
1431 Del Paso Blvd.
916/922-6792
$$

The cuisine at the Enotria Café and Wine Bar reflects both California and the Mediterranean, while the wine list (frequently considered the best in town) reflects the entire planet. Their offerings include almond-grilled meats, fresh fish, and homemade desserts. Be seated indoors or out, then shop in the wine store. The Enotria is at the forefront of renewed interest in the "Uptown" area as an arts district; it's the perfect place to go before or after a Second Saturday art walk through some of the permanent and phantom galleries of the neighborhood (see chapter 6, Museums and Galleries). They host a wine tasting and sale every Tuesday evening, and a singles wine tasting the second and fourth Thursday of the month. Cocktails, banquet facilities, and catering are available. Lunch Tue–Fri, dinner Tue–Sun. (North)

VIRGIN STURGEON
1577 Garden Hwy.
916/921-2694
$$

Here you can take advantage of exactly what ought to be taken advantage of in a river town. The Virgin Sturgeon is literally on the water, located on a barge at the edge of the Sacramento River. The Virgin Sturgeon has a history (writ small) that oddly parallels the city's own. The original barge sank in the late '70s, so the owners soldiered on beneath an improvised tent, doing business as a beer garden. While negotiating to buy another barge, it, too, sank. It was salvaged, towed back into place, and promptly burned to the water line. An interim restaurant was opened on Broadway until the present barge was purchased, and the persistence was well worth it. Walk down a converted airport gangway to find fresh fish and seafood served with imaginative touches, and enough variety to please young and old. Smoked fish appetizers are a must, or try the calamari appetizer for a preview of the light sauces that set off every dish's freshness with just the right touch. Monkfish with drawn butter passes as "poor man's lobster," but has a unique flavor not readily available at most seafood restaurants. The atmosphere is homey, like a country cabin along the river, and it once attracted ex-Governor Jerry Brown and his staff. Lunch Mon–Fri, dinner nightly, brunch Sat–Sun. & (North)

NORTHEAST

ALEXANDER'S MERITAGE
6608 Folsom-Auburn Rd.
Folsom
916/988-7000
$$$

The California/French cuisine by Chef Vincent Paul Alexander at Alexander's Meritage has been rated four stars by the *Sacramento Bee*. A full range of appetizers, with entrées such as ahi tuna, filet mignon, and live Maine lobster are served in a beautiful garden setting. They also offer a full bar and a California wine list. Lunch Tue–Fri, dinner Tue–Sun. ♿ (Northeast)

AMADEUS
2310 Fair Oaks Blvd.
916/922-7070
$$$

Directly across from Pavilions shopping center, Amadeus is part of an area sometimes called "gourmet gulch" along Fair Oaks Boulevard. Recently voted one of the best new restaurants in the area, the menu samples cuisines from throughout the Mediterranean, including French-inspired lamb skewers, assorted pastas, and steaks. Be seated indoors or out and enjoy your meal as you listen to classical music. There's a full bar. Lunch Mon–Fri, dinner nightly. ♿ (Northeast)

BANDERA
2232 Fair Oaks Blvd.
916/922-3524
$$$

A fellow-traveler with Amadeus along "gourmet gulch," Bandera features rotisserie-cooked leg of lamb, jambalaya, Seattle-style barbecued salmon, prime rib, and a wide choice of salads. A favorite in local polls, Bandera consistently gets high marks for quick service and reasonable prices for its high-quality food. Dinner nightly. ♿ (Northeast)

CAFÉ EAST MEETS WEST
1841 Howe Ave.
916/483-7062
www.cafeeastmeetswest.com
$$$

Brand new to Sacramento, Café East Meets West has a subtitle: Eurasian Fusion Cooking and Sushi Bar. This is the quintessence of California dining, with the world's cuisines coming together in unexpected harmonies. Weekly dinner specials reflect what this fusion is all about. From a recent October menu: assorted sushi with *uni* sauce, hearty seafood and spinach miso soup, Sardinian lobster salad with wasabi vinaigrette, sautéed chicken breast with white truffles and port wine glaze, Korean pear tart *tatin* with raspberry honey compote. It's probably no accident that the restaurant is located across the street from a Mercedes Benz dealership, but it's also the future of fine dining. Bring two or three wallets. Lunch Sun–Thu, dinner nightly. (Northeast)

CHINOIS CITY WOK
3535 Fair Oaks Blvd. (at Watt)
916/485-8690
$$

Though Chinese cuisine is emphasized at the Chinois City Wok, it's not the only choice. You can also get Thai basil roasted chicken breast and braised lamb shanks—a result of owner/chef David SooHoo's leadership in the "fusion" movement. His success here enabled him to open Bamboo in Midtown as well. Judged one of the best restaurants in the city by *Sacramento* magazine, the atmosphere is family-friendly. A discounted takeout menu is available. Lunch Mon–Fri, dinner nightly. ♿ (Northeast)

EAT YOUR VEGETABLES
1841 Howe Ave.
916/922-8413
$

A favorite of local vegetarians, Eat Your Vegetables attracts diners of every ilk, perhaps drawn by the

GREATER SACRAMENTO

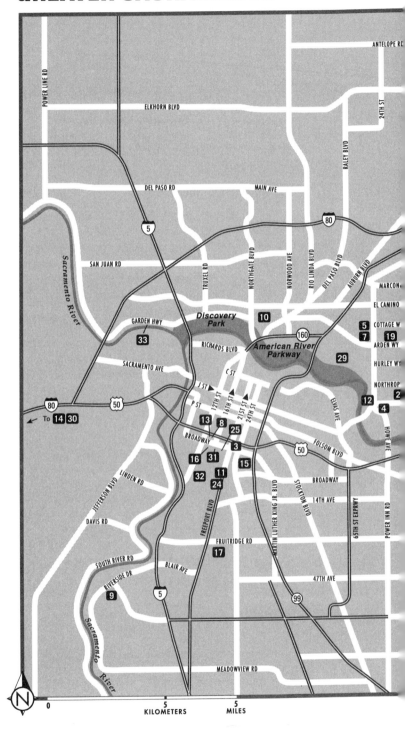

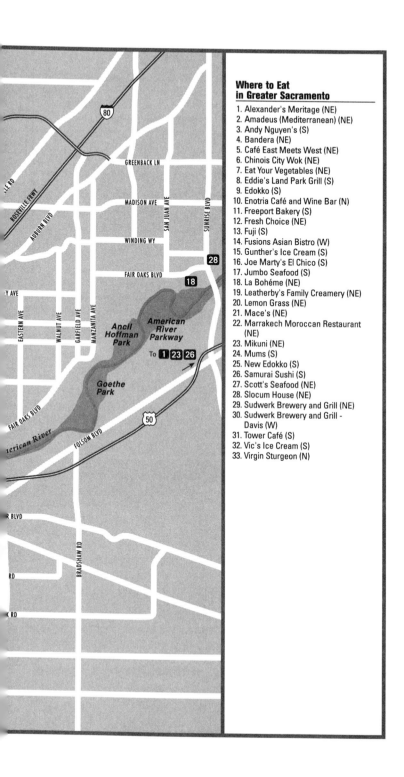

Where to Eat
in Greater Sacramento

1. Alexander's Meritage (NE)
2. Amadeus (Mediterranean) (NE)
3. Andy Nguyen's (S)
4. Bandera (NE)
5. Café East Meets West (NE)
6. Chinois City Wok (NE)
7. Eat Your Vegetables (NE)
8. Eddie's Land Park Grill (S)
9. Edokko (S)
10. Enotria Café and Wine Bar (N)
11. Freeport Bakery (S)
12. Fresh Choice (NE)
13. Fuji (S)
14. Fusions Asian Bistro (W)
15. Gunther's Ice Cream (S)
16. Joe Marty's El Chico (S)
17. Jumbo Seafood (S)
18. La Bohéme (NE)
19. Leatherby's Family Creamery (NE)
20. Lemon Grass (NE)
21. Mace's (NE)
22. Marrakech Moroccan Restaurant (NE)
23. Mikuni (NE)
24. Mums (S)
25. New Edokko (S)
26. Samurai Sushi (S)
27. Scott's Seafood (NE)
28. Slocum House (NE)
29. Sudwerk Brewery and Grill (NE)
30. Sudwerk Brewery and Grill - Davis (W)
31. Tower Café (S)
32. Vic's Ice Cream (S)
33. Virgin Sturgeon (N)

Evolution of a Bakery

Tarts and Truffles began as a traditional bakery, and, as many bakeries do in order to compete, added catered lunches to their goods. Now Tarts and Truffles offers cyberlunches. Tarts and Truffles will deliver a high quality lunch to your location for $8.95, including bottled water, plastic utensils, and a cookie. All you have to do is click on their boxed-lunch delivery site on the Internet (www.mealsatwork.com), fill out a form, and order at least five items by 4 p.m. of the day before they're needed. If you need your food the same day, you can still order it on the Web and then pick it up yourself at 5050 Arden Way (at Fair Oaks Blvd.). Call 916/488-0100 for directions.

restaurant's offer of "all you can eat." Soups, salads, baked potatoes, pastas, baked desserts made at the in-house bakery (which also turns out muffins, scones, pizza, and French bread), frozen yogurt, and fresh fruit will fill you up without filling your arteries. Lunch and dinner are served here daily. &
(Northeast)

FRESH CHOICE
535 Howe Ave.
916/649-8046
$
One of three in the area, this Fresh Choice is a place where you can go vegetarian and not suffer from lack of choice. The salad bar is said to be 60 feet long (but who's measuring?), with dessert and fruit bars as well. Baked potatoes, soups, muffins, and pastas are available and can be washed down with beer or wine if you like. Lunch and dinner daily. &
(Northeast)

LA BOHÉME
9634 Fair Oaks Blvd.
916/965-1071
$$$
The menu at La Bohéme is haute cuisine, with the ingredients, techniques, and compositions of traditional French cookery. But it's not a menu chiseled in stone. On any given night, it might offer kangaroo as one of its game dishes or, more familiarly, a rack of lamb, but prepared with a Thai curry sauce, a modern take on the tradition. Enjoy the romantic atmosphere either casually on an outdoor deck or, more formally, in the dining rooms. The essence here is classic fare sparked with adventurous sauces. "Surf and turf," for example, becomes filet mignon and prawns, cooked in a peppery cream sauce laced with sherry and roasted garlic. The large wine list covers a wide price range of mostly Californian selections, with French and Italian labels included.

Lunch Mon–Fri, dinner Mon–Sat. (Northeast)

LEATHERBY'S FAMILY CREAMERY
2333 Arden Way
916/920-8382
$

As the name indicates, Leatherby's is a family place, serving light fare such as sandwiches, burgers, soups, and salads. But the key word is dessert. Homemade treats keep Leatherby's on list after list of local favorites, especially for ice cream and their baked-on-site pies. Seating for large groups is available. Lunch and dinner daily, open late for that must-have blast of calories. & (Northeast)

LEMON GRASS CAFÉ
601 Munroe St.
916/486-4891
$$–$$$

The Sacramento *News and Review* recently pronounced Mai Pham— cookbook author and owner/chef of the Lemon Grass Café—"best chef to translate memories into food." Mai Pham has re-created her memories of a childhood spent in Vietnam into authentic experiences for the rest of us, with the cuisine of her homeland. The food of Thailand is represented as well. Pots of *pho* (a broth to which customers add meat and vegetables), *banh cuon* (rice rolls stuffed with shrimp), and *bun rieu* (rice vermicelli soup with shrimp dumplings) are just a sampling of choices on a menu cooked with ingredients fresh from local farmers' markets. Lunch Mon–Fri, dinner Mon–Sat. & (Northeast)

MACE'S
501 Pavilions Ln.
916/922-0222
$$$

The decor at Mace's is impossible to ignore—it's elegant and bizarre at the same time. If you can get past the implication that British Colonial Africa is a period in history worth duplicating, then it's a pip to walk by the massive bar and gaze at the animal heads on the wall. The food is excellent, and the Sunday brunch is especially imaginative. Veal, fresh seafood, chicken, pasta, and lamb are part of the full menu, and food is offered weekdays in the bar between lunch and dinner. You're right in the Pavilions shopping center, in the retail/gustatory flow, as it were. Lunch Mon–Fri, dinner nightly, brunch Sun. & (Northeast)

MARRAKECH MOROCCAN RESTAURANT
1833 Fulton Ave.
916/486-1944
$$$

The excellent food, exotic ambience, and belly dancing (not to mention fezzes worn by the waiters) at the Marrakech transport you across cultures. Featuring authentic Moroccan dishes, such as phyllo dough stuffed with chicken, lamb, or beef, the restaurant was voted Best Group Dining Experience in the *News and Review.* You sit on cushions around low tables and eat with your bare hands, the way your kids would like to eat every meal. The fare also includes lentil soup, lamb with eggplant, chicken with honey and prunes, couscous, and *pastilla,* a hot pastry filled with ground meat and egg and then dusted with powdered sugar. Dinner Tue–Sun. & (Northeast)

MIKUNI
4323 Hazel Ave.
916/961-2112

www.mikunisushi.com
$$

This restaurant and sushi bar celebrates a combination of "American heart and Japanese flavor." To the palate, it's all Japanese, and quite wonderful, using creative and more complex ingredients than most Japanese menus. There's also a salad bar with Mikuni's own dressings, which you can take home bottled. The American heart must refer to the bustle of this hugely popular spot. Though located in a nondescript strip mall, the joint jumps, especially on weekend evenings when patrons pile up at the bar while waiting for tables. (The place has expanded at least twice, and they've opened a second Mikuni, in Roseville, as well.) This is sushi at its finest, with seasonings that enhance the basic wasabi and shoyu. (Try the salmon skin and spicy tuna rolls.) The restaurant also features a full range of entrées, including "sea steak" (seared tuna) and combination dinners beautifully presented. Catering is available. Lunch and dinner Mon–Sat. ⅅ (Northeast)

SCOTT'S SEAFOOD
545 Munroe
Loehmann's Plaza
916/489-1822
$$$

Even though the Scott's Seafood chain started in San Francisco, Sacramentans have no trouble citing the local version of Scott's as the best seafood restaurant in town year after year. The ingredients are deeply flavorful yet still inviting to young tastes, making Scott's ideal for a family outing in which no one will be deprived. The cioppino is usually worth checking out; otherwise, go for the day's special—

freshness is the key. For non-fish eaters, try the Angus steaks. An oyster bar and a wide choice of desserts round out the experience. A second Scott's is located in Folsom. Banquet facilities are available. Lunch Mon–Sat, dinner nightly. ⅅ (Northeast)

SLOCUM HOUSE
7992 California Ave.
916/961-7211
$$$

Slocum House was voted Most Romantic Restaurant by the readers of *Sacramento* magazine. How can you beat that? Well, with the food, for starters. It's based on French cuisine, but embellished with Asian and Italian influences, all of which adds up to a New American cuisine. The setting is historical as well as romantic, with a courtyard that can accommodate 85, shaded by a century-old maple. It's like visiting a well-off family at their home, a secluded hilltop house surrounded by gardens. The menu includes Australian lamb loin, Pacific king salmon, and almond wood–grilled filet mignon. Lunch Tue–Fri, dinner Tue–Sun, brunch Sun. ⅅ (Northeast)

SOUTH

ANDY NGUYEN'S
2007 Broadway
916/736-1157
$

Jump into the Vietnamese dining experience (if you haven't already) at this unpretentious restaurant. At Andy Nguyen's, you can see the meat and seafood grilling at the table (in fact you'll do a lot of the work yourself, for a custom meal), but it's a simple enough procedure

Local Pizza Flavor

Unwilling to visit a new city without knowing where the fast-food pizza lies? Not to worry: Sacramento abounds with national franchises for pizza, some of which make a fine pie. But for a local taste, consider:

- *Original Pete's Pizza*, 916/442-6770 (East): Great for families because the kids can get an individual pizza while Mom and Dad check out the pastas.
- *Paesano's*, 916/447-8646 (East): A fine Italian restaurant with a full range of choices; consistently gets votes from locals for best pizza.
- *Pieces*, 916/441-1949 (East): Yes, you can get individual pieces of gourmet pizza pie.
- *Pizzeria Classico*, 916/721-1111 (Northeast): Run by the folks at Il Palio, a fine Italian restaurant in the area.
- *Steve's Place Pizza*, 916/920-8600 (Northeast): Considered the best place to take kids for pizza, with distractions for (and booths to contain) the little ones.
- *Zelda's Gourmet Pizza*, 916/447-1400 (East): Aims (as their name indicates) for the connoisseur, which in this case means garlic-laden, Chicago-style pizza.

for kids. Once cooked, the meats can be combined with herbs, vegetables, and fish sauce, and then wrapped in rice paper to create a "Vietnamese taco." A Thai sauce and a pineapple sauce served over sautéed shrimp or chicken are house specialties. There's a second location in Rancho Cordova. Beer and wine are available. Open daily 10 a.m. to 10 p.m. ♿ (South)

EDDIE'S LAND PARK GRILL
1517 Broadway
916/441-1297
$
Eddie's enjoys a great local reputation for breakfast, which features fried rice (better than Wheaties). Steak sandwiches, daily specials, a jalapeño burger, and a garlic burger round out the menu. Breakfast and lunch daily. ♿ (South)

EDOKKO
358 Florin Rd.
916/395-0632
NEW EDOKKO
1724 Broadway

916/448-2828

$

These restaurants are related by a complex ownership history that even some of their employees cannot explain, but their menus (and the informal atmosphere) are virtually identical. What's most important to the customer, however, is that they are the best places in town for Japanese-style noodles. Though traditional selections (tempura, sushi, and teriyaki—more than 100 items in all) are offered in simple elegance, what establishes both Edokkos as the Japanese equivalent of "good, down-home cooking" is their variety of noodle dishes. Ramen (thin noodles made from wheat flour and egg), *udon* (thick noodles made from wheat flour), and soba (thick, dark noodles made from buckwheat flour) come in a huge bowl, with a rich broth enhanced by any number of items, such as chicken, tempura, egg, and vegetables. The "Challenge Ramen" is for lovers of mouth burn, ordered from "medium hot" to "crazy hot." Lunch and dinner Mon–Sat. & (South)

FREEPORT BAKERY
2966 Freeport Blvd.
916/442-4256
$

While not a restaurant, this is a great place to start the day. An authentic European-style bakery, the Freeport offers Danish pastries, cinnamon rolls, bear claws, breadsticks, brownies, and tortes to go with your coffee or espresso.

Nestled next to Mums (and across the street from McDonald's, if vegetarianism is too scary), the bakery is owned by Walter and Marlene Goetzeler. Walter is a third-generation baker, and it's fit-

ting that here in the heart of pear country, one of his specialties is *pearfladen,* a baked, buttery pastry dough with cinnamon, ginger, and cloves flavoring a pear filling. Open from 7 a.m. Mon–Sat, from 8 a.m. Sun. & (South)

FUJI
2422 13th St. at Broadway
916/446-4135
$$

Considered by many locals to be the best Japanese restaurant in town, Fuji offers a full menu, including sushi, tempura, sukiyaki, and combination dinners. Family-owned and -operated, the restaurant's traditional atmosphere is enhanced by servers in kimonos. There is a full bar, and banquet facilities are available. Lunch Mon–Fri, dinner nightly. & (South)

GUNTHER'S ICE CREAM
2801 Franklin Blvd.
916/457-6646
$

Besting *Happy Days,* this soda shop, dating back to the '40s, is the real thing. The same so-bad-it's-good neon sign welcomes you as it did then: a soda jerk flipping ice-cream scoops over his head from hand to hand. Gunther's has unique flavors, with sandwiches available, too. Open daily from 10 a.m. until late evening. & (South)

JOE MARTY'S EL CHICO
1500 Broadway
916/448-7062
$

This was where fans of the Pacific Coast League's Sacramento Solons used to come after the game, before the Edmunds Field stadium was demolished to make way for a Target

Chef School

Did you ever get a haircut for next to nothing at the local beauty school? The same principle is at work on campus at American River College (4700 College Oak Dr.) in the Fair Oaks area. A full meal is served at lunchtime, Monday through Friday, for the prix fixe of just $10. And it's not just any meal. The Culinary Arts and Hospitality Program is training cooks, and they are working from the menus of well-known chefs. Recent offerings included recipes found in Frances Mayes's novel, Under the Tuscan Sun, *and, during another week, they reproduced the menu of the* Titanic. *Lunch is served at two seatings (11:30 a.m. and 1 p.m.) in Room 506 of the Home Economics Building. For reservations and directions, call 916/484-8526.*

parking lot. But the sports bar is still here—the kind of neighborhood joint that just feels so comfortable. The walls are covered with baseball memorabilia, a collection that began with founder Joe Marty's team photos from when he played with the San Francisco Seals. One shot shows him posing with some guy named Joe DiMaggio. Joe Marty's serves burgers, pizza, and Bloody Marys. Breakfast, lunch, and dinner daily. & (South)

JUMBO SEAFOOD
5651 Freeport Blvd.
916/391-8221
$$
Jumbo is simply one of the best Chinese restaurants in town. As you'd expect, you go there for the seafood, which includes salt-baked shrimp, sweet-and-sour whole rock cod, and lots of rich, garlicky sauces. It's

an unpretentious, brightly lit place along a commercial strip of road, but what it lacks in ambience it makes up for in flavor. Try a hot pot, a deeply flavored broth filled with a combination of meats, vegetables, seafood, and tofu. There will be a line at the door on weekend evenings. Lunch and dinner daily. & (South)

MUMS
2968 Freeport Blvd.
916/444-3015
$$
This gourmet vegetarian restaurant serves complex, interesting, and satisfying meals throughout the day, and has become a favorite place to do brunch. To those who might think a vegetarian breakfast is broccoli and wheat germ, think again. Mums serves a dish called Artichoke Hearts Benedict, which consists of

two English muffins topped with poached eggs or grilled tempeh, sautéed artichoke hearts, wilted spinach, and Gruyère cheese, and all of it covered with hollandaise. Or to go more simply, try the apple buttermilk pancakes. There's also the Avocado Rarebit: tomatoes, avocados, artichoke hearts, and jack cheese, baked on sourdough bread and topped with various sauces. Vegetarians are not suffering. Plus, you get a gallery of local artwork. They also offer vegan desserts. Catering and private party facilities are available, and there's live music on the second Wednesday and fourth Sunday of the month. Lunch Mon–Fri, dinner Mon–Sat, brunch Sat–Sun. & (South)

SAMURAI SUSHI
12251 Folsom Blvd.
(Hwy. 50 at the Hazel exit)
Rancho Cordova
916/353-1112
$$
One can only imagine what a "state-of-the-art sushi bar" might be, but they have one here. For over 40 years they've been serving an incredible variety of sushi, along with traditional dinners and udon in the dining room. Lunch Mon–Sat, dinner nightly. & (South)

TOWER CAFÉ
1518 Broadway
916/441-0222
$$
Located next to the place "where it all started" (the original Tower Records—see chapter 9, Shopping), the Tower Café has its own distinct place in the Tower compound. Featuring "world cuisine," they offer dishes from Jamaica, Africa, Brazil, or Thailand, and top them off with a

baked dessert made on the premises. Outdoor seating at the inviting "urban patio" lets you scope out the length of Broadway from beneath umbrellas. Open at 8 a.m. daily, brunch available on weekends until 2 p.m.; lunch and dinner daily. & (South)

VIC'S ICE CREAM
3199 Riverside Blvd.
916/448-0892
Family-owned and family-oriented, Vic's Ice Cream looks like a striped-awning malt shop straight out of *Ozzie and Harriet,* only it's authentic—a happy contradiction in terms. The soda fountain serves dozens of flavors of ice cream, malts, sodas, and phosphates, plus sandwiches. Vic's opened in 1947, and wall-mounted photos from the past attest that the place has not changed one iota since. Open daily. & (South)

WEST

FUSIONS ASIAN BISTRO
2171 Cowell Blvd.
Oak Shade Town Center
Davis
530/297-7100
$-$$
"Honey, let's go out for Burmese tonight." If this is not a frequently spoken sentiment in your home, it soon may be. Fusions, in the college town of Davis, blends ingredients and cooking practices of Burma with those of China, Thailand, Korea, Japan, Vietnam, and India into a truly modern take on Asian cuisine. The starting point is noodles, with plenty of vegetarian choices in the mix. For example, try "man-a-mango": ripe mango tossed with

spinach ramen noodles, lemon juice, chili flakes, and roasted garlic—a combo that imparts a sweet fruitiness rather than the hot curry effect of more traditional Burmese dishes. Fowl, seafood, and darker meats can also be ordered with the noodles, and they offer appetizers like Korean short ribs. Carefully selected wines are available to complement the sweet spiciness of the meals. Lunch and dinner daily. ♿ (West)

SUDWERK BREWERY AND GRILL
2001 Second St.
Davis
530/758-8700
$$

Forget that it's brewed all over the world—there's still a strong German association with beer. In 1999 Sudwerk was voted Best Microbrewery, as well as Best German Cuisine, by readers of *Sacramento* magazine. They've got the whole package. The Sudwerk Privatbrauerei Hübsch is bottled right in Davis. It's a fine lager and a great starting point for discovering the difference (if you don't already know) between what's brewed on these premises and what's sold over the counter at 7-Eleven. A second Sudwerk is across the street from Arden Fair Mall, next to Cal Expo (1375 Exposition Blvd., 916/925-6623; Northeast). ♿ (West)

© Tom Myers 1999

5

SIGHTS AND ATTRACTIONS

For the visitor, Sacramento is inextricable from its history. As California's first important city (it dwarfed Los Angeles soon after its inception), this commercial and agricultural center gave California its American identity, which in turn resulted in statehood. Sacramento has become a living tableau of how California came to be. Even the abundant parks reflect what was once lost (though, in some cases, happily preserved) during the explosive origins of a city born almost overnight in 1849. The Old Sacramento Historic District—the largest cluster of preserved buildings in the West—is a gathering of museums that capture the past in archives and artifacts, and the old buildings themselves are history. Regional parks and nature trails have helped keep natural history alive as well in this river valley/floodplain, with its band of riparian habitat that once wound through a grass and oak savanna. By itself, the city would offer fascinating glimpses of the local past. As California's capital, Sacramento's modern, evolving center frames that history while showcasing entertainment, culture, and recreation representative of the entire state.

All sights and attractions listed below are considered wheelchair accessible.

OLD SACRAMENTO HISTORIC DISTRICT

Saved from "improvement" (and/ or razing) in the '60s, the old west end of town is now reborn as a liv-ing museum, housing businesses, shops, restaurants, and even residences, while preserving the brick buildings which survived fire and flood (or replaced the ones that did not). More than 5 million visitors a year drop in at the visitors center, where maps for self-guided tours are found (1101 Second St.). Parking is at either the north end (beneath the freeway; enter at I St.) or the south end (in the parking structure locals refer to as "the Brick," entered from Capitol Mall), with limited street parking in Old Sac itself. A waterside Embassy Suites and new riverfront restaurants are on the way, as Old Sac thrives. The District includes the following, and much more:

B.F. HASTINGS BUILDING
Second and J Sts.
916/440-4263
www.wellsfargo.com/about /museum
An amazing amount of history occurred in this one building. It held the western terminus of the Pony Express; the first permanent home of the California Supreme Court; the first Wells Fargo office in Sacramento; the office of Theodore Judah, who designed the route of the transcontinental railroad; and the office of the Alta California State Telegraph Company, where the first transcontinental telegram doomed the Pony Express located in the same building. The offices are now restored, and admission is free. Open daily 10–5. (Central)

BIG FOUR BUILDING (HUNTINGTON, HOPKINS AND CO. HARDWARE STORE)
113 I St.
916/323-7234
www.csrmf.org
Named for the four financiers—Leland Stanford, Mark Hopkins, Collis Huntington, and Charles Crocker—who carried out Theodore Judah's grand design for a transcontinental railroad, the original building was torn down to make way for Interstate 5, then reconstructed, using the original brick, on its present site. The hardware store is a display of items a 49er might have bought on his way into the hills. There's an impressive library of reference works in the Railroad Museum upstairs, near the boardroom where Judah's idea was first proposed. Free, open daily. (Central)

CALIFORNIA MILITARY MUSEUM
1119 Second St.
916/442-2883
www.militarymuseum.org
The emphasis is on the state's militias and armed forces, from pre-statehood to the present (see chapter 6, Museums and Galleries).

TRIVIA

The Eagle's first performance was *The Spectre of the Forest*, starring Elizabeth Ray, of New Zealand's Royal Theatre. Three months later, the flood waters that destroyed the Eagle arrived during a performance, allowing the spectators to sit on railings and shove one another into the rising water for amusement until the final curtain.

Huntington, Hopkins and Co. Hardware, Old Sacramento, p. 87

Guided tours are available (make arrangements in advance). Tue–Sun 10–4. $2.25 adults, $1.50 seniors, $1 service members in uniform and children 5–12. (Central)

CALIFORNIA STATE RAILROAD MUSEUM
Second and I Sts.
916/445-7387, 916/445-6645 (recorded information)
www.csrmf.org
Finest, best, largest—it's impossible to overstate the effect this museum has on anyone who ever cared a whit about trains. Sitting almost atop the site of the first spike driven for the transcontinental railroad, the 100,000-square-foot facility houses not only vintage trains (including the first and last steam engines built by Central Pacific), but a still-working turntable with service pits where the engines are restored (see chapter 6, Museums and Galleries). Daily 10–5. $6 adults and children 13 and over, $3 children 6–12. Ticket includes admission to the passenger station below. (Central)

CENTRAL PACIFIC RAILROAD PASSENGER DEPOT
Front St. near J St.
916/455-7837
Here is the original western terminus of the transcontinental railroad. On

TRIVIA

The Pony Express's first ride began at a telegraph office on Montgomery Street in San Francisco, then continued aboard a steamboat upriver. Upon landing in Sacramento, rider Sam Hamilton remounted his pony and began the harsh journey east to Saint Joe.

OLD SACRAMENTO HISTORIC DISTRICT

Sights in Old Sacramento Historic District

1. B.F. Hastings Building
2. Big Four Building
3. California Military Museum
4. California State Railroad Museum
5. Central Pacific Railroad Passenger Depot
6. *Delta King* Hotel
7. The Discovery Museum History Center
8. Eagle Theatre
9. Lady Adams Building
10. Old Sacramento Schoolhouse
11. Pony Express Monument
12. Theodore Judah Monument
13. Travels Through Time Science Fiction Museum

the same site as the first building, this historic reconstruction replicates the ambience passengers felt in the 1870s. Vintage steam engines and passenger cars are here, brought in on tracks connected to the museum's turntable. On summer weekends (April through September) and the first weekend of every month October through December, you can leave from the CPRR Freight Depot aboard the Sacramento Southern Railroad Excursion trains. The Depot is found right next door along the waterfront shops of the embarcadero. $5 adults, $2 children 6–12. (Central)

DELTA KING HOTEL
1000 Front St.
916/444-5464
The sister ship of the *Delta Queen* (of Mississippi River fame), these two ships once plied the river between Sacramento and San Francisco, from the 1920s to the 1940s, going one way and changing places daily. The *King* is now permanently moored as a hotel and restaurant (see chapter 3, Where to Stay; and chapter 4, Where to Eat). Visitors are discouraged from wandering the decks unless they are patrons of the dining room or hotel, but the best views, in any case, are from the pier. Free (to look at). (Central)

THE DISCOVERY MUSEUM HISTORY CENTER
101 I St.
916/264-7057
www.thediscovery.org
This museum is an exact replica of the city's first City Hall and Waterworks. It features hands-on science and technology exhibits which are very interactive and educational, but don't tell anyone that

TIP

The Jazz Jubilee music sites are wheelchair accessible, and shuttle buses are equipped with lifts. Loaner wheelchairs are available in Old Sacramento and at Cal Expo. Sign-language interpreters are at selected performances, and personal FM receivers are available at the Sacramento Convention Center concert site and the Crest Theatre. Jubilee programs are published on cassette and in Braille.

(see chapter 6, Museums and Galleries; and chapter 7, Kids' Stuff). Tue–Sun 10–5, Mon 10–5 during the summer and on holidays. $5 adults, $4 seniors and children 13–17, $3 children 6–12. (Central)

EAGLE THEATRE
925 Front St. near J St.
916/323-6343 (rental), 916/445-4209 (tours), 916/207-1226 (Runaway Stage Productions), 916/445-6645, ext. 4# (scheduled theatrical performances)
The Eagle Theatre has a very special history—it was the first building constructed as a theater in California. This reproduction duplicates the theater destroyed by floods soon after its original construction (see chapter 7, Kids' Stuff). (Central)

HISTORIC AUDIO TOUR
Visitors Center
Second and K Sts.
Pick up tokens at the visitors center, or pay a bit more with quarters at nine kiosks located throughout Old Sac. A "Mark Twain" voice narrates the tour, with sound effects and tales from the Gold Rush. Learn about buildings, famous people, and business practices of the era. Daily 10–5. $4 for a set of nine

tokens, or 50 cents at each station. (Central)

HORSE-DRAWN CARRIAGES
The period ambience of Old Sac is enhanced if you climb aboard one of many available carriage rides. The south end near the schoolhouse is a turnaround point and a good place to catch them, but ask any driver you see, who will then recite narratives which take you back to the Gold Rush era as the horses clomp up and down the streets. Cowboys Carriage and wagon (916/681-3812), Elegant Dreams Carriage Service (916/441-5286), and Old Sacramento Carriage Company at 304 West M Street (916/991-6370) are the companies that transport you. Available daily 9 a.m. to 10 p.m. A 15-minute ride is $10, a trip to the state capitol and back is $50. Carriages hold six adults, covered wagons can accommodate up to 15 adults. Prices and times may vary by company, but the $10 ride is a consistent standard. (Central)

JAZZ JUBILEE
916/372-5277
nshartma@pacbell.net
This annual festival during Memorial Day weekend is centered in Old

Sac but has grown so large that it has spread to other venues around town as well. (The Firehouse Restaurant on Second Street—formerly known as Engine Company #3—is the oldest continuous showplace for the Jubilee.) Sponsored by the Sacramento Traditional Jazz Society, the Jubilee was once known as a Dixieland festival, but it now touches on all kinds of musical tastes—as long as they're jazz (you'll find blues, gospel, Latin jazz, swing, western swing, and zydeco). The event showcases more than 125 bands from around the world. Prices vary. (Central)

LADY ADAMS BUILDING
K St., between Front and Second Sts.
While not architecturally distinct from the surrounding buildings, it's interesting to know that the Lady Adams Building was the only building to survive one of the city's early devastating fires. It endured because it was constructed from the bricks that had served as ballast for the ship *Lady Adams* as she sailed around Cape Horn. Sacramentans learned this lesson well; the city was rebuilt in brick and cast iron. Free. (Central)

TRIVIA

Each year the Jubilee hosts more than 800 RVs at the Cal Expo site. Park here and enjoy this "jazz center," then catch a shuttle to Old Sac or other venues to hear even more. For Cal Expo space reservations, call 916/372-5277.

OLD SACRAMENTO SCHOOLHOUSE
Front and L Sts.
916/483-8818
This is a preserved one-room school building from the nineteenth century (see chapter 7, Kids' Stuff). Mon–Fri 10–4, Sat–Sun noon–4. Free. (Central)

PONY EXPRESS MONUMENT
Second and J Sts.
This monument is a tribute to the 80 young men who rode the 2,000-mile trail in less than 10 days to deliver mail to and from Saint Joseph, Missouri. (Central)

SECOND GREAT GOLD RUSH
Old Sacramento
Once a year, Old Sac is closed to auto traffic, its cobblestones covered with dirt, and the streets filled with "living history" characters who reenact Gold Rush days. The Rush features special entertainment, food, and arts-and-crafts demonstrations. Usually in early September. (Central)

THEODORE JUDAH MONUMENT
Second and L Sts.
Forgotten beside the financial giants dubbed "the Big Four," Judah was the visionary engineer who conceived the train route that would conquer the Sierra Nevada. (Central)

TRAVELS THROUGH TIME SCIENCE FICTION MUSEUM
1017-B Front St.
916/444-2320
Daily tours by docents will take you through 100 years of largely TV- and movie-inspired science-fiction memorabilia (see chapter 7, Kids' Stuff). (Central)

© Tom Myers 1996

The rotunda in the State Capitol, p. 94

CENTRAL

ALKALI FLAT HISTORIC HOUSES
Named for the lime deposits found in the soil, Alkali Flat, north of the downtown business district, was the first distinct residential neighborhood in the city. Governors, judges, wealthy merchants, and community leaders lived here before the wealthy drifted to other neighborhoods and Alkali Flat became a working-class area. The National Register of Historic Places lists three historic districts in this neighborhood alone, where homes might have Victorian, Queen Anne, Classical, or Craftsman styling touches. Elaborate, excessive decoration is the hallmark of the several architectural styles lumped under "Victorian." Another distinct neighborhood characteristic is the "Delta Basement" in many homes, where the first floor is elevated above street level, reached by a full story of stairs, to resist flooding. Look for these beautiful homes on 9th, 10th, and 11th Streets, between E and H Streets. The oldest remaining home in the city is the J. Neely Johnson house at 1029 F Street, built in 1854. (Central)

CALIFORNIA PEACE OFFICERS MEMORIAL
10th St. and Capitol Mall
800/937-6722
www.camemorial.org
A bronze and granite tribute to the more than 1,300 peace officers in California who've given their lives in the line of duty, this memorial has a quiet dignity next to the Library and Courts Building. It's located on the Capitol Mall circle at the west side of the capitol. (Central)

CALIFORNIA STATE ARCHIVES
1020 O St.
916/653-7715
www.ss.ca.gov
The California State Archives are housed in a massive new state building that takes up an entire

---

TRIVIA

The original state constitution was written on animal skins in both English and Spanish. Until 1879, all laws and regulations were required to be written in both languages because nine of the state's 48 "founding fathers" were Hispanic.

CENTRAL SACRAMENTO

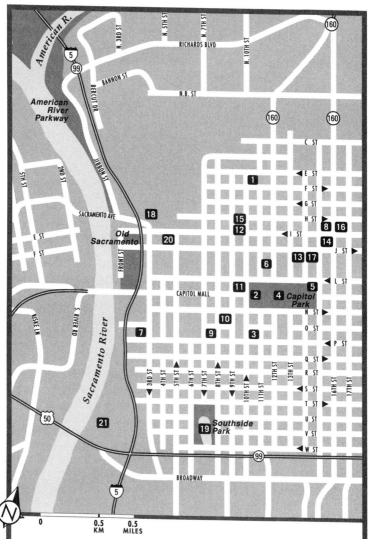

Sights and Attractions in Central Sacramento

1. Alkali Flat Historic Houses
2. California Peace Officers Memorial
3. California State Archives
4. California State Capitol and Capitol Park
5. California Vietnam Veterans Memorial
6. Cathedral of the Blessed Sacrament
7. Crocker Art Museum
8. Governor's Mansion State Historic Park
9. Heilbron House
10. Leland Stanford Museum
11. Library and Courts Buildings
12. Llewelyn Williams Mansion (Sacramento International Hostel)
13. Sacramento Convention Center
14. Sacramento Memorial Auditorium
15. Sacramento Metropolitan Arts Commission
16. Sacramento Power Station A
17. Saint Paul's Episcopal Church
18. Southern Pacific Depot/Amtrak Station
19. Southside Park
20. Sun Yat Sen Memorial
21. Towe Auto Museum

Governor's Mansion, p. 96

block and also contains the Golden State Museum. You'll find historical California documents and accessible displays including the *Constitution Wall* (see chapter 6, Museums and Galleries). Open for research Mon–Fri except holidays, 9:30–4. (Central)

CALIFORNIA STATE CAPITOL AND CAPITOL PARK
10th and L Sts.
916/324-0333
www.assembly.ca.gov
The capitol dominates the city's center, not with height but grandeur. Built in the 1860s and '70s, its gold-tipped dome soars above classical columns and pediments, which glow white in the intense California sun. Even while hemmed in by state office buildings on all sides, the capitol maintains a stateliness, with ample grounds, including Capitol Park, where flowers and trees from throughout the world have been planted in a symbolic gesture (see chapter 8, Parks, Gardens, and Rec-

reation Areas). Tours begin in the basement, in room B-27, on the hour. Also in the basement are museum rooms, which document not only the history of the building's construction, but the huge task (completed in the 1980s) of renovating, as well as seismically retrofitting, the capitol. The building was gutted and completely reconstructed from the inside out, and the museum displays are a primer on construction techniques from an era of grand architectural embellishment. Upstairs are the real

TRIVIA

All the interior hardware in the Governor's Mansion is original. The ornamental bronze was installed for the first owner, Albert Gallatin, who was the Huntington, Hopkins and Co. Hardware president. He got a deal.

prizes of restoration: rescued marble mosaic floors, hand-carved staircases, and rooms preserved as they were at the turn of the last century. It's amazing to see the desk where the secretary of state once signed driver's licenses, one at a time, or where the treasurer opened his office safe to fund the state's business. It would be worth the price of admission (if there were one—the tour is free) just to see Jerry Brown's official portrait mounted next to George Deukmejian's, Brown's staid successor. Tour guides enjoy asking schoolkids if Brown's semi-abstract portrait makes him appear to have a different personality from the other governors. Indeed. Daily 9–5. (Central)

CALIFORNIA VIETNAM
VETERANS MEMORIAL
15th St. and Capitol Mall
(east end of Capitol Park)

Built entirely with donations, the memorial is a moving tribute to the dead and missing from that war. Shiny black granite panels are engraved with the names of the 5,822 Californians who gave their lives, and full-relief bronze figures depict a scene of the conflict's daily life. (Central)

CATHEDRAL OF THE
BLESSED SACRAMENT
11th and K Sts.
916/444-3071
At the east end of the K Street Mall, just down the block from the Convention Center and Hyatt Regency, stands the gigantic Catholic church modeled after L'Église de la Trinité in Paris. Some of the stained-glass windows are from fifteenth-century Austria, and inside the cathedral hangs a reproduction of Raphael's *Sistine Madonna,* which was given

---

A City of Terra-cotta

If you're a sharp-eyed observer of architectural detail, Sacramento will become an endless field trip for you, thanks to the terra-cotta embellishments of Gladding, McBean and Co. The clay used for terra-cotta (and for bricks as well) is a local natural resource ("terra-cotta" literally means "burnt earth"). The substance can be shaped into ornamentation or tiles (and then fired), or it can be sprayed as a veneer that convincingly imitates granite. It's been used abundantly in all these ways by Gladding, McBean and Co., especially in buildings made before World War II. Doing business since 1875 and still around, the company has been hired by architects throughout the world and is prominent in every major California city. Take a moment to look for gargoyles, shields, relief sculptures, and initialed crests throughout Sacramento.

---

to the wife of Leland Stanford by the King of Saxony. Until the 1960s it was the largest cathedral west of the Mississippi. Visitors are welcome daily. Free. (Central)

THE CROCKER ART MUSEUM
216 O St.
916/264-5423
The Crocker is Sacramento's only public museum devoted to the visual arts (see chapter 6, Museums and Galleries). It's also worth a look purely for its value as an architectural treasure from Sacramento's Victorian era. Tue–Sun 10–5, Thu 10–9; closed major holidays. $5.50 adults, $4.50 seniors, $3 youths 7–17. (Central)

GOVERNOR'S MANSION STATE HISTORIC PARK
16th and H Sts.
916/323-3047
This 15-room Victorian mansion with 14-foot ceilings was good enough for 13 previous governors, but not for Nancy Reagan, who declared it a firetrap. (In fairness, the state fire marshal had declared the house unsafe as early as 1941.) Refurbished for tours, the mansion contains artifacts reflecting the tastes of previous governors and first ladies, including oriental rugs, Italian marble fireplaces, chandeliers, and French mirrors. Daily tours on the hour 10–4. $3 adults and children 13 and over, $1.50 children 6–12. (Central)

HEILBRON HOUSE
704 O St.
916/446-5133
Heilbron House is a beautiful example of the Second Empire style of Victorian architecture built in 1884. It was designed by the same architect who built the Governor's Mansion. Heilbron House has also been a restaurant and a bank, and is currently La Raza Bookstore Galeria Posada, the gallery and gift shop for Latino and Native American artists (see chapter 6, Museums and Galleries). (Central)

LELAND STANFORD MANSION
Eighth and N Sts.
916/445-4209, 916/324-0575
(tour information)
www.Cal-parks.ca.gov/districts/goldrush/lsmshp.htm
Leland Stanford was a railroad baron, governor of California, and U.S. senator, but it was as a successful dry-goods merchant that he purchased what was then simply a two-story house. The mansion became a tribute to Sacramentan adaptability: flooded chronically, Stanford had the house jacked up a full story, then topped with an additional story and a mansard roof. The house served as a temporary state capitol for years. Be sure to call first before

TRIVIA

Patrick Manogue, a successful gold miner, used his riches to finance his study at a seminary in Paris. By 1881 he had not only returned to America, but had become a bishop overseeing construction of the Cathedral of the Blessed Sacrament. He never heard the four bells, which weigh over six tons: They tolled for the first time at the bishop's funeral in 1889.

trying a tour, as extensive renovation has been ongoing to restore its past splendor. Tours available Tuesdays and Thursdays at 12:15 p.m.; Saturdays at 12:15 and 1:30 p.m.; and by appointment. (Central)

LIBRARY AND COURTS BUILDING
914 Capitol Mall (opposite the capitol on the west side)
916/654-0261
Paired with what was once called State Office Building No. 1 (now known as the Jesse Unruh Building), these two structures were the first response to the capitol building's inability to contain the growing needs of state government. Their massive, neoclassical presence is often missed by those circling the block to get a better look at the capitol. But go inside the Library and Courts building. There is hidden splendor here most Sacramentans know little about: carved eucalyptus walls, marble columns, Grecian statues and lamps, and murals of famous warriors (in the Memorial Vestibule). The pediments on the buildings' exteriors depict symbols of California's agricultural and mineral wealth. The third floor reading room features a mural of the state's development by Maynard Dixon. The state supreme court holds session here twice a year. Free. (Central)

Leland Stanford Mansion

© Tom Myers 1998

The kitchen and pantry of the Governor's Mansion were destroyed in 1917 when an assassin attempted to dynamite Governor William Dennison Stephens. Members of the International Workers of the World (the IWW, or "Wobblies") were accused but never convicted.

LIBRARY AND COURTS BUILDING II
900 N St.
916/654-0261

A new annex to the original, this Library and Courts building contains the Braille and Talking Book Library Reading Room (916/654-0640), and next to it is a fragrance garden. For further reading, the Rare Materials Room is open to the public, and the California History Room has rotating exhibits, an extensive photograph collection, and microfilms of virtually every newspaper ever published in the state. Free. (Central)

LLEWELYN WILLIAMS MANSION
900 H St.
916/443-1691

Now better known as the Sacramento International Hostel, the Llewelyn Williams Mansion is a gorgeous example of restoration and preservation. It was moved from across the street to make way for a high-rise that was never built, and now may have to move back to its original site, as the City Hall looks to expand. It is, however, still a low-mileage house. (Central)

SACRAMENTO CONVENTION CENTER
J St. between 13th and 15th Sts.
916/264-5291 (main)
916/264-5181 (box office)
www.sacto.org/dwntwn/convctr

Hard fought by preservationists at its inception, the Sacramento Convention Center displaced a number of old structures. But the center is now an accepted fact and was recently expanded. Its sheer busyness has had a symbiotic effect on the immediate neighborhood, and the opening of several new (or relocated) restaurants, the IMAX Theater, and the Hyatt (and its surrounding shops) has made this a retail and entertainment focal point of the city. Immediately next door is the Sacramento Community Center Theater, the city's finest performing-arts center. Across the street is the Sacramento Memorial Auditorium. (Central)

SACRAMENTO MEMORIAL AUDITORIUM
15th and J Sts.

Erected to memorialize those killed in World War I, this massive brick structure, in a blend of Mediterranean styles sometimes called Byzantine, was recently renovated and now stands as one of the premier venues for concerts and sporting events in the city. The ghosts of past performers Jimi Hendrix and Will Rogers might be here, amidst some of the finest examples of Gladding, McBean and Co.'s terra-cotta embellishments. Only a block from the Convention Center, it typifies the juxtaposition of old and new that gives downtown its special charm. It's also an official state historical landmark, because during World War II it was used as a detention center for Japanese Americans while concentration camps were being built. (Central)

SACRAMENTO METROPOLITAN ARTS COMMISSION
800 10th St., Ste. 1
916/264-5558
www.sacto.org
The commission offers public art tours of the downtown district, plus they offer information on the region's arts in general. Groups of 20 or more should call for a group tour. Free. (Central)

SACRAMENTO POWER STATION A
16th and I Sts.
This was the receiving end of the first transmission of electricity from the Folsom Powerhouse in 1895, when 11,000 volts traveled along what was then the longest power line in the world. Power

Station A distributed that power throughout Sacramento, and still stands today as a functioning part of the city's power grid. For the immediate future a renovation aimed at restoring public access to the interior of the building prohibits tours. (Central)

SAINT PAUL'S EPISCOPAL CHURCH
1430 J St.
916/446-2620
Tiffany stained-glass windows and a rare Johnson Tracker organ embellish Sacramento's oldest church. Hard against the Convention Center, Saint Paul's holds its own as a dignified building, appearing almost as if it were carved from rock. (Central)

SOUTHERN PACIFIC DEPOT/ AMTRAK STATION
Fifth and I Sts.
Built in the 1920s and now a national historic landmark, the Southern Pacific Depot is in danger of disappearing, at least as a functioning

Sacramento Convention Center

Pat Cosgrove

Skyline Sensations

California Environmental Protection Agency, 10th and I Sts.

As of this writing, the new Cal EPA building is still unfinished, but promises to be one of the most prominent landmarks in the Sacramento skyline. The white-sided thrust will provide a dramatic contrast to the Beaux Arts City Hall and Central Library a block away. The intention is to give it a dramatically lit presence, capable of being picked out at night from miles away across the broad, flat Sacramento Valley. (Central)

Elks Building/California Life Insurance Building, 921/926 11th St.

Standing opposite one another on the 900 block of 11th Street, these two buildings once were the only outstanding features of Sacramento's skyline. The Elks Building, at 921, emulates the New York City style of a graduated tower at its peak—the only building of its kind in Sacramento. The Insurance Building, at 926, was Sacramento's first skyscraper at the time of its construction, and the tallest structure from here to Portland, Oregon. A two-story French chateau sits atop the main structure. Together, in the 1920s, these buildings could be seen for miles by the approaching motorist. (Central)

Esquire Plaza, 1201 K St.

The Esquire Plaza has been central to the revitalization of the east end of the K Street Mall. With its restaurants and IMAX Theater, the Plaza building is distinct in two rather different ways. On its western end is a round, dome-topped tower that echoes the capitol dome; its nickname, however ("the Ban Roll-On Building") is not nearly as glamorous. On the eastern end, a blue neon "zip" running vertically up the building's corner is the closest thing to a central landmark the city has. This "blue streak" is visible for miles at night, from almost any direction. (Central)

Pyramid Buidling, Riverfront, West Sacramento

Whether approaching Sacramento on Interstate 5 from the north or the south, the one building that snatches a driver's attention from the rest of the skyline is the bizarre pyramidal shape that sits directly opposite Old Sac on the West Sacramento side of the river. For better or worse, it's now impossible to imagine the city without this stack of pizza boxes glowing in the mind's eye. Though it was originally built as the Money

Store's home office, their new corporate owner turned off the lights that kept all four sides of the Mayan-like ziggurat shining through the night. Recently, the lights have been turned back on (following corporate fortunes, one must suppose). It will soon be less isolated and obtrusive, as the next-door neighbor, Raley Field (home of the Triple-A River Cats baseball team) attracts new businesses and restaurants. (Central)

Renaissance Tower, 810 K St.

Dubbed (with no affection whatsoever) the "Darth Vader" building, the Renaissance Tower was the tallest structure in the city when it was erected in 1989. Its dark presence has a brooding effect, and though its lobby level ought to be one of the highlights of the K Street Mall, there's nobody home. Still, it provides part of the big-city aura Sacramento has only recently taken on. (Central)

Tower Bridge

Sacramento's history has always been linked to San Francisco's, and the Tower Bridge has been, since it opened in the '30s, the gateway to Sacramento for visitors from the Bay. If you can catch a view of the bridge in action as it lifts its middle section to allow ships to pass below, it's quite a sight. Even when stationary it provides an impressive frame for Capitol Mall, especially since the mall's redevelopment as a stately approach to the capitol. Inspired by the design of the Golden Gate Bridge, Tower Bridge is a stouter, more workman-like rendition, and may be the only thing in town named "Tower" that didn't begin with a drugstore record bin. (Central)

U.S. Bank Building, 980 Ninth St.

The U.S. Bank Building is a fine example of what modern architecture can do by looking back, just a little. This new skyscraper emulates the classic New York City high-rises of the 1930s. The coloring blends with the older brick and terra-cotta buildings of the surrounding blocks, while embellishments include bronze cougars at the front entry, marble lobby floors, and lobby murals by Richard Piccolo. (Central)

Wells Fargo Center, 400 Capitol Mall

Reigning champ of the bigger-than-you race to raise the skyline profile, this elegant building houses both the Wells Fargo History Museum (916/440-4161) and the Il Fornaio restaurant at ground level. (Central)

The original *Spirit of Sacramento* was lost to fire in 1996. Its replacement was a paddle wheeler named the *Becky Thatcher* from Cincinnati. To reach Sacramento, the new *Spirit* sailed down the Mississippi, through the Gulf of Mexico and the Panama Canal, then up the coast to San Francisco Bay and the Sacramento River—an 8,500-mile trip its current owners liken to "driving your car from San Francisco to New York and back to San Francisco at seven miles per hour."

train station. Union Pacific has purchased Southern Pacific, and proposes to sell a good portion of the land surrounding the depot to developers, who in turn are proposing a mixed-use (commercial/residential/ retail) complex. This will be in dispute for some time, as there is considerable argument that such a development would compete with, and diminish the role of, retail in the Downtown area. Recent proposals have been turned down. Highlights of the depot include a Gold Rush mural high above the spacious open floor (depicting the driving of the Golden Spike that completed the transcontinental railroad), a 44-foot-high ceiling, marble floors, and oak benches. If, as the city has counterproposed, the depot becomes a hub of train, light-rail, and other public transportation, then Sacramento will not have abandoned this portion of its legacy. (Central)

SOUTHSIDE PARK
Between Sixth and Eighth Sts., T and W Sts.
Southside Park is in a beautiful downtown setting, with tall trees, tennis and basketball courts, a large pond, and lots of joggers. It's also host to the Cinco de Mayo Festival (see chapter 8, Parks, Gardens, and Recreation Areas). (Central)

SUN YAT SEN MEMORIAL
Chinatown Mall between Third and Fifth Sts., J and I Sts.
916/441-7180
The original Chinatown was the site of one of the first completed redevelopments of Downtown. Here you'll now find a plaza, surrounded by imposing, red-trimmed buildings, and the Sun Yat Sen Memorial, which is not so much a tourist destination as it is a cultural center for the current Chinese community. An imposing Dr. Sun Yat Sen statue memorializes the author of the first Chinese constitution. He wrote the document, in part, while visiting Chinese communities in Sacramento and the Delta. Afterward, he returned to China and, following the fall of the Manchu dynasty, was elected China's first president. There is also a Confucian temple, landscaped with Asian plants and trees; a courtyard (at the city's original street level); a gift shop; and a restaurant. Memorial Hall contains a library of historical documents, as well as a museum with brush paint-

EAST SACRAMENTO

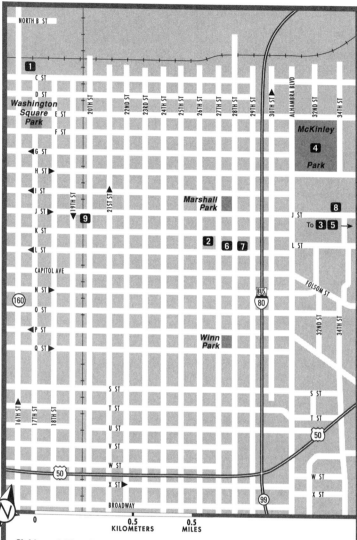

Sights and Attractions in East Sacramento

1. Blue Diamond Growers Visitor Center
2. California State Indian Museum
3. Fab Forties Neighborhood
4. McKinley Park
5. Sacramento State University Campus
6. Sutter's Fort State Historic Park
7. Tavern Building
8. Turn Verein Hall
9. Western Pacific Railroad Passenger Station

ings, bronzes, pottery, and jewelry. Tue–Sat 1–3. Call first to make sure the Memorial Hall is open. (Central)

TOWE AUTO MUSEUM
2200 Front St.
916/442-6802
The Towe Auto Museum has vintage cars displayed in cultural vignettes that will give kids (or grandkids) a feel for the era in which the car was driven. (See chapter 6, Museums and Galleries.) It's at the southern end of Front Street, just below Old Sacramento. Open daily 10–6. $6 adults, $2.50 youths 14–18, $1 children 5–13. (Central)

EAST

BLUE DIAMOND GROWERS STORE
1701 C St.
916/446-8439
www.bluediamondgrowers.com
At this visitors center, you can learn about the nation's largest almond-growing region in a delicious way, with their tasting room, store, and a video that has replaced the tour. Once owned by Del Monte and one of the largest canneries in the world, the building is now on the National Register of Historic Places. Mon–Fri 10–5, Sat 10–4. Free. (East)

CALIFORNIA STATE INDIAN MUSEUM
2618 K St.
916/324-0971
Arts-and-crafts exhibits vividly illustrate the abundance of nature and the wide-ranging ways it was put to use by the original peoples of California. The displays, exhibits, and photographs capture something close to paradise, before it was lost. Immediately next to Sutter's Fort. (See chapter 6, Museums and Galleries.) Open daily, 10–5. Nominal fee. (East)

THE FAB FORTIES NEIGHBORHOOD
Low-40s-numbered Aves.
between J St. and Folsom
Beginning in the 1910s and '20s, residential neighborhoods began a steady push to the east of downtown. The powerful and wealthy began to build in this neighborhood, often using architects who had designed downtown business buildings. This building surge came at the end of the excesses of the various styles referred to as Victorian, and while Colonial Revival and Craftsman styles were already in use, architects were still casting about for a distinctively American

---

T I P

There are always specially priced days or nights at the California State Fair, and several local retailers (often supermarket chains) have discounted deals available through their outlets. Check the *Sacramento Bee* for ads anytime during August and right up until the fair closes.

On inauguration day, 1861, governor-elect Stanford left his flooded home in a rowboat and later returned through a second-story window.

way of designing homes. As a result of this search, the "Fab Forties"—so named because of their location in low-40s-numbered avenues between J Street and Folsom—became a mix of many other revival styles. You'll find English cottages, Tudor estates, Dutch farmhouses, Mediterranean villas, and Craftsman and Norman Revival houses. It was here that wealthy friends ensconced the Reagans when Nancy declared the old Governor's Mansion a firetrap. (East)

MCKINLEY PARK
Between H St., Alhambra Blvd., McKinley Blvd., and 33rd St.
Named in the wake of the assassination of the president, McKinley Park, which many consider to be the city's most beautiful park, is a favorite jogging site and the home of elaborate gardens and play areas (see chapter 8, Parks, Gardens, and Recreation Areas). (East)

SACRAMENTO STATE UNIVERSITY CAMPUS
6000 J St.
916/278-6011
Officially known as California State University, Sacramento (CSUS), "Sac State" is largely a commuter campus, but nevertheless has a beautiful wooded setting along the American River. Call the general information number to find out about art exhibits, theater performances, concerts, films, sporting events, and lectures, all of which are open to the public (see chapter 10, Sports and Recreation, for activities at the CSUS Aquatics Center). A fun landmark to see is the Guy West Bridge, a miniature version of the Golden Gate Bridge that spans the river for pedestrians. (East)

SUTTER'S FORT STATE HISTORIC PARK
2701 L St.
916/445-4422
Sutter's Fort is located just above the riverbank, at the spot where John Sutter first stepped from his boat to found New Helvetia. As early as the end of the nineteenth century, Sacramentans realized the importance of their own historical legacy. The fort's ruined walls were reconstructed and the site was saved from a plan to put a street through it. Today, self-guided tours give a feel for life in Sutter's time, and the exhibits feature cooper and blacksmith shops, a bakery, a prison, the dining room and living quarters, and livestock quarters. On special Pioneer Demonstration Days, craftspeople demonstrate the skills that made life at the fort possible. Daily 10–5; last self-guided audio tour at 4:15. $3 adults and children 12 and over, $1.50 children 6–11 (fees slightly higher during Living History Days, when local actors portray early settlers). (East)

TAVERN BUILDING
2801 Capitol Ave.
Originally a one-story brick brew-

ery, the Tavern Building was re-modeled in 1922 as a four-story, English period revival. It's a rather massive showcase of Tudor-style architecture. It's also noteworthy for housing one of the finest restaurants in town, Biba (see chapter 4, Where to Eat). (East)

TURN VEREIN HALL
3349 J St.
916/442-7360
Turn Verein, translated (roughly) from the German, means "gymnastics gathering," and this social and athletic hall was the kind of male club established in most U.S. communities where Germans had settled. This one, however, was the first of its kind on the Pacific coast, and dates to 1854. The ornate entrance medallion is a beautiful example of Gladding, McBean and Co.'s terra-cotta work. (East)

WESTERN PACIFIC RAILROAD PASSENGER STATION
1910 J St.
Ask almost any Sacramentan where this building is and you'll get a blank stare in return. But ask where Midtown's Old Spaghetti Factory is and they'll point you right here. Built in 1909, in the Mission Revival style that evokes California's history, this is a beautiful relic of early railroad architecture. The restaurant has occupied the building since 1970. (East)

NORTH

AMERICAN RIVER PARKWAY
There are many entrances to the American River Parkway. The bike trail begins in Discovery Park off the Garden Highway, near the meeting point of the American and Sacramento Rivers. This park is covered in more detail in chapter 8, Parks, Gardens, and Recreation Areas, but it's worth mentioning again and again. When the building of the Folsom Dam upstream tamed the American River and added instant value to the flood-prone land immediately across from downtown, it would have been easy to give the land over to developers for solid cash. Sacramentans, however, had the foresight to preserve this land and create instead a parkway five times the size of San Francisco's Golden Gate Park, protecting for all time the natural habitat that greeted the first European settlers. The Parkway extends all the way to Folsom. (North)

GIBSON RANCH COUNTY PARK
8552 Gibson Ranch Rd.
Elverta
916/991-7592
This is a most unusual county facility, in that it's a working ranch that features tours of the facilities, the pastures, the animals, and offers horse-drawn hayrides. It contains, among many other things, an extensive equestrian facility (see chapter 8, Parks, Gardens and Recreation Areas; and chapter 7, Kids' Stuff). (North)

NORTHEAST

CALIFORNIA EXPOSITION AND STATE FAIR (CAL EXPO)
1600 Exposition Blvd.
916/263-FAIR, 916/263-3000
(general information and events)
www.bigfun.org
Cal Expo is the site of Waterworld

USA aquatic park and Cal Expo harness racing, but the big annual attraction here is the California State Fair. For roughly two-and-one-half weeks leading up to Labor Day, the gigantic showcase, spread over 700 acres, hops with activity. Each year almost a million visitors see live entertainment from famous names and home-state groups alike, a carnival with state-of-the-art midway rides designed to separate you from your stomach (or at least your popcorn), plus a rodeo, petting zoos, farm-animal exhibits and competitions, and galleries of statewide arts and crafts. It's guaranteed to be at the hottest time of the year, so drink your slushees and walk through the misting stations. Admission prices vary, based on the multiple packages available. Ride tickets are sold separately inside the gates. Cal Expo also serves as the venue for anything to do with animals or things that go for speed (like motocross and car and boat shows), which, along with home and garden shows, auctions, the Sacramento County Fair (916/263-2975), sportsmen's expos, and concerts in the amphitheater, keep the place busy all year. (Northeast)

THE DISCOVERY MUSEUM OF SCIENCE AND CHALLENGER

SPACE CENTER
3615 Auburn Blvd.
916/575-3941, 916/485-8836 (group reservations), 916/264-7057
www.thediscovery.org
This hands-on learning museum features a simulated mission control, a planetarium, displays about Native Americans of the Sacramento Valley, an animal hall, an adjoining outdoor nature area, and much more (see chapter 7, Kids' Stuff; or chapter 6, Museums and Galleries). Tue–Fri 12–5, Sat–Sun 10–5. $5 adults, $4 seniors and children 13–17, $3 children 6–12. (Northeast)

EFFIE YEAW NATURE CENTER
Ancil Hoffman Regional Park
6700 Tarshes Dr.armichael
916/489-4918
The Effie Yeaw Nature Center is a great place to see the area's natural flora and fauna, on trails or in exhibits. (See also chapter 7, Kids' Stuff.) Mar–Oct daily 9–5, Nov–Feb daily 9–4. $4 parking fee. (Northeast)

FOLSOM CITY ZOO
Folsom City Park
Folsom and Stafford St.
916/985-7347
This "misfit" zoo is where exotic pets and native North American animals who cannot return to the

Parking for the Old City Cemetery is just inside the cemetery gates, which you enter along Broadway between 9th and 10th Streets. The Odd Fellows and Masonic cemeteries are immediately south of the Old City Cemetery along Riverside Boulevard—be sure not to pull in there instead.

GREATER SACRAMENTO

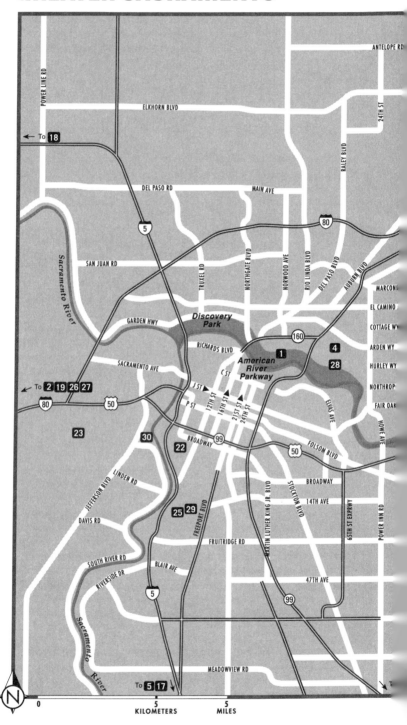

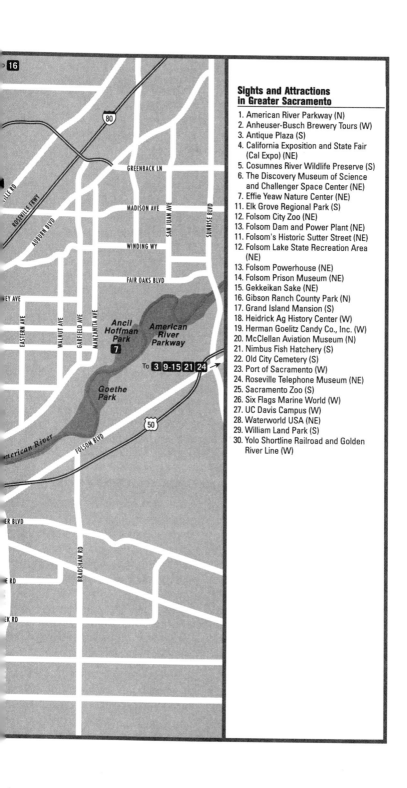

Sights and Attractions in Greater Sacramento

1. American River Parkway (N)
2. Anheuser-Busch Brewery Tours (W)
3. Antique Plaza (S)
4. California Exposition and State Fair (Cal Expo) (NE)
5. Cosumnes River Wildlife Preserve (S)
6. The Discovery Museum of Science and Challenger Space Center (NE)
7. Effie Yeaw Nature Center (NE)
11. Elk Grove Regional Park (S)
12. Folsom City Zoo (NE)
13. Folsom Dam and Power Plant (NE)
11. Folsom's Historic Sutter Street (NE)
12. Folsom Lake State Recreation Area (NE)
13. Folsom Powerhouse (NE)
14. Folsom Prison Museum (NE)
15. Gekkeikan Sake (NE)
16. Gibson Ranch County Park (N)
17. Grand Island Mansion (S)
18. Heidrick Ag History Center (W)
19. Herman Goelitz Candy Co., Inc. (W)
20. McClellan Aviation Museum (N)
21. Nimbus Fish Hatchery (S)
22. Old City Cemetery (S)
23. Port of Sacramento (W)
24. Roseville Telephone Museum (NE)
25. Sacramento Zoo (S)
26. Six Flags Marine World (W)
27. UC Davis Campus (W)
28. Waterworld USA (NE)
29. William Land Park (S)
30. Yolo Shortline Railroad and Golden River Line (W)

wild are cared for. (See also chapter 7, Kids' Stuff.) Daily Tue–Sun. Small admission charge. (Northeast)

FOLSOM DAM AND POWER PLANT
7794 Folsom Dam Rd.
Folsom
916/989-7275

The Folsom Dam and Power Plant helps keep Sacramento safe from flooding. Though it only generates a small percentage of the city's electricity, it also shunts a portion of the American River to farmlands. Guided tours last about 90 minutes (Tue–Sat at 10 a.m. and 1 p.m.). You'll see the floodgates, the giant turbines and dynamos, and, from the dam tower, a panoramic view of the reservoir, which is the Folsom State Recreation Area. Shorter tours are available, and all require reservations. Free. (Northeast)

FOLSOM LAKE STATE RECREATION AREA
7806 Folsom-Auburn Rd.
Folsom
916/988-0205

Literally millions of people come here year-round to swim, fish, ski, camp, picnic, boat, bicycle, and enjoy the outdoors (see chapter 8, Parks, Gardens, and Recreation Areas). (Northeast)

FOLSOM POWERHOUSE
Corner of Leidesdorff and Riley
916/985-0205

Not to be confused with Folsom's dam and power plant, this is the historic installation that first sent a surge of electricity south to Sacramento in 1895, the longest distance usable alternating current had

ever traveled. A 40-minute tour is available, or you can stroll at your leisure. Free. (Northeast)

FOLSOM PRISON MUSEUM
Folsom Prison
End of Natoma St.
800/821-6443, 916/985-2561
ext. 4589

Yes, it's the place Johnny Cash sang about. And no, Johnny didn't really do time there (see chapter 6, Museums and Galleries). Open daily 10–4. $1 ages 13 and older. (Northeast)

FOLSOM'S HISTORIC SUTTER STREET

Antique stores, gift shops, and nice little restaurants make a fun afternoon of wandering and browsing in this preserved section of "Old Town Folsom." The buildings in Old Town date from the nineteenth century and include the History Museum and the oldest railroad turntable in California. (The Sacramento-to-Folsom track was the first railroad in the West.) The visitors center is in the Historic Train Depot at 200 Wool Street. Head east on U.S. 50, exit at Folsom Boulevard, and drive north into town. (Northeast)

GEKKEIKAN SAKE
1136 Sibley St.
Folsom
916/985-3111
www.gekkeikan-sake.com

The tasting room, Japanese gardens, and koi pond at Gekkeikan Sake create a beautiful atmosphere for viewing the sake-making process. A self-guided one-hour tour with complimentary samples is offered. Open Mon–Fri 10–4:30. (Northeast)

Top Ten Reasons to Visit Sacramento

by Lucy Steffens, director of public relations, Sacramento Convention and Visitors Bureau

1. **Old Sacramento**, the 28-acre historic area along the Sacramento River with the largest concentration of historic buildings in California.
2. **The California State Railroad Museum,** the largest interpretive railroad museum in North America.
3. A tour of the **California State Capitol,** reflecting turn-of-the-last-century splendor after a $68-million restoration.
4. A bike or run along the 26-mile **American River Parkway** from Old Sacramento to Folsom Lake.
5. A visit to the **Crocker Art Museum,** the oldest art museum west of the Mississippi, housing a fabulous collection of early California paintings and master drawings.
6. Catching a **Sacramento Kings** game at Arco Arena with the most enthusiastic fans in the NBA.
7. A **whitewater rafting** adventure on the American River.
8. Watching Triple-A baseball action at Raley Field, the brand new home of the **Sacramento River Cats.**
9. A leisurely drive through the **Sacramento Delta towns.**
10. An orange freeze from **Merlino's.**

MCCLELLAN AVIATION MUSEUM
3204 Palm Ave.
North Highlands
916/643-3192
The McClellan Aviation Museum features indoor exhibits and an outdoor collection of vintage and historically significant military aircraft (see chapter 6, Museums and Galleries). Open Mon–Sat 9–3. Free. (Northeast)

ROSEVILLE TELEPHONE MUSEUM
106 Vernon St.
Roseville
916/786-1621
The Roseville Telephone Museum showcases phone technology, from its invention to the present (see chapter 7, Kids' Stuff). Group tours Mon–Fri 9–5; also open Sat 10–4. $1 ages 13 and older. (Northeast)

SOUTH

ANTIQUE PLAZA
11395 Folsom Blvd.
Rancho Cordova
916/852-8517 (fax)
www.antiqueplazaonline.com
With 300 dealers and 85,000 square feet, this is California's largest antique mall (see chapter 9, Shopping). (South)

COSUMNES RIVER WILDLIFE PRESERVE
6500 Desmond Rd.
Galt
916/684-2816
Just as the name suggests, this is truly a wild preserve. Its riparian environment and wetlands are a vital part of the migrating routes of uncountable species of birds (see chapter 8, Parks, Gardens, and Recreation Areas). Trails open daily during daylight hours, visitors center open weekends 10–4. (South)

ELK GROVE REGIONAL PARK
Elk Grove-Florin Rd.,
South of Elk Grove Blvd.
916/685-3908
Elk Grove is Sacramento County's second-most-popular park, after the American River Parkway. It's huge and full of facilities for picnicking and organized sports (see chapter 8, Parks, Gardens, and Recreation Areas). (South)

GRAND ISLAND MANSION
Grand Island Rd., on Steamboat
Slough (three miles south of
Hwy. 160)
916/775-1705
At first glance, this 58-room residence seems to have risen out of the ground near antebellum Atlanta (or even Mediterranean France), but not Sacramento. Even so, visitors who ease down a long driveway lined with towering junipers that echo the columned architecture will get a solid feel for another era on the Delta. Jean Harlow and Earl Stanley Gardner were once frequent guests, and the mansion's been a movie location several times. Built in 1917 by a German financier for his wife, who missed the glamour of San Francisco, the four-story, 24,000-square-foot villa still hosts weddings and corporate retreats, and even overnight stays. The Delta is a destination in itself (see chapter 13, Day Trips), but if you're only going to see one thing, come here. Jay Gatsby would have. Though it's a privately owned, unoccupied house now, Sunday brunch is served to the public (the only day the mansion is open), and reservations are recommended. (South)

NIMBUS FISH HATCHERY
2001 Nimbus Rd.
Rancho Cordova
916/358-2820
The Nimbus Fish Hatchery is a great place to watch salmon and trout spawn. Daily 7–3. Free, with fish food available for a nickel (see chapter 7, Kids' Stuff). (South)

OLD CITY CEMETERY
10th St. and Broadway
916/264-5621, 916/448-0811 (tours)
916/554-7508 (fax)
www.jps.net/occc/cemetery.htm
Sacramento's original cemetery—more accurately, New Helvetia's—now lies beneath Sutter Middle School, near Alhambra. The Sacramento City Cemetery occupies land donated by John Sutter at a time when area residents were

There are dozens of buildings (too numerous to list) worth seeing in the various parts of Sacramento. Contact the Sacramento Convention and Visitors Bureau (1303 J St., Ste. 600, 916/264-7777) for a brochure entitled "Sacramento's Historic Architecture." It suggests detailed walking tours and gives excellent information on the buildings, their histories, what to look for, and where to find them. Included are house tours in "Bungalow Row," "Poverty Ridge," and "Boulevard Park," as well as walks through Alkali Flats, the capitol area, and Downtown.

desperate to inter those felled by cholera. Indeed, one grave marker is dedicated simply, "To the memory of the cholera victims, 1852," with no name or number.

Historians can only guess how many may rest in all the trenches dedicated to them, with perhaps 50 to a grave, and probably totaling between 600 and 800. The cemetery was largely filled by 1900, and touring there now is more a fun history lesson than a somber remembrance. John Sutter Jr., Mark Hopkins, three governors, and Judge Edwin and his wife Margaret Crocker (of Crocker Art Museum fame) are all here, along with Alexander Hamilton's son, who died seeking gold.

Self-guided tours are offered daily, while docent-led tours occur periodically throughout the year on Saturday mornings and Wednesday evenings. Some theme tours are offered (reservations and a donation are required). Private tours may also be scheduled. Brochures can be picked up in the office at the Broadway entrance. There is nothing unsettling here regarding death and dying (see chapter 7, Kids' Stuff). Daily 7–4:30, with extended summer hours. Free, with donations for restoration welcome. (South)

SACRAMENTO ZOO
William Land Park
3930 West Land Park Dr.
916/264-5888 (main)
916/264-8561 (groups and catering)
www.saczoo.com
This is a complete—if small-scale—zoo specializing in endangered species (see chapter 7, Kids' Stuff). Open daily 10–5. Call for admission prices. (South)

WILLIAM LAND PARK
Bordered by Freeport Blvd., Sutterville Rd., West Land Park Dr., and 13th Ave.
Locally known as Land Park, this urban oasis is home to the zoo, Funderland, and Fairytale Town. Its wide-open grassy areas and beautiful towering trees are relaxing to drive or stroll through. The intense greenery attracted builders of some of the most beautiful homes in the city, and the park has given its name to the surrounding Land Park neighborhood. (see chapter 7, Kids' Stuff; and chapter 8, Parks, Gardens, and Recreation Areas.) (South)

WEST

ANHEUSER-BUSCH
BREWERY TOURS

3101 Busch Dr.
Fairfield
707/429-7595
Part of the Homer Simpson Memorial Tour (see Hershey's Tour, chapter 7 Kids' Stuff), this is where you get to see the stuff made. Fairfield is a good hour west of the city, right along Interstate 80; in fact, you can see the looming plant from the highway. The brewery offers a film about the Clydesdales, videos about the brewing process, plus fermentation vats, bottling lines, a gift shop, and free samples of beer. There are also soft drinks and snacks at the end of the road. Open Sept–May Tue–Sat, Jun–Aug Mon–Sat; tours offered every hour on the hour 9–4. Free. (West)

HEIDRICK AG HISTORY CENTER
1962 Hays Ln.
Woodland
530/666-9700, 530/666-9712 (fax)
www.aghistory.org
The "Ag" here is, of course, agriculture. Located in the booming town of Woodland, just northwest of Sacramento, the Heidrick Ag History Center is near the junction of Interstate 5 and County Road 102. The center combines the Fred C. Heidrick Antique Ag Collection and the Hays Antique Truck Museum. They are both recognized as the largest of their kind anywhere (see chapter 7, Kids' Stuff). Easter–Labor Day Mon–Fri 10–5, Sat 10–6, Sun 10–4; Labor Day–Easter Wed–Fri 10–5, Sat 10–6, Sun 10–4; closed Dec 24–Jan 1. $6 adults, $5 seniors, $4 kids 6–14. (West)

HERMAN GOELITZ
CANDY CO., INC.
2400 North Watney Way

Fairfield
707/428-2838
This is the Jelly Belly Tour (see chapter 7, Kids' Stuff). Though the Herman Goelitz Candy Company is more than an hour west on Interstate 80 from Sacramento, it can be combined with the Anheuser-Busch tour to cover most major vices. Tours daily 9–3. Free. (West)

PORT OF SACRAMENTO
2895 Industrial Blvd.
West Sacramento
916/371-8000
www.portofsacramento.com
Although it has never lived up to original ambitions, the deepwater channel and dredged-out basin of Port Sacramento does attract ships from around the world. A brochure with a self-guided tour is available at the main gate, which is reached by exiting south from Interstate 80 in West Sac onto Harbor Boulevard and following the gate. It's open daily, as much as 24 hours a day, depending on the ships in port. Guided tours may be arranged in advance. Free. (West)

SIX FLAGS MARINE WORLD
Marine World Pkwy.
Vallejo
707/643-ORCA
More a day trip than a local attraction, Six Flags Marine World is nevertheless easily reachable for a full day's worth of fun (see chapter 7, Kids' Stuff). Open year-round. (West)

UNIVERSITY OF CALIFORNIA, DAVIS
UCD exit from I-80
Davis
800/752-0881
One of the preeminent campuses

of the University of California system, UCD began as an agricultural school and still leads the field, so to speak, in aggie research. It is also home to one of the leading veterinary schools in the nation and the California Primate Research Center. It's physically the largest of the UC campuses, and the walk through the UC Davis Arboretum along Putah Creek is beautiful.

Annual events open to the public include Picnic Day in April. Thousands of people come to view parades, floats, exhibits, animal shows, and the best wiener dog race in the history of dachshunds. The campus is also one the area's best venues for performing arts, art galleries, and lectures. The surrounding town of Davis has a distinct flavor, especially in the sections close to campus, where environmental design (including solar-energized housing), farmers markets, and the massive use of bicycles give the old downtown a great deal of charm. (West)

YOLO SHORTLINE RAILROAD AND GOLDEN RIVER LINE

800/942-6387
www.ysrr.com
The Yolo Shortline and the Golden River Line offer a May-through-October schedule of historic train and paddle-wheeler river cruises. Lunch, dinner, or pizza is served, depending on which trip you take. Add an Old West Great Train Robbery show if you'd like, or just go on a sightseeing trip. Fares vary according to meals and excursions chosen. Reservations are required for all trips on which food is served. Group rates and private charters are available. (West)

CITY TOURS

CAL-EVENTS TOURS AND SPECIAL EVENTS
777 Campus Commons Rd., Ste. 200
916/924-8661
916/920-0448 (fax)
Cal-Events offers personally designed historical tours of Sacramento, the gold country, or the wine country. Groups only.

CKS KIMURA AGENCY

TRIVIA

Want to see the Sacramento River of 75 or so years ago? Rent videos, if you can find them, of the following films in which the Sacramento portrayed other rivers, especially the Mississippi:
Showboat (Universal, 1935)
Huckleberry Finn (Paramount, 1931)
Tom Sawyer (Paramount, 1930)
The Michigan Kid (Universal, 1928)
Steamboat Bill Jr. (Keaton, 1927)
The Volga Boatman (DeMille, 1925)
Tess of the D'Urbervilles (MGM, 1924)
The Iron Horse (Fox, 1924)

1700 Opper Ave.
916/456-0686
The CKS Kimura Agency's Japanese translation services will help you plan business or personal travel anywhere in the area, as well as arrange business negotiations.

FRONTIER TOURS/SACRAMENTO
GRAY LINE SIGHTSEEING TOURS
2600 North Ave.
800/356-9838
916/927-2877 (fax)
www.frontiertours.com
This company offers mini- or large charter buses for convention groups, sightseeing tours, and shuttle services.

LANDMARK TOURS
2641 Cottage Way, Ste. 5
800/895-0055, 916/482-2900,
916/482-3166 (fax)
Landmark Tours offers full-service travel and reception services with customized itineraries and touring programs, as well as meet-and-greet and convention services.

RIVER OTTER TAXI COMPANY
917 Seventh St.
916/448-4333
In warm weather, a great way to tour the waterfront is in one of the River Otter Taxi Company's small (24-passenger) boats. They also provide a shuttle service from Old Sac to various restaurants along the river.

FERRIES/STEAMBOATS

SPIRIT OF SACRAMENTO AND
MATTHEW MCKINLEY
L St. Landing on Front St.
(sales office at 110 L St.)
800/433-0262, 916/552-2933
www.oldsacriverboat.com
Dubbed "the Victorian paddle wheelers," these two boats provide year-round cruises with dining, dancing, and sightseeing. Prices vary according to which tour you choose. Group rates are available, and if you can get 25 or more friends together you can make up your own cruise.

VALLEJO BAYLINK FERRIES
495 Mare Island Way, Vallejo
877/64-FERRY, 707/64-FERRY
707/649-3471 (fax)
www.baylinkferry.com
If you'd like to make a day trip to San Francisco without the parking nightmare, and can get yourself to Vallejo, you can board a ferry (a high-speed catamaran) in Vallejo that docks at the foot of San Francisco's Market Street. From there you can hook up with BART or MUNI service, or walk to Fisherman's Wharf and Pier 39. By the end of 2001, there is a chance that a former commuters' bus link from Sacramento and Davis will be restored to the Vallejo ferries, making the Sacramento–San Francisco excursion once again car-free.

6

MUSEUMS AND GALLERIES

History is everywhere in Sacramento (it's the subject of other chapters as well as this one), and the best museums in town not only remind visitors of the past, but have become interactive with the present and future. Any consideration of area museums must begin with the Crocker Art Museum. It was the first of its kind west of the Mississippi and was founded by Edwin Crocker, the legal counsel to railroading's Big Four. Crocker used his wealth in the early 1870s to scour Europe for great works and was so successful that the museum has been battling ever since for enough display space to show its treasures. Traditional art museums beyond the Crocker, however, are almost nonexistent. This deficit is remedied by a very active gallery community that sustains the local art scene: regionally and nationally known artists are displayed in dozens of small showplaces, which often combine exhibition space with picture framing and retail supplies. History, on the other hand, is generously covered by various museums and given a unique context by each. The Golden State Museum sums it up nicely with its organizing themes: the Place, the People, the Politics, the Promise. One might say, in fact, that these are the treasures of Sacramento's entire museum and arts community.

ART MUSEUMS

CROCKER ART MUSEUM
216 O St.
916/264-5423
Philanthropist, abolitionist, lawyer, state supreme court justice—Edwin B. Crocker was all these things. When a stroke ended his active attorney days, he set off for Europe with his entire family and returned with hundreds of paintings and

Crocker Art Museum

master drawings which took up whole carloads in his expedition's triumphant return. By collecting not just old masters but also contemporary Californian art, Asian art, ceramics, photography, and Victorian decorative arts, Crocker amassed holdings that rivaled any private collection in the nation at that time. The museum began as a gallery annex added to his home (one of the oldest residences still standing in the city) and today holds over 9,000 works. The eclectic archives allow current exhibit directors to show contemporary art and at the same time trace developments through time which led to that expression. Tue–Sun 10–5, Thu 10–9; closed major holidays. $5.50 adults, $4.50 seniors, $3 youths 7–17. (Central)

SUN YAT SEN MEMORIAL
Chinatown Mall between Third and Fifth Sts. and J and I Sts.
916/441-7180
Not so much tourist destination as cultural center for the Chinese

community (see chapter 5, Sights and Attractions), the Memorial Hall is both a history museum relating to Dr. Sun Yat Sen's ascension to the presidency of China as well as a museum of Chinese art, including brush paintings, bronzes, pottery, and jewelry. Tue–Sat 1–3. Call first to make sure the Memorial Hall is open. (Central)

SCIENCE AND HISTORY MUSEUMS

CALIFORNIA MILITARY MUSEUM
1119 Second St.
916/442-2883
www.militarymuseum.org
A legislative act authorized the California National Guard to establish a military museum, and the result is this three-story Old Sac building filled with military memorabilia arranged in chronological order from 1775 to the present. It contains one of the largest collections of military long-arms in the western United States. Today's M-16, for example, traces its ancestry to the British "Brown Bess" of the American Revolution. But this museum is not just about weapons; it's about the dedicated people who sacrificed their lives for their country. The museum's oldest artifacts are from the 1770s, when the Spanish were establishing the mission/presidio system throughout California. Dozens of their swords, writings, helmets, and guns, including an 1842 Dragoon pistol, fill the exhibit. A large part of the museum is dedicated to the Civil War: There were more volunteers per capita in the Union Army from California than from any other state. Exhibits honor all branches of the military—with

an emphasis on the roles Californians played—beginning with the American Revolution and through the Gulf War and Bosnia. Guided tours are available (make arrangements in advance). Tue–Sun 10–4. $2.25 adults, $1.50 seniors, $1 service members in uniform and children 5–12. (Central)

CALIFORNIA STATE ARCHIVES
1020 O St.
916/653-7715

California has taken its own history seriously from the moment of its inception. The first legislature charged the Secretary of State to receive any and all documents which chronicled the government's activities, and the State Archives continues that tradition. This state-of-the-art facility has six floors of stacks and new facilities for the preservation, reproduction, and research use of archival materials. Interactive exhibits and educational programs are

The Image of Sacramento

Can there be such a thing as a quintessential image for an entire region, across time, place, and culture? Perhpas not, but one candidate comes to mind: Picture yourself before a canvas divided roughly in half, in two broad horizontal bands, with rhythmic thrusts at right angles along the border between upper and lower expanses, all rendered with intense earth tones. This is the palpable reality of the Sacramento Valley—flat land beneath a big sky, the two realms knitted together at the horizon by towering trees along rivers and levees. No one produces this imagery better than Gregory Kondos, the Sacramento artist with perhaps the biggest national reputation. Even if you're newly arrived, chances are you've already seen his work. The front entrance of the airport's new Terminal A has a magnificent series of panels designed by Kondos, in colored and etched transom-glass panels depicting the Sacramento River as it moves through the Delta.

on the first two floors. While the building also holds the Golden State Museum (see below), the larger portion of it is given over to archival collections on topics such as California Constitutions, election and political campaigns, governors, railroads, prisons, oral histories, and genealogical material. Open to the public for research Mon–Fri except holidays, 9:30–4. (Central)

CALIFORNIA STATE CAPITOL MUSEUM
10th and L Sts.
916/324-0333
www.assembly.ca.gov

The capitol was built in the 1860s and '70s, with a gold-tipped copper dome that emulates the nation's Capitol and compares favorably with it in grandeur. The tour is well worth taking (see chapter 5, Sights and Attractions); don't miss the museum in the basement. Exhibits here document not only the history of the building's construction, but the huge task of renovation completed in the 1980s, which included retrofitting the building seismically. The building was gutted and completely reconstructed from the inside out, and the museum displays are a primer on

construction techniques from an era of grand architectural embellishment. Modern workers rediscovered (or, in some cases, reinvented) the methods that produced the original building. The renovation was, at the time, the largest and most expensive remodeling project ever undertaken. Daily 9–5. Free. (Central)

CALIFORNIA STATE INDIAN MUSEUM
2618 K St.
916/324-0539

This is the first state-run museum to devote itself entirely to Native American culture, and the arts and crafts exhibits here vividly illustrate the lifestyle of the original peoples of California, as well as the native plants and animals they relied upon for survival. Highlights include hunting and fishing implements, basketry (with some incredible miniature works), ceremonial dance regalia, sacred objects, headdresses, bow-and-arrow sets, musical instruments, a hand-carved canoe, and even early photographs. One exhibit retells the story of Ishi, the last survivor of the Yahi tribe, and there are some hands-on displays, such as the mortar and pestle in front. It's located next to Sutter's Fort. Open daily 10–5. $2 adults, $1 children 6–12. (East)

CALIFORNIA STATE RAILROAD MUSEUM
Second and I Sts.
Old Sacramento
916/445-7387, 916/445-6645 (recorded information)
www.csrmf.org

As the largest interpretive museum of its kind in North America, the Railroad Museum will deeply affect anyone who ever cared a whit about trains. The first spike driven for the transcontinental railroad was hammered into the ground about a block away and the 100,000-square-foot facility houses not only vintage trains (including the first and last steam engines built by Central Pacific), but a still-working turntable with service pits where the engines are restored. There are 21 locomotives (among them a million-pound steam engine) and 46 exhibits, and even more of each when a rail fair is in town. "Interactive" takes on new meaning when kids can climb through cars from past rail lines and feel a sleeping car rocking on its tracks as they pass mannequins "asleep" in their berths, or see the slots where mail was sorted while the trains carried these bags of letters through the night. Be sure to watch the movie in the museum's theater first, and then go to the top level where beautiful model trains are displayed. During summer rail festivals, locomotives even from across the oceans might be on display. Take a ride along the river on a working steam-engine train during the summer (see chapter 5, Sights and Attractions). Plans are in the works for a railroad technology museum to be built in the adjacent rail yards, where brick buildings in which the engines, rails, and rolling stock were built from scratch for the transcontinental railroad still

stand. Daily 10–5. $6 adults and children over age 12, $3 children 6–12. (Central)

THE DISCOVERY MUSEUM HISTORY CENTER
101 I St.
Old Sacramento
916/264-7057
www.thediscovery.org
The Discovery Museum is housed in a replica of the city's first City Hall and Waterworks Building (1854), in which a huge 200,000-gallon storage tank was used to create the first municipally owned water system in California—especially useful in a town that would regularly burn to the ground. Exhibits are largely on loan from the City of Sacramento History and Science Division. The division has collected artifacts from commercial, governmental, and domestic life, and not only preserves these artifacts but creates ever-changing programs, and continues to collect the history of the city. A highlight is the Gold Gallery, showcasing interactive kiosks and multimedia stations, gold specimens, and simulated environments that teach the history of mining and of gold itself. There are special programs for kids (see chapter 7, Kids' Stuff). Tue–Sun 10–5, Mon 10–5 during the summer and on holidays. $5 adults, $4 seniors and children 13–17, $3 children 6–12. (Central)

TIP

Collection descriptions can be obtained through the State Archives' Web site. Try www.ss.ca.gov/archives/archives.htm, or e-mail for information (ArchivesWeb@ss.ca.gov) on the more than 100 million documents, 20,000 maps and drawings, 250,000 photographs, and thousands of video and audio recordings.

THE DISCOVERY MUSEUM OF SCIENCE AND CHALLENGER SPACE CENTER
3615 Auburn Blvd.
916/575-3941, 916/485-8836 (group reservations), 916/264-7057
www.thediscovery.org

This hands-on learning museum features a simulated Mission Control where flights into space are created for "crew members." Though it is primarily aimed at kids, there is also an adult "community flight" on the third Wednesday of the month for additional cost. "Flights" include a "Voyage to Mars" and "Rendezvous with Comet Halley in 2061." The "missions" require teamwork and even local corporations have found the flights to be unique training experiences in staff cooperation. The museum also features the area's only planetarium, as well as displays about Native Americans of the Sacramento Valley, an animal hall, and an adjoining outdoor nature area with a short trail that winds through miniature natural environments including a creek and pond. (You don't have to enter the museum to enjoy the nature trail, but if you don't encounter much wildlife, come inside to see reptiles and bugs, among other animals.) Natural history displays include crystals, minerals, rock formations, and fossils. Tue–Fri 12–5, Sat–Sun 10–5. $5 adults, $4 seniors and children 13–17, $3 children 6–12. (Northeast)

GOLDEN STATE MUSEUM
1020 O St. (California State Archives Building)
916/653-7524

"High-tech" and "interactive" are the first two adjectives associated with this brand new museum. The four galleries each have themes: the Place, the People, the Politics, and the Promise. Their multimedia exhibits make use of the vast archives stored next door to produce tableaus of California history. Audio tours through personal CD players and headsets (including kids' versions), multiscreen video displays, a hologram of naturalist John Muir, computers, and re-creations of local landmarks make this a compelling experience. In one re-creation, Posey's Café restaurant, an old Ronald Reagan hangout, plays back political debates through the booths' jukeboxes. Even the building's exterior is a wonder: The Constitution Wall in the courtyard was built to include 36 words from the Constitution in various levels of relief, so that as the sun moves through the sky, different words appear to come and go, along with the shifting shadows. Tue–Sat 10–5, Sun 12–5. $6.50 adults, $5 seniors, $3.50 children 6–13. Admission includes audio guide program. (Central)

GOVERNOR'S MANSION STATE HISTORIC PARK
16th and H Sts.

T I P

The Sacramento County Museum Network has a hotline of recorded information covering hours, locations, and special events. Call 916/947-4478.

916/323-3047
Nancy Reagan likened this 15-room Victorian mansion to a funeral parlor, and declared it a firetrap. While it may have felt like a mausoleum to a family with young kids, its restoration as a museum for artifacts preserved from almost a century of use serves as a powerful reminder of the wealth that surrounded Sacramento's founding. Splendor is the thing; original owner Albert Gallatin estimated the value of the 1877 Victorian at $75,000, in a day when the average home cost $700 to build. Oriental rugs, Italian marble fireplaces, chandeliers, and French mirrors completed the effect. The built-in swimming pool was constructed for Pat Brown after reporters discovered that his regular routine was to cross the street in his swim trunks to take a dip in the neighboring hotel pool. To this day, since the Reagan's departure to a home rented for them in the East Sac "Fab Forties" neighborhood, California governors make their own housing arrangements. Daily tours on the hour 10–4. $3 adults and children 13 and over, $1.50 children 6–12. (Central)

**LELAND STANFORD MANSION
Eighth and N Sts.**

Golden State Museum

Golden State Museum

The downstairs breakfast room in the Governor's Mansion is where Governor Pat Brown declined John F. Kennedy's invitation to be his presidential running mate.

916/445-4209, 916/324-0575 (tour information) www.Cal-parks.ca.gov/districts /goldrush/lsmshp.htm

Leland Stanford was one of the Big Four of transcontinental railroad fame and later founded Stanford University. While he was still a successful Sacramento dry-goods merchant, he purchased what was then a two-story house. To withstand chronic flooding, Stanford had the house jacked up a full story, then topped with an additional story and a mansard roof. The mansion now boasts 44 rooms and 19,000 square feet. The house served as a temporary state capitol for years and was a children's home for some time. Be sure to call first before visiting, as extensive renovations have been ongoing to restore the building's past splendor. Tours during the restoration process emphasize the archaeological search for clues to the mansion's past. (Central)

SUTTER'S FORT STATE HISTORIC PARK 2701 L St. 916/445-4422

Sutter's Fort was the beginning of all that came after, the place where Sacramento was created. After building the fort and trading post with the labor of Native Americans

Annual Art Events

During Chalk it Up to Sacramento on Labor Day weekend, artists from throughout the region gather at Fremont Park (at 15th and P Streets) to each color a square of sidewalk with pastels. Chalk it Up raises funds for arts-education programs for kids in Sacramento County. The works of more than 100 artists and galleries are viewed by more than 40,000 visitors during the Waterfront Art Festival in Old Sacramento, usually in early May. Wine, food, and entertainment are served to complement the art. The Crocker Art Museum holds an Annual Art Auction in June that includes an art preview, music, and an outdoor supper, all followed by an auction. If you're intimidated by the process, attend the Crocker Art Museum's New Collectors' Symposium in late May to get up to speed.

and Hawaiians, John Sutter prospered until the site was largely destroyed by the lawless gold miners who ripped through his property in 1849. The fort's walls have been reconstructed, and today self-guided tours give a feel for life in Sutter's time. The exhibits feature cooper and blacksmith shops, a bakery, prison, a doctor's office with instruments of the time, the dining room and living quarters, and livestock quarters. Daily 10–5; last self-guided audio tour at 4:15. $3 adults and children 12 and over, $1.50 children 6–11. Fees slightly higher during Living History Days, when local actors portray early settlers and cheerfully talk to visitors about Sacramento's history. (East)

WELLS FARGO HISTORY MUSEUM
400 Capitol Mall
916/440-4161
From the street, this Chippendale-topped skyscraper looks like just another part of the business and political district's skyline, but at ground level Wells Fargo maintains a museum that highlights the bank's own place in Sacramento history. A Concord stagecoach is fully restored in its fiery red glory, and there are also a hand-painted safe, antique gold-mining equipment, and one of the early telegraphs, all from the Gold Rush days. A second Wells Fargo History Museum is at 1000 2nd Street in Old Sacramento. Mon–Fri 9–5. Free. (Central)

OTHER MUSEUMS

FOLSOM PRISON MUSEUM
Folsom Prison, Prison Rd.
off East Natoma St.
800/821-6443, 916/985-2561

ext. 4589
Yes, it's the place Johnny Cash sang about. And no, Johnny didn't really do time here, but "Sam the Prisoner"—a talking mannequin—will tell you about life for those who did. "The end of the world" to its inmates, this somber, granite, castlelike structure was built in 1878 and has a history of gruesome treatment of its prisoners, who were not model citizens. A hobby shop sells artwork by the prisoners, including jewelry, woodwork, wooden toys, and paintings. The museum includes exhibits on prison life, such as a 10-barrel Gatling gun that was used to patrol the grounds before the walls reached their present height. Daily 10–4. $1 ages 13 and older. (Northeast)

HEIDRICK AG HISTORY CENTER
1962 Hays Ln.
Woodland
530/666-9700, 530/666-9712 (fax)
www.aghistory.org
This agriculture museum is located in Woodland, just northwest of Sacramento. The center combines the Fred C. Heidrick Antique Ag Collection and the Hays Antique Truck Museum, recognized together as the largest of their kind anywhere (see chapter 7, Kids' Stuff). Gold and

TRIVIA

A free-standing bathtub with clawed feet in the Governors' Mansion has its toenails painted bright red. This was the work of Kathleen Brown, daughter of Edmund (Pat) Brown and sister of Jerry.

railroads had their part in Sacramento history, but agriculture and the machines that made its gigantic scale possible are the enduring threads from the Sacramento Valley's past that were woven into each era. Easter–Labor Day Mon–Fri 10–5, Sat 10–6, Sun 10–4; Labor Day–Easter Wed–Fri 10–5, Sat 10–6, Sun 10–4; also closed Dec 24–Jan 1. $6 adults, $5 seniors, $4 kids 6–14. (West)

MCCLELLAN AVIATION MUSEUM
3204 Palm Ave.
North Highlands
916/643-3192

Situated on the McClellan Air Force Base, which is gradually being converted to civilian use, the McClellan Aviation Museum has three indoor facilities and a wonderful outdoor collection of 32 restored airplanes. There are vintage aircraft that predate the base, and dozens of planes that had historical roles when the base was in greatest use. Inside are instrument trainers and displays on such things as the history of the Air Force uniform. The building also contains displays of pilot headgear, exhibits on the famous Doolittle Tokyo Raid, a chronological lineup of several aircraft engines, and a vast collection of models and art-

work depicting airplanes through the years. Some of the most popular aircraft are: the North American F-100D "Super Sabre"; the first Soviet MiG-21 on permanent display in this country; the Lockheed EC-121D "Warning Star"; and the Fairchild-Republic 10A "Thunderbolt II (Warthog)," which was used prominently during Desert Storm. For the time being, this is still a working air base, so you'll first have to stop at the visitors center to get a pass and show proof of insurance, car registration, and a current driver's license. Use the Palm Avenue Gate, off Watt Avenue. Mon–Fri 9–3, Sat 9–4, Sun noon–4. Free. (North)

TOWE AUTO MUSEUM
2200 Front St.
916/442-6802

"Memory Lane" and "Dreams" are the operative themes here. While the vintage cars are spectacular enough, they're displayed in cultural vignettes that will give kids (or grandkids) a feel for the era in which the car was driven. The Dream of Cool and The Dream of Speed are two of the many exhibits that will give adults and youngsters a chance to connect—or get the oldsters laughed at—as nostalgia for the twentieth century overwhelms the visitor. Mannequins wear the garb of the era and props fill out small dioramas that connect a car with the culture that produced it. The museum also has a gift shop, video programs, and a research library. Private parties can be arranged. Group discounts and guided tours with volunteer docents are available. It's at the southern end of Front Street just below Old Sacramento. Daily 10–6. $6 adults, $2.50 youths 14–18, $1 children 5–13. (Central)

ROSEVILLE TELEPHONE MUSEUM
106 Vernon St.
Roseville
916/786-1621
The Roseville Telephone Museum provides yet another opportunity for parents and grandparents to set themselves up for derisive comments from their thoroughly modern youngsters (the ones with cell phones grafted onto their ears). Four galleries display telephone technology, from its inception in the 1890s to the present. Grow nostalgic, or em-

barrassed, as your kids see how you used to let your fingers do the walking. Group tours Mon–Fri 9–5; also open Sat 10–4. $1 ages 13 and older. (Northeast)

GALLERIES

The great majority of art-viewing in the Sacramento region is available within galleries rather than museums. The galleries themselves have organized a way to make small, diverse venues more accessible with what is now known as "Second Saturdays." On the second Saturday evening of each month, participating galleries coordinate their hours (frequently from six to nine) and stay open, often with simultaneous receptions for new showings and artists. The nature of the city makes this relatively easy: In Midtown, particularly, the gallery district can be walked, and many galleries can be easily visited in one ambling stroll. Area restaurants

Towe Auto Museum

Art on Foot

If you'd like to experience a surprising variety of contemporary, folk, and ethnic art, then "Second Saturday" is the way to go. The daunting thing about gallery-hopping in most cities is the urban sprawl, but in Sacramento—especially in Downtown and Midtown—you can do so on foot. The following itinerary will help you navigate 20 galleries in the city's central area on a walking tour. The art walk starts on the north end of Capitol Park, goes east, then west, and ends in Old Sacramento, with a variety of restaurants along the way just as rich and surprising as the art.

1. **The Crate/Artists Contemporary Gallery,** 1200 K St., Hyatt Regency building
2. **Thomas A. Oldham Gallery,** 1729 L St.
3. **Barton Gallery,** 1723 I St.
4. **b. Sakata Garo,** 923 20th St.
5. **WEAVE Works,** 919 20th St.
6. **Platinum West Gallery,** 1018 22nd St.
7. **Still Life Gallery,** 2231 J St.
8. **Studio 1109,** 1109 22nd St.
9. **Fire & Rain,** 1014 24th St.
10. **Jon Gabriel's,** 2408 J St.
11. **Ensoul,** 2421-1/2 J St.
12. **Big Art,** 1928 L St.
13. **Blooming Art,** 1901 Capitol Ave.
14. **Thistle Dew Gallery,** 1901 P St.
15. **Excentrique Functional Art Gallery,** 1409 R St.
16. **Art Foundry Gallery,** 1021 R St.
17. **La Raza Bookstore Galeria Posada,** 704 O St.
18. **Crocker Art Museum,** 216 O St.
19. **750 Gallery,** 719-1/2 J St.
20. **Artists' Collaborative Gallery,** 1007 Second St.

cooperate as well, so that one can wander through the galleries with dozens or even hundreds of fellow residents and visitors and then enjoy a late dinner seated along the avenues of this livable urban setting. It's part of what makes Sacramento special.

ART FOUNDRY GALLERY
1025 R St.
916/444-2787
This is both a fine-arts gallery and a working bronze foundry. As you might expect, sculpture is featured, but so is painting, very often in exhibits in which the artist works in both media. Styles range from classical to abstract expressionist. Located in "the Building" (see chapter 9, Shopping), a restored nineteenth-century brick warehouse. (Central)

THE ARTERY
207 G St.
Davis
530/758-8330
www.ArteryArt.com
As a showcase for Northern California artists (particularly those in the Davis area), the Artery has been around as an artists' cooperative and retail store for over 25 years. It features decorative and functional ceramics, as well as other traditional media by members. Each spring the Artery sponsors the California Clay Competition, a statewide juried exhibition. (West)

ARTISTS' COLLABORATIVE GALLERY
1007 Second St.
Old Sacramento
916/444-3764
The Artists' Collaborative Gallery was founded over 20 years ago. Member artists display their own work, which includes fine arts as well as traditional crafts like glassworks, hand-painted silks, and ceramics (see chapter 9, Shopping). (Central)

BARTON GALLERY
1723 I St.
916/443-4025
www.sacarts.com
In exhibitions that rotate monthly, the Barton Gallery features unknown local artists who work with the human figure. Owner Gregory Barton also has a permanent collection of his own bronze sculptures, and the gallery includes an outdoor sculpture garden and open-studio

Contact the Sacramento Gallery Association (Deidre Trudeau of Via Graphics, 916/783-6185) to obtain a "Second Saturday" guide with maps of the areas that coordinate their showings—Del Paso Boulevard, Midtown/Downtown, Arden/University, and Fair Oaks/Carmichael. The map will show only SGA members, but there are many others to see as well, and they will all be listed, by address, in the *Sacramento Bee* and the *News and Review.* Also, the town of Davis has a "Second Friday" so as not to compete head-to-head with Sacramento. In addition, the foothill town of Auburn has "Second Thursday" every other month, and Placerville has "Third Saturday" monthly.

figure drawing opportunities. An Italian restaurant (Michelangelo's) on the premises makes it easy to eat and stroll during Second Saturday art walks. (East)

b. SAKATA GARO
923 20th St.
916/447-4276

The purpose of this gallery is stated as: "Connecting the visions and thoughts of the artist with the public." Here, you'll often find provocative written support for the exhibitions, which serves an educational function, and works from throughout the world in a wide array of media. (East)

CAMERA/ARTS
712 57th St.
916/736-3084

Camera/Arts, located next to the Darkroom Gallery (see below), features local and regional photography. (East)

CHROMA GALLERY
10030 Fair Oaks Blvd.
916/966-6020
www.thechromagallery.com

This is Sacramento's plein-air gallery, featuring more than 30 painters who work to capture the light and color of the region. Emulating the techniques and results of the Impressionists, the member artists bring individual vision to the intense natural ambience of their main subject—the Sacramento Valley. (Northeast)

THE CRATE/ARTISTS CONTEMPORARY GALLERY
1200 K St. #9
916/446-3694

This gallery is the oldest in Sacramento and fits in well with the retail crafts found at the base of the Hyatt Regency. Original works by both established and new artists are on display. (Central)

THE DARKROOM GALLERY
708 57th St.
916/454-4906

The Darkroom Gallery showcases fine art and experimental photography by local artists. (Northeast)

DOIRON GALLERY
1625 Del Paso Blvd.
916/564-4433
www.doirongallery.com

Part of the resurgent Uptown neighborhood along Del Paso in North Sacramento, the Doiron features everything from fine arts to wearable and functional art for the home. Big enough to exhibit local, regional, and national artists, the gallery also has four studio artists who demonstrate their crafts. (North)

ENCINA ART GALLERY
1400 Bell Ave. (Encina High School Campus)
916/971-5881

The Encina Art Gallery is worth a special note because curator/artist Suzanne Adan and director/art instructor Michael Stevens have brought serious art exhibits onto a high school campus, where students can have daily exposure to the work of local and national artists. (Northeast)

ENSOUL
2421-1/2 J St.
916/446-3908

Passing on the street, you might think it's a framing shop, but look closer. The emphasis at Ensoul is on African American and Southwestern artwork, and their motto is "From

A New Kind of Venue

*Amidst the sensory overload of today's popular culture, there is now an art exhibition space where the viewer can be stimulated by more than the eye. The "art bar" concept has come to Sacramento, and it's more than just paintings hanging in a restaurant at the **Pegase Art Bar** (916/920-1616) adjacent to the Himovitz Gallery. Art is on the walls, but sculpture stands among the dining tables too, and the furnishings are designed by prominent local artists. Even the tables feature artworks beneath the glass tabletops, so you can enjoy an intimate view of new works while sampling "world fusion" cuisine and sipping fine wine.*

our soul to your heart." Demetrice Cheathon, an artist represented in collections across the nation, is featured. (East)

EXCENTRIQUE FUNCTIONAL ART GALLERY
1409 R St.
916/446-1786
Contemporary art furniture is finding a wider niche lately, as galleries have discovered that modern three-dimensional design is more understandable when it also has a working place in the home. New shows monthly include sculpture and mixed-media works. (Central)

MICHAEL HIMOVITZ GALLERY
1616 Del Paso Blvd. ("Building on the Boulevard")
916/929-7896
Often cited as being both hip and New York–style, the Himovitz is one of the most prominent area galleries. It's at the center of the Uptown arts district, in the "Building on the Boulevard." (North)

JGLENN GALLERY
604 Fourth St.
Davis
530/757-2292
Both established and emerging Northern Californian artists are featured in this intimate gallery space located in a historic building. (West)

JOHN NATSOULAS GALLERY
140 F St.
Davis
530/756-3938
The John Natsoulas Gallery features contemporary sculpture and paintings by Bay Area figurative and abstract expressionists and by artists of the Sacramento Valley. (West)

LA RAZA BOOKSTORE GALERIA POSADA
704 O St.
916/446-5133
Focused on Latino and American Indian artists, La Raza is in a historically significant building, the Heilbron House (though looking for new space). (Central)

Solomon Dubnick Gallery shows the work of Jeff Myers.

MATRIXARTS
1518 Del Paso Blvd.
916/923-9118
Matrixarts, a nonprofit gallery, supports outreach through both exhibitions and education programs. "Empowering artists, serving the community" is their motto. Women artists are featured. (North)

PHANTOM GALLERIES
492 Arden Way
916/922-ARTS
Phantom Galleries is a rotating collection that temporarily occupies various unused buildings in the Uptown arts district, primarily along Del Paso Boulevard. (North)

PLATINUM WEST GALLERY
1018 22nd St.
916/448-3725
Platinum West is a photography gallery featuring turn-of-the-century (nineteenth into twentieth, that is) photographic processes, such as platinum/palladium prints on hand-coated paper. (East)

750 GALLERY
719-1/2 J St.
916/758-8912
As a cooperative, 750 Gallery's local artists have been working on the contemporary cutting edge for 15 years. Group and individual shows of unconventional and experimental art are offered. (Central)

SOLOMON DUBNICK GALLERY
2131 Northrop Ave.
916/920-4547
A nationally prominent gallery, the Solomon Dubnick Gallery made its reputation primarily with Northern California artists, some just emerging and others well established. (Northeast)

SMITH GALLERY
2650 Marconi Ave.
916/481-1455
www.smithgallery.com
Specializing in works by artists in Sacramento and the surrounding region, the Smith Gallery showcases original paintings and limited-edition

prints, often emphasizing the area's landscape, cityscape, and river views. (Northeast)

SMUD ART GALLERY
6310 S St.
916/264-5558
Not your everyday venue, the Sacramento Municipal Utilities District lends its customer-service lobby to art-gallery purposes for both student and professional exhibits. (East)

TOWER GALLERY
484 Howe Ave.

916/924-1001
Tower Gallery shows original works by local and regional artists, plus signed limited-edition prints by both local and internationally exhibited artists. They have a different show each month. (Northeast)

VENTANA GALLERY
552 Pavilions Ln. (Pavilions shopping center)
916/920-9562, 916/920-8346 (fax)
Ventana—window, in Spanish—serves both emerging and widely recognized artists working in a vast range of media including painting,

Top Ten Favorites of a New Arrival

by Lial Jones, who recently arrived from the Delaware Art Museum to become the director of the Crocker Art Museum

1. **The arts.** Del Paso gallery district, the Crocker Art Museum (of course), La Raza . . . the list goes on.
2. **The history.** Sacramento was a crossroad to the Sierras, bringing in people from all over the world.
3. **The river.** You're never too far from a bit of nature. Take a walk, go biking—escape.
4. **The festivals.** Festival de la Familia, Pacific Rim, Summerfest, outdoor concerts, farmers markets.
5. **The trees.** Sacramento has more trees per capita than any other urban area in the world—except Paris, France.
6. **The cemetery** on Broadway (especially on Halloween).
7. **The contrasts.** New and old at the same time. The juxtaposition of Old Sac to modern structures in a city being reborn.
8. **The food.** We have a broad range of incredible places to eat.
9. **The sports.** Kings, Monarchs, and River Cats.
10. **The location.** We're a short drive from many other great destinations, and a great place to come home to after a day trip.

sculpture, and limited-edition prints. Regular patrons enjoy exclusive showings throughout the year. (Northeast)

WILD ARTS
231 G St. #8
Davis
530/758-8170
Wild Arts owner Susan Hargrove is a painter and sculptor herself and has owned a number of area galleries in the past. She has created a place for "fun, functional, affordable art pieces." National as well as regional artists provide whimsical objects, furnishings, jewelry, and other contemporary art. (West)

PUBLIC ART

Art in Public Places is a program sponsored by the Sacramento Metropolitan Arts Commission (SMAC). Each year 15 to 25 artists are chosen to receive grants that help them design, make, and install their work in public spaces. The program is funded with a 2 percent charge to area developers, one of the highest such rates in the nation. While there is no dominating, city-defining, landmark work of art on the order of, say, Calder's *Flamingo* at the Federal Center in Chicago, there are many human-scaled works throughout Sacramento commissioned by SMAC, many of which are carefully integrated with the surrounding architecture. The wonderful glass panels at the airport's Terminal A by Gregory Kondos, iron sculpture by Kathy Noonan at several light-rail stations, and public art placed at the Central Library and Downtown Plaza, including the sculptures outside the convention center, are a few examples. SMAC docents offer monthly tours of the downtown-area artworks (call 916/264-5558).

© Tom Myers 1998

7

KIDS' STUFF

Sacramento is a great place to be a salmon or a native human. The high percentage of offspring who leave in their youth only to return to spawn is testimony to an inner drive to get back to someplace that feels right. (The human adults survive the reproduction process in better shape than do the salmon.) Time and again the newcomer here will meet someone who was born and raised a Sacramentan, left for greener pastures or brighter lights, and then came back to raise their own families. It's a place to feel comfortable, and for the restlessly ambitious that may not be good enough. But for parents, it's something to give back, a chance to offer their children the experience of growing up involved and valued, in a family-oriented community where kids and learning and the outdoors come together. Some places just feel like home, and here the more than 120 city parks and more than 2,000 acres (not even counting the 5,000 acres of the American River Parkway) of both developed and natural land have a lot to do with that feeling. Sacramento may not be overrun by mega-amusement parks with show-business themes, but kids can enjoy the best the Golden State has to offer in history, culture, and nature.

All locations below are considered wheelchair accessible.

ANIMALS AND THE GREAT OUTDOORS

AMERICAN RIVER PARKWAY

This park is covered in more detail in chapter 8, Parks, Gardens, and Recreation Areas, but it's worth noting here because it offers so much recreational space and so many facilities for children. Older kids have the 23-mile greenbelt to bike or skate through. You will also find picnic grounds all along the Parkway, and several businesses that offer rafting trips from the Sunrise Bridge area downriver to Goethe Park, a gentle trip kids of all ages can enjoy until they're ready to roar down the whitewater forks of the American River. There are also horse rentals for the equestrian trails, archery, boat launches, and almost limitless hiking choices—enough activities to keep kids occupied for years. The are many entrance points to the American River Parkway. The bike trail begins in Discovery Park off the Garden Highway near the meeting point of the American and Sacramento Rivers. (C, E, N, NE)

COSUMNES RIVER WILDLIFE PRESERVE
6500 Desmond Rd.
Galt
916/684-2816

As the name suggests, Cosumnes is truly a wild preserve. Its riparian environment and wetlands are a vital part of the migrating routes of uncountable species of birds (see also Parks, Gardens, and Recreation Areas). Though there is a visitors center (open weekends 10–4), the preserve has no permanent facilities, so be prepared to pack out everything you might bring in. Ducks, geese, deer, beavers, and even river otters may be spotted. Take Interstate 5 south to Twin Cities Road west. Then take Franklin Road south and turn left on Des-

mond Road to park. Open daylight hours. Free. (South)

EFFIE YEAW NATURE CENTER
Ancil Hoffman Regional Park
6700 Tarshes Dr.
Carmichael
916/489-4918

The Effie Yeaw Nature Center was named for a Carmichael teacher who emphasized the importance of nature to pupils throughout her teaching career. Effie Yeaw ("rhymes with jaw," she would say) is now an interpretive park and education center within Ancil Hoffman Park, which is along the north side of the American River. Call for information on ongoing programs for adults and kids, then visit exhibits of native plants and animals, including live displays and dioramas. The center offers games, campfire programs, films, demonstrations, and self-guided walking tours along nature trails. There are also free guided tours by park rangers available on weekend afternoons and by reservation. Beyond the Nature Center itself, Hoffman Park has its own wild pleasures. It's a place where kids can observe firsthand a healthy riparian environment as they spot deer, wild turkeys, hawks, water fowl, foxes, raccoons, possums, squirrels, and much more while following the river along trails shaded by woods still preserved in pristine condition (this land was

TRIVIA

Salmon aren't the only anadromous fish of the American River. Striped bass, shad, white sturgeon, lamprey eel, and steelhead trout also leave the freshwater river to spend part of their life cycle at sea.

The Sacramento Recreation and Community Programs offer activity choices for kids too numerous to list—sports, arts and crafts, performing arts, martial arts, piano lessons, you name it—for low fees. Find their printed directories at the Central Library or any of its branches. While you're there, check out the libraries' story times, puppet shows, and music programs.

highly valued by its private owners as protection for their farms against the river's floods). You pay a low admission fee for your car as you enter Hoffman Park, then the Nature Center is free. It's also a good place to buy native plants. Mar–Oct daily 9–5, Nov–Feb daily 9–4. $4 parking fee. (Northeast)

FOLSOM CITY ZOO
Folsom and Stafford St.
Folsom City Park
916/985-7347
The Folsom Zoo has been called the "misfit zoo" because it features wild animals (such as mountain lions, wolves, and bears) native to California and other parts of North America that no one else wants, and who, because of injuries or illness, or because they were kept as pets, can be nursed back to health but not returned to the wild. This is a small place but a great resource for helping children understand the precarious relationship between humans and nature. Daily Tue–Sun. Small admission charge. (South)

GIBSON RANCH COUNTY PARK
8552 Gibson Ranch Rd.
Elverta
916/991-7592
This county facility is a working ranch. The 326-acre area was once a Mexican land grant (Rancho del Paso) and was homesteaded in the 1870s. Farm animals can be fed and petted, and kids can check out displays of antique farm equipment, buggies, a carriage shop, an old ranch house, and a blacksmithy. There is also a swimming hole surrounded by grass and sand, as well as changing areas with showers. You and the kids can fish an 18-acre pond, ride the equestrian trails, have a picnic, and camp by day or overnight. (North)

MCKINLEY PARK
Between H St., Alhambra Blvd.,
McKinley Blvd., and 33rd St.
At the juncture of Midtown and East Sac, McKinley Park is considered by many to be one of the most beautiful neighborhood parks in town. The park is a favorite for all, while kids will especially like the newly refurbished tot-lots, which have loads of structures to climb on, and the duck pond. (East)

NIMBUS FISH HATCHERY
2001 Nimbus Rd.
Rancho Cordova
916/358-2820
Though open year-round, the action here really heats up from October

Backpacking and Hiking Trails for Kids

Bill McMillon, with his son Kevin, has written a book called Best Hikes with Children around Sacramento. *Remarkably, there are no fewer than 15 trails listed that are within 20 miles of downtown Sacramento. While urban, and especially suburban, growth is advancing by leaps and bounds, many pockets of nature have been preserved, and Sacramento's largely flat topography helps keep trails accessible even to the very young. McMillon's book is published by the Mountaineers and is worth seeking out to discover the many different ways kids can have direct contact with the region's land and its creatures.*

to December because that's when the oceangoing salmon return to their birthplace to spawn and start their life cycle all over again. (Steelheads make the same journey roughly January through March.) Kids can see the fish close-up and marvel at the power of instinct as the fish fight their way upstream. The human hand interferes with nature's process here because construction of the flood-controlling dam made it necessary. The adult salmon who make it as far as the fish ladder are gathered and killed, and their eggs and sperm are harvested. Though this will seem cruel to children, the fish were, after all, on their way to die, and this human aid guarantees that millions of smolt will be released in the Delta during spring to make their way back to the Pacific. (The edible fish are donated to various agencies.) From U.S. 50 East, take the Hazel Avenue exit north. Go left on Gold Country Boulevard and follow the signs to the hatchery. It's adjacent to the American River Fish Hatchery (2101 Nimbus Rd., 916/355-0896), a smaller facility where the Department of Fish and Game raises the trout they use to stock streams and lakes throughout the state. Open daily. Free. (South)

SACRAMENTO ZOO
3930 West Land Park Dr.
William Land Park
916/264-5888, 916/264-8561
(groups and catering)
www.saczoo.com

This is a small, urban zoo that has suffered in its inability to expand to accommodate modern developments in animal care. Rather than give in to physical restrictions, however, a dedicated staff has focused on working with endangered species, as funding permits the zoo to slowly rehabilitate itself. A recent makeover of available space is the "Pandamonium" exhibit of red pandas, the giant panda's cousin.

Birds, primates, monkeys, lions, giraffes, tigers, and other exotic cats are all here, as is a reptile house. It's all laid out amidst high trees and ponds for a beautiful wooded effect, even if many of the exhibits are still concrete bunkers. Endangered-species exhibits include the snow leopard and the golden-headed, lion tamarin (a kind of monkey). Check their calendar for numerous special nights, including some that give a behind-the-scenes look at how the animals are maintained. Open daily 10–5. Call for admission prices. (South)

SILVER BEND–KIRTLAND FARMS
34600 South River Rd.
Clarksburg
916/665-1410

A tour of a working farm, including a pumpkin patch in the fall, a ride on a miniature train, a hay-bale maze, farm animals, picnic grounds, and in season it becomes a cut-your-own Christmas tree farm. A popular spot for field trips by Sacramento-area

Sacramento Zoo

© Tom Myers 1998

elementary schools, where kids get to hear a talk about Pilgrims and harvests. From the city take Freeport Boulevard south (it's also called Highway 160) to the signs for the Freeport Bridge. Cross over the Sacramento River here, then proceed south to Silver Bend. Open June–December, although they're closed in November to get ready for the Christmas season, which starts right after Thanksgiving. A small admission charge during October and December weekends, otherwise free, from late morning until sundown. (South)

UNIVERSITY OF CALIFORNIA, DAVIS, ARBORETUM
Main Campus along Putah Creek
916/752-2498

The 2.5 miles of paths and lawns at this arboretum can be used to walk, run, picnic, and, most of all, to observe this great collection of trees, shrubs, herbs, and riverbank flora. Older kids might enjoy the annual Spring Battle of the Bands (part of a larger event called Picnic Day, a sort of open house for the entire campus). University marching bands strut and oompah their stuff, and the battle is won by the band which plays the longest without repeating itself. Take the Old Davis Road exit off Interstate 80, park on the south edge of the campus (a small parking office along Old Davis Road will have a helpful attendant with campus maps), then simply walk into the heart of the campus grounds and follow the creek. Parking fees, but no admission charge. (West)

UNIVERSITY OF CALIFORNIA, DAVIS, RAPTOR CENTER
Old Davis Rd., two miles south of campus

530/752-6091
The California Raptor Center offers both guided and self-guided tours through exhibits of several dozen species of birds of prey. These birds can't, for various reasons, be released into the wild, but they help the rest of us learn about their world. Educational programs help kids "meet" eagles, falcons, owls, and others, and learn what indicator species can tell environmentalists about the habitat we all share. Open weekdays. (West)

WILLIAM LAND PARK
Bordered by Freeport Blvd.,
Sutterville Rd., West Land Park
Dr., and 13th Ave.
This is a great place to let the tiny ones run free, especially during the warm months. While the park is home to the zoo, Funderland, and Fairytale Town, it also has wide-open grassy areas, beautiful towering trees, shady tot-lots, picnic grounds with barbecue pits, a wading pool, gardens, an outdoor stage (where "Shakespeare in the Park" is performed during the summer), a duck pond, a golf course (where kids are encouraged to get involved), and softball diamonds. (South)

WITTER RANCH HISTORIC FARM
3480 Witter Way
916/927-4116
The ranch house at Witter Ranch

was built in 1934, while the outbuildings date from 1920, and they are all on the National Register of Historical Places. Kids can see what farm life might have been like for any era from 1915 through the 1950s. They can churn butter, feed animals, use a washboard, and make small crafts. Large groups are encouraged (usually a school field trip, but several-family groups are welcomed as well). Call ahead for an appointment. Some of the supervising adults in the group go first to get oriented and then become capable of running the tour themselves, although at least one staff member will come along, too. (North)

MUSEUMS AND LIBRARIES

CALIFORNIA STATE CAPITOL
AND CAPITOL PARK
10th and L Sts.
916/324-0333
Kids of all ages will marvel at the interior of the capitol building's rotunda and dome. The small museum space in the basement offers budding architects insight as to how big buildings are put together, now and historically. The urban park surrounding the building provides a terrific walking and looking experience. Tree, flower, and plant species from around the world were deliberately cultivated, often received as gifts from visiting dignitaries. Call for

T
I
P

Got a teen who's out of sorts and looking for connections? Try the Web site www.sacteens.org for lists of clubs and activities at local high schools, calendars of teen events, and chat rooms.

children's programs. Open daily 9–5. Free. (Central)

CALIFORNIA STATE INDIAN MUSEUM
2618 K St.
916/324-0971
While the museum is serious in tone, kids will enjoy the exposure to an authentic culture untainted by old-movie absurdities. Here, among exhibits and hands-on displays, kids can appreciate the close ties between humans and nature which existed before increasing settlement of the West brought an end to peaceful and long-lived Native American societies (see also chapter 6, Museums and Galleries). Open daily 10–5. Nominal fee. (East)

CALIFORNIA STATE RAILROAD MUSEUM
Second and I Sts.
Old Sacramento
916/445-7387, 916/445-6645 (recorded information)
www.csrmf.org
With walk-through exhibits, gigantic restored steam engines, model layouts and cars, period-dressed mannequins and room to run from locomotive to locomotive, it's impossible to overstate the effect this museum has on any child who ever gave trains a moment's thought. One of the finest places in the country to combine history and fun (see chapter 6, Museums and Galleries). Open daily 10–5. $3 children 6–12, all others $6. (Central)

CROCKER ART MUSEUM
216 O St.
916/264-5423
Sacramento's primary visual art museum is covered in greater detail in chapter 6, Museums and Galleries.

It's worth calling in for ongoing programs for kids. A typical summer program in the past was "Art Blast: Hands-On Art Activities." These programs are held on Saturday afternoons, free of charge with museum admission. There are also Family Sundays, which in the past have featured puppet theater, among other events. For serious young artists, there are Art Masters classes for kids ages 8 through 12. Tue–Sun 10–5, Thu 10–9; closed major holidays. $5.50 adults, $4.50 seniors, $3 youths 7–17. (Central)

THE DISCOVERY MUSEUM HISTORY CENTER
101 I St.
Old Sacramento
916/264-7057
www.thediscovery.org
The center offers history, of course, plus interactive science and technology exhibits. Kids will gawk at a gigantic gold nugget. A print shop from the 1860s has been duplicated. It's very educational, but don't tell the kids. California history slips enjoyably by, from Native American times to the present (see chapter 6, Museums and Galleries). There are programs for crafts and storytelling offered specifically for kids. In the summer, classes are available for grades one through seven, covering topics such as cooking, chemistry, astronomy, geology, and dinosaurs, here and at the Science Center (see below). Tue–Sun 10–5, Mon 10–5 during the summer and on holidays. $5 adults, $4 seniors and youths 13–17, $3 children 6–12. (Central)

THE DISCOVERY MUSEUM OF SCIENCE AND CHALLENGER SPACE CENTER
3615 Auburn Blvd.

916/575-3941, 916/485-8836 (group reservations), 916/264-7057 www.thediscovery.org

The Challenger Centers, found nationwide, are a living memorial to the crew members who perished in the shuttle flight of 1986. This hands-on learning museum features a simulated Mission Control where flights into space are created for "crew members." Though the simulation is aimed primarily at kids, there is also an adult "community flight" on the third Wednesday of the month for additional cost. A class field trip favorite, students learn to solve in-flight problems with math, science, and technology, relying on team-

Where to Skate

*The ice-skating experience hasn't really caught on in Sacramento as much as it has in Southern California. **Skatetown** in Roseville (916/783-8550) seems to have a lock on hockey activity. The next full-size rink is in Reno, Nevada. **Iceland Skating Rink** (916/925-3121), in the North Sac arts district, is an old and cozy facility for free-skating, but it's not adequate for hockey. From late fall through winter, a holiday tradition is the **Holiday Ice Rink** (916/329-7235) at St. Rose of Lima Park, where outdoor ice is kept fitfully frozen. It's at the meeting place of the K Street Mall and the Downtown Plaza.*

*Inline skating, on the other hand, offers a greater variety of choices. **Cal Skate University** (916/688-5868) has been around for a while and offers skating times for all ages but emphasizes social nights, which makes it a favorite for area teens who want to boogie to dance music under the special lighting effects. Young teens also favor **Kings Skate Country** (916/363-2643), which has two locations in the area. The newest venue is the squeaky-clean **Laguna Skates** (916/691-1800), subtitled a "Family Fun Center." It's a big place, with a video arcade, climbing wall, birthday-party area, and pizza parlor. They have a wide variety of music and programs— some for tots, some for teens, and some for hockey players, as well as parent/child games on Saturday mornings. Rolling mascots add to the party atmosphere. Roller hockey can also be found at the **River City Roller Hockey Arena** (916/386-9990) and **The Rink** (916/852-6795) in Rancho Cordova.*

work to save their missions. The simulation is likened more to participating in a play than being on an amusement park thrill ride. The museum also features a planetarium, displays about Native Americans of the Sacramento Valley, an animal hall, and an adjoining outdoor nature area with a short trail that winds through miniature natural environments including a creek and pond. (You don't have to enter the museum to enjoy the nature trail.) Tue–Fri 12–5, Sat–Sun 10–5. $5 adults, $4 seniors and youths 13–17, $3 children 6–12. (Northeast)

HEIDRICK AG HISTORY CENTER
1962 Hays Ln.
Woodland
530/666-9700, 530/666-9712 (fax)
www.aghistory.org
The "Ag" here is agriculture, in a big way. In Woodland, just northwest of Sacramento, the History Center combines the Fred C. Heidrick Antique Ag Collection and the Hays Antique Truck Museum near the junction of Interstate 5 and Road 102. Together they are recognized as the largest of their kind anywhere. Kids can marvel at carefully preserved relics of both agriculture and the commercial trucking industry, and see the machines that helped grow our food and ship it around the world. (Okay, it's sort of a guy thing, but not necessarily.) With over 130,000 square feet of display space, the center uses interactive computer stations to keep things up-to-date, and toy manufacturer Ertl sponsors a Playzone where kids can get their hands on model farms. Easter–Labor Day Mon–Fri 10–5, Sat 10–6, Sun 10–4; Labor Day–Easter Wed–Fri 10–5, Sat 10–6, Sun 10–4; also closed Dec 24–Jan 1. $6 adults, $5 seniors, $4 kids 6–14. (West)

MCCLELLAN AVIATION MUSEUM
3204 Palm Ave.
North Highlands
916/643-3192
Situated on the McClellan Air Force Base, the Aviation Museum has three indoor facilities and a wonderful outdoor collection of 32 restored military airplanes for future Top Gun candidates to explore. There are vintage aircraft that predate the base and dozens of planes that had historical roles in America's air wars, including a Soviet MiG and the "Warthog" bomber that was still in use during Desert Storm. Inside are displays such as the history of the Air Force uniform and "the children's room," which contains, among many things, hands-on F-101B and T-28 instrument trainers. This is still a working air base, so you'll first have to stop at the visitors center to get a pass and show proof of insurance, car registration, and a current driver's license. Use the Palm Avenue Gate, off Watt Avenue. Mon–Fri 9–3, Sat 9–4, Sun 12–4. Free. (North)

OLD SACRAMENTO SCHOOLHOUSE
Front and L Sts.
Old Sacramento
916/483-8818
The Old Sacramento Schoolhouse serves as a fieldtrip destination for kids from the entire state of California. The one-room schoolhouse has been preserved faithfully from the nineteenth century, and costumed docents hold "class" to dramatize how children of a bygone era were expected to behave. The desks come with writing slates, and the

posted rules for how teachers were to conduct their lives in order to remain employed and avoid scandal are a real hoot. Every kid will want to pull the rope and ring the belfry's school bell. Mon–Fri 10–4, Sat–Sun noon–4. Free. (Central)

ROSEVILLE TELEPHONE MUSEUM
106 Vernon St.
Roseville
916/786-1621
The Roseville Telephone Museum offers four galleries displaying telephone technology, from its inception in the 1890s to the present. Your kids will see how you used to let your fingers do the walking—though at least you can prove you weren't using tom-toms or blowing conch shells to communicate when you were their age. Group tours Mon–Fri 9–5; also open Sat 10–4. $1 ages 13 and older. (Northeast)

SUTTER'S FORT STATE HISTORIC PARK
2701 L St.

916/445-4422
See chapter 5, Sights and Attractions. Open daily 10–5. $1.50 children 6–11, $3 ages 12 and up; fees slightly higher during Living History Days. (East)

TRAVELS THROUGH TIME SCIENCE FICTION MUSEUM
1017-B Front St.
Old Sacramento
916/444-2320
Daily tours by docents will take you through 100 years of largely TV- and movie-inspired science fiction memorabilia. The basement museum (at Sacramento's original street level before the city was raised) begins with the Galactic Imports Store, where fans of *Star Trek, Star Wars,* and other popular series will thrill at the merchandise for sale—figures, toys, and other licensed knick-knacks. The inexpensive tour then takes you through Jules Verne dioramas and on to H. G. Wells treats, such as a re-creation of the time machine from the book and movie of the same name and a staged crash

---

Taming Testosterone

Got a birthday-party problem? Got hyper males who can't sit still? **Prime Time** *(at 530/877-6517 or www.primetimeinteractive.com) bills itself as "Northern California's rental choice for inflatable interactive games, inflatable Velcro walls, sumo wrestling, giant slides, jump houses, obstacle courses, bungee runs, jousting, and more. . . ." This year the company is introducing 20-foot-round water trampolines, mini golf, a 25-foot climbing mountain, sky dancers, and water slides. Beats the heck out of pin-the-tail-on-the-donkey.*

---

of the Martian ship from *War of the Worlds*. Buck Rogers, Flash Gordon—they're all here, in a modest, fun setting. Small admission charge; discounts for seniors, students, and children under 17. Call for hours. (Central)

TOWE AUTO MUSEUM
2200 Front St.
916/442-6802
While the vintage cars are spectacular enough, they're displayed in cultural vignettes that will give kids (or grandkids) a feel for the era in which the car was driven (see Museums and Galleries). It's at the southern end of Front Street just below Old Sacramento. Open daily 10–6. $6 adults, $2.50 youths 14–18, $1 kids 5–13. (Central)

PUPPETS AND THEATER

CHAUTAUQUA PLAYHOUSE
5325 Engle Rd.
Carmichael
916/489-7529
This respected community theater produces an equal number of plays for adults and children throughout the season. (Northeast)

CITY THEATRE AT SACRAMENTO CITY COLLEGE
"Storytime Theatre"
3835 Freeport Blvd.
916/558-2228
"Storytime Theatre" is a student-run production company that offers frequent presentations for kids. Call for schedule. (South)

EAGLE THEATRE
(RUNAWAY STAGE PRODUCTIONS)
925 Front St., Old Sacramento

916/445-6645, ext. 4#
Adjacent to the State Railroad Museum in Old Sacramento, the Eagle Theatre can claim a special history of its own: It was the first building constructed as a theater in California. The original Eagle was lost to floods over a century ago, but this faithful reproduction has become the home of kids' theater on weekends and special historical presentations during festival times in Old Sac. (Central)

FAIRYTALE TOWN PUPPET THEATER
1501 Sutterville Rd.
916/264-5233
(See "Theme Parks," below.) Call for seasonal schedules. (South)

FANTASY THEATRE
2711 B St.
916/443-5391
This is actually a part of the Busfield brothers' B Street Theatre (see chapter 11, Performing Arts). They claim to be the most productive and popular theater for children in Northern California and strive to bring the same level of professionalism to contemporary theater for kids as they do for adults. (East)

GARBEAU'S FAMILY THEATRE
12401 Folsom Blvd.
Rancho Cordova
916/985-6361
www.garbeaus.com
See chapter 12, Nightlife. Saturday dinner matinees. (South)

RIVER CITY THEATRE COMPANY
8194 Belvedere Ave.
916/457-7282
This is a nonprofit children's theater

Top Ten Reasons a Sacramento Native Came Back

by Vicki Hallberg, who grew up in Sacramento, and later lived in both Los Angeles and San Francisco. She returned home to raise her family because:

1. More affordable housing.

2. Traffic far less overwhelming.

3. Proximity to San Francisco and Lake Tahoe, and it's an even shorter distance to outdoor recreation—water and snow skiing, rafting, hiking, and fishing.

4. Recreation and entertainment—parks, restaurants, movies, etc.—are easily available and not overcrowded.

5. You can park your car (see San Francisco, above).

6. A safer urban environment than other major California cities.

7. You might actually see people you know in public places, and see friends and neighbors in the news—it's easy to feel you're part of the community.

8. Ethnic diversity.

9. You're ten minutes away from open and rural areas from any-where in the city.

10. Easy access to public facilities and activities, a convenient airport, and you'll actually know someone who attends Kings games.

workshop. The workshops lead to a Broadway musical production. (South)

T STREET THEATRE
4623 T St.
Coloma Community Center
916/264-8890
Part of the City of Sacramento's Recreation and Community Program, the "T Street Players" perform any-thing from fairy tales to comedic farces at the Coloma Community Center. (East)

STORES KIDS LOVE

THE CANDY BARREL
1006 Second St.
Old Sacramento
916/446-5196
This shop has not just one, but liter-ally dozens of barrels filled to the brim in a nineteenth-century set-ting. You'll find taffy mostly, but also every other kind of candy. School groups from all over the state make pilgrimages to Sacramento to bask in the historical significance of their

capital. What the kids remember when they get home is the Candy Barrel. (Central)

CAPITOL AQUARIUM
1920 29th St.
916/452-5556
The selection of fish and water turtles is so large here that it becomes not just a store, but a display of nature—a fish zoo. Tanks of fresh- and saltwater fish are so numerous that they're identified by row and number on the "Catch of the Day" sign that lists daily special sales. There are residents of the store who've been there for years, including one slow-moving creature as big as a boom box who likes to rub noses with curious visitors on the other side of the glass. (East)

THE COUNTRY BEAR
1028 Second St.
Old Sacramento
916/441-3407
This is a teddy-bear store mainly, but has collectibles of many other kinds as well. There are also robots, tin toys, and die-cast replicas. (Central)

DISCOVERY ZONE FUNCENTER
6351 Mack Rd.
916/688-7529
The Funcenter is not so much a store as a for-profit playground. It's a safe indoor play area, full of things to crawl up, through, and down, as well as fall into. "Coaches" supervise the play (which parents can join if they like) and also help put on birthday parties, which include in-house food (pizza, hot dogs, soft drinks), a cake, and tokens for the arcade games. (South)

OLD CITY KITES
1201 Front St.
Old Sacramento
916/443-3478
Old City Kites features other toys as well (Frisbees, boomerangs, yo-yos), but where else could you go to find so many kites in one place?

The Candy Barrel, Old Sacramento

TIP

University of California, Davis, Sacramento State, and most if not all of the local community colleges offer more than enough summer camp activities to keep your child busy until school starts again. Contact the individual campuses, especially for sports camps.

Kite flying is the perfect pastime for the "City of the Delta Breeze." (Central)

UNDERGROUND RAILROAD
128 J St.
Old Sacramento
916/443-7777
There are several fine model-train stores in the region, but the Underground Railroad has the ideal location, one where you can continue the magical feeling imparted by the Railroad Museum. The gift shop is modest, but the train layout isn't: Miniature re-creations of trains and towns from throughout the state fill one of the largest layouts in the country. More a model museum than a store, there's a small admission charge, but one of the payoffs is hands-on control of some of the rolling stock. You have to look for the place, because "underground" refers to its basement location. (Central)

UNIVERSITY ART
2601 J St.
916/443-5721
In addition to all the supplies the young artist might need for creation in any medium, University Art stocks many kinds of kits, games, and toys for hands-on manipulation. They also have paints, stamps, puz-

zles, markers, and any kind of paper in tablet or journal form. If for some reason you can't find what you want here, go across the street and a block west to Art Ellis Art Supplies, a more traditional art shop. While aimed at the serious artist, it will nevertheless entice a young artist who loves to get his or her hands on fine materials and make the stuff of imagination become real. (East)

THEME AND AMUSEMENT PARKS

COUNTRY CLUB LANES
2600 Watt Ave.
916/483-5105
This can be thought of as an indoor amusement park, with bowling, Lazer Tag, video games. A one-stop place for several activities, but call first as this enormously popular venue is often booked for parties. Lazer Tag is open year-round, with the longest hours in the summer: weekdays noon–midnight, weekends noon–2 a.m. Bowling is open 24 hours. Costs vary according to the activities you choose. (Northeast)

FAIRYTALE TOWN
AND FUNDERLAND
3901 Land Park Dr.
916/264-7462, 916/264-7061

(birthday party reservations)
www.fairytaletown.org
Fairytale Town has been a place to run, climb, and imagine for more than 40 years. Their structures are re-creations of fairy-tale settings, where little ones can pretend themselves right into their favorite stories. There are also scheduled arts-and-crafts activities, puppet theater, storytelling, and animal demonstrations. Birthday parties can be held in King Arthur's Castle or Sherwood Forest. It's directly across from the Sacramento Zoo entrance, inside William Land Park. Jan–Feb weekends 10–4, Mar–Sept daily 9–4, Oct–Dec daily 10–4. $3.75 adults, $3.50 kids 3–12.

Funderland is an amusement park in miniature, with eight scaled-down rides that won't frighten the very young. Birthday packages include an unlimited number of rides, but within a time limit. An independent pony-ride track is right next door, where the action is slow enough that parents can walk alongside tots as they ride. Hours vary seasonally; in summer, Mon–Fri 11–5, Sat–Sun 10–6. Admission is free, rides cost $1.(South)

GOLFLAND/SUNSPLASH
1893 Taylor Rd.
Roseville
916/784-1273
www.golfland-sunsplash.com
This is a water park (with slides and a wave pool) combined with two miniature golf courses. You can pile it on with other amusements as well, including Lazer Tag and more than 200 arcade games. Open weekends only during the school year; during the summer, golf is open daily 11–7, Lazer Tag Mon–Fri and Sun 10–10, Sat 8 a.m. to midnight. Group rates are available. (Northeast)

SCANDIA FAMILY FUN CENTER
5070 Hillsdale Blvd.
916/331-5757
www.scandiafamilyfun.com
Primarily a miniature-golf complex

Fairytale Town in Land Park

(with two 18-hole courses), Scandia also has bumper boats, Indy-style race cars, batting cages, and a video arcade. Golf is $5.95, and a ride package is $15.80, but prices will vary by activity. Generally open weekdays 10–10 and weekends 10 a.m.–11 p.m., plus an hour is added to the end of the day during summer. (Northeast)

SIX FLAGS MARINE WORLD
Marine World Pkwy.
Vallejo
707/643-ORCA
Formerly Marine World/Africa USA, the old title was more indicative of the unique combination of attractions: It's an oceanarium, a wildlife park, and an amusement park with thrill rides. It features a butterfly house, aquariums, performing sea mammals, play areas, waterskiing shows, a variety of food venues, gift shops, and—if you're inspired by the acrobatic whales and dolphins—roller coasters. This can easily fill an entire day with activity. It's really only loosely a Sacramento attraction, as it requires a good 75-minute drive out of the city (southwest along Interstate 80, more than halfway to San Francisco), but you can still do it without staying overnight in Vallejo. $36 adults, $24 kids 4–12 over 48 inches tall, $18 kids 3–12 under 48 inches tall, $27 seniors. Two-day and season passes available, and the season pass will also admit you to Waterworld USA at Cal Expo (see below). Always call first for hours. Generally, open daily in the summer, weekends during the school year. Usually open by 9 or 10 a.m., to 8 p.m. weeknights, later at night on weekends and holidays. $7 parking. (West)

WATERWORLD USA
1600 Exposition Blvd.
(inside Cal Expo)
916/924-3747, 916/924-0556
Surf's up in River City. The wave tank at Waterworld USA is Northern California's largest. This is not the kind of gigantic water park one might find in Southern California. While it has a limited variety of water slides compared to, say, Wild Rivers in Orange County, it's still a great way to beat the 100-plus-degree heat of Sacramento and

Fishing for Beginners

Between the American and Sacramento Rivers and the maze of Delta sloughs, there is fishing everywhere in the region. Kids can get started during the winter, courtesy of the California Department of Fish and Game, when the Department stocks rainbow trout in eight area ponds. A free fishing clinic is then taught at each location on a rotating basis, January through April during selected Saturdays from 8:30 until noon. Rods, reels, bait, and tackle are provided. Call 916/358-2872 for scheduled locations.

Waterworld USA

offers a few attractions that will take your breath away. One drop is nearly vertical—when they warn you not to try to stand or sit up on the way down, don't. Group and convention rates are available. Open daily Memorial Day–Labor Day, generally 10:30 a.m.–6 p.m. Closing times vary as summer days lengthen. Call to verify. $18 adults, $13 kids 3–12, $10 seniors. $5 parking. (Northeast)

TOURS

CAL STATE RECYCLING CENTER
6000 J St. (on the Sac State campus)
916/278-7301
While this may sound rather uninviting at first, it's a recycling/community garden/composting program where kids who are taught to take care of the planet in school can see it actually being done and culminating in organic produce. Picnic facilities and restrooms are available. Tours by appointment (call first). Free. (East)

CREATIVE PLAY PUPPETS
1881 Walters Ct., Ste. C
Fairfield
707/428-1828
Young ones will enjoy seeing how felt puppets are made, in the only factory of its kind in the United States. Moving from station to station, kids see how the puppets are cut and assembled. This is an hour's drive west on Interstate 80 and could be combined with the Jelly Belly tour, also in Fairfield (see below). Open daily. Free. (West)

FOLSOM DAM
AND POWER PLANT
7794 Folsom Dam Rd.
Folsom
916/989-7275
This is the structure that keeps life in Sacramento safe from flooding. It's also where a small percentage of the city's electricity is generated at the same time a portion of the

American River is shunted to farmlands. Guided tours last about 90 minutes (Tue–Sat; call for times.) Shorter tours are available, and all require reservations (see chapter 5, Sights and Attractions). Free. (South)

HERSHEY'S VISITOR CENTER
120 S. Sierra Ave.
Oakdale
209/848-8126
Eleven acres of chocolate will reduce anyone to a Homer Simpson–shaped puddle. See Kisses and Reese's Peanut Butter Cups come to life. It's quite a drive (halfway to Yosemite). Take Highway 99 south out of the city to Manteca, then go east on Highway 120 to Oakdale. Open daily except for most holidays. (South)

JELLY BELLY/HERMAN GOELITZ CANDY COMPANY
2400 North Watney Way
Fairfield
800/953-5592, 707/428-2838
www.jellybelly.com
Home of the "gourmet" jelly bean, this is where the famous Jelly Belly candy is born. Kids can see the whole process, from cooking to packaging. It's best to arrange a tour as far in advance as possible. It's an hour's drive west on Interstate 80. (West)

OLD CITY CEMETERY
Main gate at 10th and Broadway
916/448-0811
There are more than 25,000 dead here. Most kids find cemeteries either fascinating or totally creepy, but the emphasis at Sacramento City Cemetery is on history and quirky characters. Death is, of course, a topic, but in a nonthreatening way, as the tour guides focus on lively stories and this cemetery was filled up decades ago (there'll be no surprise caskets). Famous founders, politicians, and victims of past disasters all have their places. Tours can be self-guided or taken with docents, some of whom provide paper for tombstone rubbings on designated markers the kids have to find (like in a scavenger hunt). (See also chapter 5, Sights

---

Tower of Youth

For over six years, budding filmmakers and other young artists have been involved in Bill Bronston's arts group, which showcases visual arts, music, dance, video, theater, and radio and television production. Talented area youth ages 14 to 21 have put on plays and hosted events such as an All-Youth Film and Education Day, showcasing their own films and guest speakers while gathering information on topics like the University of Southern California's Film School. Call 916/922-0100 or log onto www.towerofyouth.org.

and Attractions.) Park just inside the cemetery gates, which you enter on Broadway. Daily 7–4:30, with extended summer hours. Free, with donations for restoration welcome. (South)

SACRAMENTO BEE
2100 Q St.
916/321-1785

While kids won't be able to stop the presses, they'll be able to see them in action. The newsroom is covered, too, plus they'll get to see words become print on the giant machinery. Tours are offered twice daily; call ahead for reservations. Children must be at least fourth graders. Free. Limited street parking; visitor lots at 21st and Q Streets and at 22nd and Q Streets. (East)

TV STATION TOURS

Several area stations offer tours. All of them are free and all require reservations, often weeks in advance. Notably:

- KOVR Channel 13 (916/374-1313): Groups should be of 10 or more. Schedule at least a month ahead of time. Located in West Sacramento.

- KVIE Channel 6 Public Television (916/929-5843): Tours are usually offered on Wednesdays and Thursdays. At least two families must be in the tour, which accommodates up to 20 people. This new state-of-the-art building is one of the largest studios in Northern California. Editing and post-production technology are highlights. Please have at least one adult for every five kids.

- KXTV Channel 10 (916/441-2345): Be a junior reporter here. Tour stops include the newsroom, the assignment desk, the live control room, and the Chromakey studio, where they electronically "key" people into different backgrounds. Tuesdays and Thursdays are the preferred tour days.

- KTXL Fox 40 (916/454-4422): This is the site of the Fox Kids' Club. The news set is included as well, as is the Public Affairs set.

OTHER DIVERSIONS

ALPINE SKI AND SNOWBOARD CLUB
4601 Francis Ct.
916/737-SNOW
www.hittheslopes.org

Supervised day trips at ski resorts, lasting 4, 8, or 10 weekend days (either Saturday or Sunday programs), including transportation, lift passes, and instruction from beginner to advanced levels in skiing and snowboarding. Parents—they've done this since 1965 (into their third generation of skiers) and have adult trips as well. (South)

GRANITE ARCH CLIMBING CENTER AND CHALLENGE COURSE
11335 Folsom Blvd.

Rancho Cordova
916/852-ROCK
www.granitearch.com
The folks here claim that their climbing center is the biggest in the west. They have 17,000 square feet of hand-sculpted rock climbing walls, 36 feet high. The center also has climbing leagues, outside field trips, mobile climbing walls that you can rent, and programs for youngsters as little as three. Their personal trainers teach (among other things) aid climbing, ice climbing, big-wall climbing, and placement of natural protection. Oct–Apr Mon–Sat 11–10, Sun 11–6; May–Sept Mon–Fri 11–10, Sat 9 a.m. –10 p.m., Sun 9–6. $20 adult pass with gear rental, $16 students, $12 kids under 12. (South)

ROCKNASIUM,
THE CLIMBING GYM
720 Olive Dr. #Z
Davis
530/757-2902
www.rocknasium.com
To quote from this climbing center's Web site: "Rocknasium offers over 7,000 square feet of climbing surface with many natural features, including aretes, cracks, dikes, an arch, and a bouldering cave. Over 4,000 square feet of the gym is available for bouldering, allowing for a nearly endless variety of boulder problems [including] Rocknasium's unique bouldering circuit. If your desires go higher than that, we have 24 top ropes and 2,000 square feet of lead climbing to satisfy you." Phew. Mon–Fri 11–11, Sat 10–9, Sun 10–6. $18 adult pass with gear rental, $14 students, $12 kids 12 and under. (West)

SAFETYVILLE, USA
3909 Bradshaw Rd.
916/366-7233
Unique in our country, Safetyville is a one-third-scale town where kids can get a preview of driver's training. Street signs, traffic signals, and police and fire stations are all on their level so they can learn, in a fun way, about pedestrian, bicycle, skateboard, and vehicle safety in the "streets," as well as the difference between safe and dangerous strangers, water safety, and electrical safety. They also receive some drug and alcohol education. The program is for kids in preschool and up to third grade. Birthday parties are available. Evenings, Apr–Oct. Small admission charge. (South)

© Tom Myers 1995

8

PARKS, GARDENS, AND RECREATION AREAS

Sacramento is fortunate in its geographical beauty. The river was named first, in 1808 when Gabriel Moraga gazed at the oak-clustered river plain and said it was like a holy sacrament. The region is also fortunate in that its inhabitants have had a preservationist attitude toward that beauty, at least from the time when the gold-mad miners realized their dreams of mineral wealth would not, literally, pan out. From the time of the city's founding by John Sutter Jr., park space has always been set aside amidst the commercially valuable lots of the street grid, and all of those public plazas exist to this day. (This accounts for the city's self-image as both the City of Trees and Camellia City.) But above all of Sacramento's natural treasures, the American River Parkway is its crown jewel—a 5,000-acre, 23-mile-long band of preserved riverbank and park space visited by more than five million people each year. And just up the road from Sacramento is Folsom Lake State Recreation Area, one of the finest water-activity parks in the nation. From wild wetlands to tot-lots, Sacramentans possess a wealth of parkland that keeps them in close touch with nature.

All described locations are considered wheelchair accessible.

AMERICAN RIVER PARKWAY

From the confluence of the American and Sacramento Rivers, to the

Folsom Lake State Recreation Area, with numerous access points.

Until the 1950s, the Parkway was largely undeveloped land, a riparian habitat preserved almost by default because of regular flooding. When the Folsom Dam was completed and flooding was brought under control, the region's planners resisted a great temptation to give this suddenly desirable land over to developers. Instead, the Parkway was set aside for all time, creating a 12-square-mile greenbelt five times the size of either San Francisco's Golden Gate Park or New York City's Central Park. The Parkway's recreational riches are too vast to cover in detail here, as an entire book could be written about what a biker or hiker might encounter along its trails. In fact, that book has been written and published by the American River Natural History Association, and it's entitled Biking and Hiking the American River Parkway. It covers every step of the 32-mile, paved Jedediah Smith National Recreation Trail, which goes more or less through the center of the Parkway, beginning to end, and is usually referred to more simply as the American River Parkway Bike Trail. Various chapters cover the flora and fauna, special stops, side trips, and convenient access points.

The Parkway trail also serves equestrians, and a recent refurbishing of the trail enabled in-line skaters to share this great resource for the first time, on a one-year trial basis. The entire trail has been widened to a 12-foot-wide Class I standard for bike trails, with four-foot jogging paths added to either side for almost the entire length of the trail. New restrooms, entry kiosks, docks, boat ramps, and a fishing pier are among the brand new amenities added to this pride of the city.

The Bike Parkway is continuous from Old Sacramento to Folsom. A feel for how much the entire greenbelt has to offer can be glimpsed by viewing it as a series of parks-within-the-park, including Ancil Hoffman, Discovery, Glen Hall, and Goethe Park.

ANCIL HOFFMAN PARK

On the north side of the American River, Ancil Hoffman is a place where hikers can observe firsthand a healthy riparian environment as they spot deer, wild turkeys, hawks, water fowl, foxes, raccoons, opossums, squirrels, and much more while following the river along trails shaded by woods still preserved in pristine condition (this land was highly valued by its private owners as protection for their farms against the river's floods). It's also the site of the Effie Yeaw Nature Center (see Kids' Stuff). You pay a four-dollar fee for your car as you enter Hoffman Park, then the Nature Center is free. It's also a good place to buy native plants, as well as the location of the Ancil Hoffman Golf Course. Enter on Tarshes Drive off California Avenue, in Carmichael. (Northeast)

DISCOVERY PARK

At the confluence of the American and the Sacramento, this is the West End starting point of the bike trail. Discovery Park's 275 acres are devoted to boat launching, a loading dock, huge picnic areas, archery

The National Skate Patrol

To ensure that skating passes its trial period, the in-line skating activists, who lobbied for years to be allowed access to the Parkway, have also formed a local chapter of the National Skate Patrol to monitor skaters and distribute safety information. These volunteers will make sure skaters are going in the right direction, headphones-free and able to stop (or, if necessary, fall down).

ranges, and easy access to all the trail's uses as well as to the American River itself. This is also the historical site of Pushune, a village of the Nisenan Indians, who still inhabited the area in John Sutter's time. Enter off Richards Boulevard near Interstate 5 or from the Garden Highway. (Central and North)

GLEN HALL PARK AND PARADISE BEACH

This park and beach is on the south side of the river, just above the Sac State campus where the river bends at Cal Expo. Glen Hall is a city park with baseball fields, picnic tables, a swimming pool, tennis courts, and showers. It's adjacent to the most popular swimming spot in the Parkway, Paradise Beach, a sandy strip that draws a lot of students. Enter at Carlson Drive. (East)

GOETHE PARK

In the local pronunciation, Goethe

Discovery Park

© Tom Myers 1999

American River Bike Trail

rhymes with "matey." This grassy and wooded park has picnic facilities under giant oaks that make for a pleasant shelter even in summer heat. There are also riding and hiking trails and easy access to the bike trail (which crosses the river here on a pedestrian bridge). It's a popular spot for fishermen and the downriver pickup spot for raft rentals coming from the Sunrise area. Enter from Rod Beaudry, north of Folsom Boulevard. (South)

CAPITOL PARK
Between 10th and 15th,
L and N Sts.
As the California state capital, Sacramento has been the govern-

mental and agricultural center of a huge economy that has been inextricably bound to world interests since its inception. And here in the City of Trees, there is no better symbol of Sacramento's ties to the world than Capitol Park. Hundreds of species of trees and plants were brought here from every climate in the world. Some of the highlights include: a bunya-bunya tree from Australia, with 30-pound cones; deodar cedars, which, though common throughout the city now, were first dug up in the Himalayas and then shipped around Cape Horn in 1870; a sugar maple given by then–Prime Minister of Canada, Pierre Trudeau; a grove of trees,

The California Department of Parks and Recreation has a statewide campsite reservation number: 800/444-7275.

now sadly at the ends of their life spans, dug up as saplings from Civil War battlefields and replanted to honor the fallen; sequoias and coastal redwoods, which grow remarkably well in the city; a dawn redwood, which is a deciduous cousin from China, thought until recently to be extinct; a grove of camellias, the official city flower (Camellia City is another common nickname for Sacramento). Kids and adults alike have fun finding the markers identifying the plants, and the greenery provides a cool respite from traffic and heat. Many state employees enjoy bringing their lunches to the park benches and picnic areas during the week. (Central)

CHARLES C. JENSEN BOTANICAL GARDENS
8250 Fair Oaks Blvd.
916/944-2025, 916/485-5322 (group tours)
The Charles C. Jensen Botanical Gardens are strictly for viewing and have no recreational facilities. It's a quiet place to wander and appreciate the gardens. Open daily from 8 a.m. to sunset. Free. (Northeast)

COSUMNES RIVER WILDLIFE PRESERVE
6500 Desmond Rd.
Galt
916/684-2816
As the name suggests, this is truly a wild preserve. The Cosumnes is the only undammed river in the Central Valley, so the overflowing banks are unimpeded, creating a 4,500-acre riparian environment and wetlands that are a vital part of the migrating routes of uncountable species of birds (bring your binoculars). Egrets and herons in particular are a wonderful sight, motionless on one leg in shallow water until they fold back their necks and fly elegantly away. This is possibly your best opportunity to see what Sacramento Valley looked like when the first European settlers arrived. The Willow Slough Nature Trail Loop winds along the Cosumnes River through the wetlands and is always open. There is a visitors center open from 10 to 4 on weekends with exhibits, but no permanent facilities, so be prepared to pack out everything you might bring in. Ducks, geese, deer, beavers, and even river otters may be spotted. A one-mile boardwalk is wheelchair accessible, and there is canoe and kayak river access. Take Interstate 5 south to Twin Cities Road west. Then take Franklin Road south and turn left on Desmond Road to park. (The trailhead is on Franklin before you reach Desmond.) Open daylight hours. Free. (South)

CURTIS PARK
Between W. and E. Curtis Dr., Sutterville and Curtis Way
This long strip of a park is just east of the Sacramento City College campus. Tennis and basketball courts,

---

TRIVIA

Sacramento's native valley oak, also called the California white oak, grows only in California. It can live from 300 to 500 years, reach heights of 150 feet, and is the largest oak in North America.

---

a tot-lot, jogging trail, and softball diamond make it a neighborhood recreation spot. (South)

DEL PASO PARK
Entrance at Auburn Blvd. and Fulton Ave.

One of the largest parks in the region, Del Paso is big enough to hold the 27-hole Haggin Oaks golf complex. It also contains lighted ball fields, a nature area, a playground, equestrian trails and arenas, a trap-shooting area, and hiking trails. The trail along Arcade Creek is an excellent bird-watching area. (Northeast)

ELK GROVE REGIONAL PARK
Hwy. 99 at Elk Grove Florin Rd.
Elk Grove
916/685-3908

One of the most visited parks in the county, Elk Grove has all the amenities for a family picnic: barbecues, tot-lots, ponds, shade trees, tennis courts, wide-open spaces, and an island in the middle of a three-acre lake where summer concerts are held. It also has the county's largest softball complex, a swimming

pool and bathhouse, and a lighted horse arena. The lake is stocked with game fish. For history buffs, the Rhoads School, a restored one-room schoolhouse (built in 1872), was moved here from the Sloughhouse area. On the first weekend in May is the annual Elk Grove Western Festival, with a parade, arts and crafts, a petting zoo, music and dance, and food booths. (South)

FOLSOM LAKE
STATE RECREATION AREA
7806 Folsom-Auburn Rd.
Folsom
916/988-0205

At Folsom Lake State Recreation Area, the numbers alone are impressive: 18,000 acres, including 10,000 acres of water surface; 80 miles of trails; nine miles of concrete and earth wing dams; and 75 miles of lake shoreline, extending 15 miles up the north fork of the American River and 10.5 miles up the south fork. Folsom Lake is artificial, yet it's still the third-largest lake in the state. The warm-weather activities are boundless: waterskiing,

In the past 10 years there have been 32 drownings at Folsom Lake and Lake Natoma. None of these fatalities occurred where lifeguards were present. The implications are obvious.

swimming, hiking, horseback riding, nature studies, camping, picnicking, fishing, sailing, boating, and windsurfing. Beal's Point, just one beach area along the lake, has lifeguard services, grassy picnic grounds, overnight camping, a snack bar, and equipment rentals, including pedal boats, sailboards, sailboats, personal watercraft, canoes, volleyball sets, rowboats, shade canopies, and rafts. They even guarantee to have windsurfers up and sailing within two hours of a lesson. Beal's Point is also the terminus of the American River Parkway Bike Trail, almost 32 miles from its beginning in Discovery Park.

The surrounding hills are covered in the spring with wildflowers, and spiked with various oak species and a few tough pines. Beware of poison oak—"leaves of three, let it be"—because it's quite common. Park rangers will help you identify it. Wildlife is abundant: jackrabbits, bobcats, raccoons, skunks, deer, raptors, quail, wild turkeys, and opossums. There are occasional sightings of rattlesnakes—leave them alone.

Facilities at the lake include Shadow Glen Riding Stables, Sac State's Aquatic Center (for both, see Sports and Recreation), the historic Folsom Powerhouse and Folsom Dam (for tours of both, see Kids' Stuff), and Folsom Lake Marina. Campgrounds are available at Beal's Point and at Peninsula Campground, which has sites for trailers (there are no hookups, but they do have a sanitary dump station). Boat camping is allowed for self-contained black and gray water systems after you register at Granite Bay or the marina, where you will receive directions to approved mooring sites. Beach your boat for overnight camping ashore only at Peninsula Campground.

Fishermen will find bass, trout, catfish, bullhead, sunfish (including crappie and bluegill), and crayfish. From October through March, trout and salmon make their run. Anyone 16 or older must have a valid California fishing license in their possession and may take fish by hook and line only. (Northeast)

GIBSON RANCH COUNTY PARK
8552 Gibson Ranch Rd.
Elverta
916/991-7592
Located north of Downtown, Gibson Ranch County Park is a favorite destination for school field trips, on which kids can learn how a working

TRIVIA

Looking for bocce ball? Try East Portal Park at 51st and M Streets.

ranch operates. Guided farm tours for folks of all ages teach farming techniques and the care of animals. Horse-drawn hayrides tour the pastures to see the larger stock animals. Equestrian classes complement the trails available for riding, plus there are complete boarding services and a lighted arena. Seasonal activities include a pumpkin patch tour and Harvest Festival in the fall, an Easter egg hunt in the spring, and an annual Civil War reenactment. There is also lake fishing and camping by day or overnight. (North)

MCKINLEY PARK
Between H St., Alhambra Blvd., McKinley Blvd., and 33rd St.
At the juncture of Midtown and East Sac, McKinley Park is considered by many to be one of the most beautiful neighborhood parks in town. A city park since 1902, these 36 acres include a clubhouse and a swimming pool. Kids will especially like the newly refurbished tot-lots, which have loads of structures to climb on, and the pond where they can feed the ducks. Adults enjoy jogging and using the facilities for baseball, horseshoes, basketball, and tennis. The park is also home to a library branch, as well as the Shepard Garden and Arts Center, which has one of the most beautiful rose gardens in the area. With more than 190 species in full bloom by June, this has been a favorite spot for weddings for years. (East)

MILLER PARK
West end of Broadway, at the Sacramento River
Just south of Old Sacramento and just north of the Towe Auto Museum, Miller Park includes the Sacramento Marina, which is in a lagoon connected to the river. You'll find picnic tables, a barbecue pit, shade trees, restrooms, a seasonal snack bar, and a free public boat launch. It's a nice green place at the heart of the city. (South)

NIMBUS FISH HATCHERY
2001 Nimbus Rd.
Rancho Cordova
916/358-2820
This is a place for visitors to see fish close-up and marvel at the power of instinct, as anadromous salmon and steelhead fight their way upstream. Nature is meddled with here, because construction of the flood-controlling dam made it necessary. The harvesting process for sperm and eggs guarantees that millions of smolt will be hatched, raised, and then released in the Delta during spring to make their way back to the Pacific. (The edible fish are donated to various agencies.) From U.S. 50 East, take the Hazel Avenue exit north. Go left on Gold Country Boulevard and follow the signs to the hatchery. It's adjacent to the American River Fish Hatchery (2101 Nimbus Rd., 916/355-0896), a smaller facility where the Department of Fish and Game raises the trout they use to stock streams and lakes through-

TRIVIA

By 1986, the Folsom Dam was estimated to have already saved the area $4.7 billion in flood damages.

out the state. Both hatcheries overlook the river from atop a cliff. (See chapter 7, Kids' Stuff.) Open daily. Free. (South)

RANCHO SECO PARK
Twin Cities Rd. (State Hwy. 104), roughly 15 miles east of Hwy. 99

Though you'll cavort in the shadows of twin cooling towers, the nuclear power plant here was decommissioned years ago after it became known as "Rancho Mistako" and was literally voted out of the power grid. The site now includes a 400-acre park that surrounds a large lake used for sailing, windsurfing, and fishing. There are boat-launching ramps (no powerboats allowed), docks, food and fishing-tackle concessions, picnic grounds, and a swimming beach. The lake is stocked with game fish. There are 18 RV sites with hookups, 20 tent sites, and one group site. (South)

SOUTHSIDE PARK
Between Sixth and Eighth Sts., T St. and Business Hwy. 80

Though close-in to downtown and within sight of busy highway traffic, Southside Park maintains a serene setting, with tall trees and a small lake surrounded by jogging trails. Lighted tennis courts, basketball courts, and pond fishing make it a recreational fun spot, and it's the site

of summer music and ethnic festivals. (Central)

STONE LAKES NATIONAL WILDLIFE REFUGE
Interstate 5 at Elk Grove Blvd.

Until recently, Stone Lakes National Wildlife Refuge was jointly administered by the state government and Sacramento County. Federal funds have been slow in coming for development, but some hiking, especially for bird watchers, is available in this vast area just south of the city. Fall and winter, especially, are migration times for waterfowl and other birds, and many species, such as Canada

McKinley Park

Pat Cosgrove

geese, rest here until their northern homelands thaw out in spring. Take the Elk Grove Boulevard exit off Interstate 5 and go west. (South)

UNIVERSITY OF CALIFORNIA, DAVIS, ARBORETUM
Main Campus along Putah Creek
916/752-2498
The arboretum is cared for by a university with agricultural origins and state-of-the-art horticultural interests. Not surprisingly, it is a showcase, serving as a "living museum," an outdoor classroom, a public garden with over 4,000 tree and plant species, and a retreat for rest or recreation. The specialties here include the plants of the Valley's inland Mediterranean climate. Take the Old Davis Road exit off Interstate 80, park on the south edge of the campus (a small parking office along Old Davis Road will have a helpful attendant with campus maps), and then simply walk into the heart of the campus grounds following the creek. Parking fees, but no admission charge. (West)

UNIVERSITY OF CALIFORNIA, DAVIS, RAPTOR CENTER
Old Davis Rd., two miles south of campus
530/752-6091
The Raptor Center offers both guided and self-guided tours through a museum and exhibits of several dozen species of birds of prey. Though the scientists can release over 60 percent of the more than 250 injured and orphaned birds of prey they receive each year, those that can't, for various reasons, be released into the wild help the rest of us learn about their world. Eagles, falcons, owls, and others can be visited at this one-of-a-kind resource where invaluable

CA Raptor Center

A resident of the Raptor Center

hands-on training is given to wildlife scientists. Open weekdays. (West)

WILLIAM LAND PARK
Bordered by Freeport Blvd., Sutterville Rd., West Land Park Dr., and 13th Ave.
Located on reclaimed marshland purchased with money donated by an early mayor of Sacramento, this park is known to locals simply as Land Park. It's a great place for tiny ones, especially during the warm months, as the park is home to the zoo, Funderland, and Fairytale Town (see chapter 7, Kids' Stuff). There's even a city-run preschool, Tiny Tot Time. Land Park is a green oasis in the midst of a beautiful urban neighborhood, and includes a botanical garden and groves of camellias and azaleas. Parking is along the streets that wind through the park and can be hard to come by when Sacramento City College classes are in session, as students walk to class from their cars in the park. (South)

© Tom Myers 2000

9

SHOPPING

When the city of Sacramento exploded into existence during the Gold Rush, the world began to pour through its streets, and it's still happening, at least in the central city areas, where you can find ethnically flavored shops from the Pacific Rim, South America, Africa, Europe, and Asia. Suburban Sacramento, however, is like suburban anywhere, full of strip malls and massive shopping centers, and only becoming more so as subdivisions sprout along the highway corridors leading away from the city's center.

Sacramento has played out most of the classical urban cycles of decay and rebirth. Throughout the nineteenth and early-twentieth centuries, the merchandized soul of its founding was sustained at the waterfront, while the rest of the city expanded confidently eastward. Then, in close correspondence with the growth of car culture, the central city declined as customers moved farther north, east, and south, radiating into the suburbs. In the last few decades, however, the city has made great strides in reclaiming its urban core.

Although "renewal" during the 1960s usually meant knocking things flat and starting all over again, more recently it has meant making the city's historical legacy work in new ways. Retail developers have been gradually gaining more confidence about returning to the city and to older suburban areas. There's also been a public investment of more than $225 million on or near K Street alone. Baby boomers and "empty nesters" with disposable income are moving into the old neighborhoods to experience the heart of this livable city in which beautiful and affordable homes exist within walking distance of terrific restaurants, eclectic shops, and live entertainment.

This has not been at the expense of suburban development. The region is growing rapidly, particularly in the Natomas area between Downtown and the airport, which is so new it doesn't yet have its own retail identity (except to say that more big boxes are on the way). It's also growing in the Laguna/Elk Grove area to the south and along the Interstate 80 and U.S. 50 corridors that lead northeast into the Sierra foothills. Here, you'll find the stucco shopping malls typical of modern suburbs across the country, as these growing communities struggle with their own plans for greater or lesser rates of increased sprawl and congestion.

SHOPPING DISTRICTS

OLD SACRAMENTO HISTORIC DISTRICT

Old Sac's museums and monuments reflect the Gold Rush in their preservation of artifacts and names. So do the district's rows of shops, which are housed in handsomely restored nineteenth-century buildings along wooden walkways. The brick exterior and interior walls are largely unchanged since they were first built to replace the wooden structures that burned down so readily in the 1850s. There are more than 100 shops bursting with antiques, novelty items, gifts, toys, crafts, souvenirs, and old-fashioned candy barrels, as well as more serious art-gallery offerings. Shopping can also be combined with the constant street activity in Old Sac, such as living-history events, a jazz jubilee, ethnic-food festivals, a Pacific Rim street festival, antique shows, railroad festivals, concerts, and even outdoor movies in the balmy summertime.

Visitors to Old Sacramento can casually stroll down cobblestone streets, lit in the evening by electrified reproductions of the original gas lamps, and then stop for a meal

at one of numerous restaurants. After dinner, they can catch live music and comedy acts. Though it may have a tourist-trap atmosphere, there's authenticity here, too: These really are the buildings—right down to the brick and mortar—that witnessed major dramatic events. And many of the shops' names reflect the door-to-the-world history that Sacramento has lived out ever since John Sutter Jr. hired William Tecumseh Sherman to map the city's street grid. You'll find names like the Scottish Castle, Hero Chinese Arts and Crafts Company, the Russian Collection, Peruvian Crafts, Ecuador and More, Maxine's Native American Art, and Arts D'Afrique.

ARTISTS' COLLABORATIVE GALLERY
1007 Second St.
916/444-3764
www.gogh.com/acg.
Founded in 1978, this cooperative of more than 40 regional artists and craftspeople provides an outlet for local work. Because members staff the store themselves, prices are lower than they would be in a traditional retail setting. On display are fine arts and contemporary crafts, glass, hand-painted silk, jewelry, paintings, photography, pottery, weavings, and woodwork. Each month there's a special showing upstairs in addition to the regular displays. (Central)

DISCOVER CALIFORNIA!
114 J St.
916/443-8275
This is a little like visiting a miniature State Fair—for the "state" of NorCal. Food, wine, and custom-designed gift packs are the main business,

with handcrafted gifts and country home decor featuring the work of more than 60 local artists and crafters, plus Sacramento and California souvenirs and gifts. The foods and wines all come from Northern California, yet there's a delightfully wide and bizarre choice of specialty items (like salsa), and a big wine selection. This is your number one source for chocolate pasta and Big Ass beer. (Central)

THE ELDER CRAFTSMAN
130 J St.
916/264-7762

The city supports this shop to develop and market fine arts and crafts created by the Sacramento area's senior community. As of this writing, one of the craftsmen is 98 years old. A brochure description says the shop "enables them to be physically productive, reinforcing their value as members of society and contributing to the economic structure of the Sacramento community," but c'mon, this is fun stuff. The crafts tend toward kitschy Americana, but there are wonderfully carved wooden toy trains, planes, boats and cars (look for a wooden aircraft carrier whose deck is drilled for cribbage), and bins of knitted throws your Grandma might have forgotten to make for you. Where else are you going to find handmade toast pullers? (Central)

GALLERY OF
THE AMERICAN WEST
121 K St.
916/446-6662

The Gallery of the American West is one of the country's finest Native American shops and has been in Old Sac for over 20 years. The store features some of the most famous American Indian potters, jewelers, weavers, and carvers. It handles the highest-quality Native American handmade pieces at what are called reservation or artist retail prices. There are beautiful Navajo blankets and a nice selection of books to help you understand the crafts and the people who made them. The pottery features the Pueblo tribes of the Southwest, but also represents the work of the native peoples of California and Mexico. These are not trinkets and souvenirs but serious crafts, and the cost reflects that. You'll also find a number of Western-themed paintings. (Central)

MY BEST FRIEND'S BARKERY
1050 Front St., Ste. 120
916/448-FIDO, 916/448-3439 (fax)

All right, we've all been insane about our pets at one time or another. Or all the time. But here, canine retail reaches its zenith: Bakery treats are handmade and baked fresh daily with your dog's health and happiness in mind

Shopping in Old Sacramento

© Tom Myers 1997

(though you're likely to feel better, too). Check out the cheesecakes and birthday cakes (for dogs, of course). Although it's part of the Public Market (see below), you can't miss the shop—it's the one with the six-foot-tall yellow fire hydrant outside. The Barkery also carries the latest in dog apparel and gift ideas for your best friend, such as dog-themed art, dog perfumes (no, don't go there), and down-to-earth ideas such as seatbelt harnesses, life preservers, decorative ceramic dog dishes, and winter coats. Less down-to-earth items include dog beds shaped like roadsters, and bags and pillows with stitched mottoes such as "My dog is my baby" and "One can never have too many dogs." Those of the feline persuasion can visit the Cat House on K Street. Woof. (Central)

OLD SACRAMENTO PUBLIC MARKET
Front St. between K and L Sts.
Located along the waterfront, the Public Market is open year-round (closed Mondays only). These multiple vendors have taken over the old Union Pacific railroad depot at river's edge. Aki's Ranch Market offers produce and flowers, and with Apodaca Natural Foods, the Italian Importing Company, the Joe Laszlo Smoked Fish Store, Ole Country Market, and Produce Junction pitching in, there's a farmers' market atmosphere with the convenience items of a small general store as well. Takeout food counters provide deli sandwiches or more global tastes such as pitas and light Indonesian dishes at the Indo Café. Shop the world and go home with fresh edibles. (Central)

DOWNTOWN
The Downtown Plaza shopping center covers several blocks from Fourth to Seventh Streets, between K and L Streets. It anchors the west end of the core of the Sacramento urban retail district. The pedestrian-only K Street Mall connects the Downtown Plaza to the core's east-end anchor—the new Esquire Plaza at 13th Street, which is at the juncture of the Hyatt Regency, several

There is a surprising amount of street parking in the Old Sacramento Historic District if you go off-hours—that is, during non-meal times when the local population is most likely to visit. The city has recently decided to add parking meters to Old Sac, which is good for merchants and bad for ambience, so bring quarters. Covered parking structures are at the north end near the Railroad Museum (enter on I St., beneath Interstate 5), or at the extreme south end. At the latter, you'll enter just past the "One Capitol Mall" building on your right, which is large and modern with green tinted windows. Be sure to hug the right side and take the nondescript turning lane into either the district's streets themselves (by angling left after the turn) or into the brick parking structure. Otherwise you'll end up crossing Tower Bridge into West Sacramento and miss Old Sac entirely.

Old Sacramento Public Market

restaurants, the Convention Center, the IMAX Theater, and soon a gigantic Sheraton. The Downtown Plaza feels like somebody dropped a suburban shopping center into the city from the sky. It has two Macy's department stores and two levels of shops, restaurants, and entertainment (see Major Shopping Malls, below).

The K Street Mall, by contrast, gives Downtown a storefront flavor, for better or for worse. It's an entertaining walk from one end of the mall to the other, though in years past it was a gauntlet run among panhandlers. The developers of the strong retail anchors at either end are now trying to fill the space in between with stores of equal quality. A Starbucks and a 24 Hour Fitness have just opened, and there's also a light-rail line down the middle of K Street. Beyond that, the owners of the Downtown Plaza have submitted proposals to expand new retail space into surrounding blocks. The city has closed several single-room occu-

pancy hotels in the area to reduce loitering, and public events like Summerfest (a kind of Thursday-night street fair) and the outdoor skating rink at St. Rose of Lima Park (open during winter months) are bringing locals back to the mall to mingle with vendors and musicians for a family-oriented, festive feeling.

THE BUILDING
1021 R St.
The Building is like a downtown version of mall convenience, where a combination of several small shops add up to a one-stop gift center with all sorts of selections. Arareity Jewelers, Clarice's Jewelry Design, Mount Shasta Naturals Aromatherapy, Tea Cozy, Rumpelstiltskin, and the Art Foundry Gallery offer you things to see, wear, and experience, while you become a little more peaceful in the process. (Central)

CHINA TOWN GIFTS
Chinatown Mall, 423 J St.
916/448-6465, 916/448-8969 (fax)
Asian art, both old and new, and

books on feng shui and Buddhism fill this delightful, eclectic gift shop. There are also beautiful ceramics, some clothing, and carved jewelry, even a stone garden lamp. Set below street level beneath the stately Chinese architecture of the Chinatown Mall, China Town Gifts is set off by shaped pines, bamboo plants, and ginkgo trees. The courtyard outside the store is from another world where even the phone booth has a pagoda-style tile roof, and you might never even know it was there because the mall is curiously undeveloped for retail, considering its prime location next to both the Downtown Plaza and Old Sacramento. Only the gift store and the Half Moon Restaurant entice pedestrians from above, making this a midday retreat worth seeking out, even if just once. (Central)

COMICS AND COMIX
900 K St.
916/442-5142
This store seems to have every comic ever published. It was voted best place to buy comics by the readers of Sacramento's *News and Review*. They also have toys on related themes (like Pokémon), T-shirts, graphic novels, and fantasy genre paperbacks, but mostly there are racks and racks of comics. Many are gruesome, vio-

lent, and sexual, but Betty and Veronica live here, too. (Central)

THE CRATE/ARTISTS CONTEMPORARY GALLERY
Hyatt Regency Plaza
1200 K St. Mall, #9
916/446-3694, 916/441-4136 (fax)
This store features a combination of fine arts-and-crafts galleries for the upscale buyer of paintings, prints, sculpture, pottery, jewelry, wood, glass, and children's toys. The Crate/Artists Contemporary Gallery is in the tonier east end of the K Street Mall where it meets the Convention Center. It's surrounded by boutiques and restaurants and is a fun place to stroll, rest in the shade at a bistro table, or shop, of course. (Central)

DAVIS & COMPANY
1015 Eighth St.
916/443-1741
Located a block north of K Street, Davis & Company is a hard store to categorize, but fascinating. It's filled with urns, vases, framed mirrors, ceramic and carved statuary, and odd icons—things which, if you stuck them in a garden or a corner of a room might make that space look just right, though you wouldn't know you were looking for the object until you came here. There are antiques, small pieces of furniture, and unique tableware (including dish sets with

Asian designs and tea and sake sets). It's a little bit of everything that "accessorizes." You could try it for a different kind of bridal registration. Be sure to take advantage of their free gift-wrap service and free delivery (within Sacramento). And don't let the retail area around it put you off: Davis & Company shares space on the block with empty storefronts and looks a bit out of place, but it's an easy walk from the Downtown Plaza. (Central)

GOLDEN STATE MUSEUM STORE
10th and O Sts.
916/653-0650

The Golden State Museum Store is in the capitol area, several blocks south of Capitol Mall. The museum itself is organized around four themes, all designed to explore what is uniquely Californian: the Place, the People, the Politics, and the Promise. The Museum Store, located inside the building, plays off these themes, especially in its book section, which offers anthologies of California writers and books on travel and nature, as well as selections for children. Expect museum quality in the store's handmade ceramics and glass, educational toys and games, cards, prints, desk accessories, and jewelry. They also have specialty foods. The museum is inexpensive (see chapter 6, Museums and Galleries), but you don't have to buy a ticket to enter the store. Tue–Sat 10–5, Sun noon–5. (Central)

New Faces

The Pacific Plaza has just opened at the corner of Stockton Boulevard and 65th Street in south Sacramento just north of Florin Mall. It's a new shopping center with grand plans, something American business does best. But this center is intended as a regional magnet for shoppers as far away as Lake Tahoe and Fresno because it will serve a long-overlooked Asian market. With 45 planned tenants, the Pacific Plaza will be the newest player in what is already called the "Asian business district" along Stockton Boulevard between Florin and Fruitridge. Its focus will be on food: The Plaza anchor will be Shun Fat, a Southern California–based chain of Chinese supermarkets. The region's Asian population has tripled in the past two decades, including Chinese, Filipino, Japanese, Vietnamese, Hmong, Indian, Laotian, Pacific Islanders, and others. The ultimate goal is not only to become a center for Asian commerce, but to draw everyone else, too—another Sacramento door open to the world.

TIP

Burned out on rack after rack of unaffordable glitz at the malls? Try the used, vintage, and consignment community. Auntie Mame's (2598 21st St., 916/456-1719), and Trés Chic (2228 J St., 916/444-3668) are places to start. Funkier trips might be to Cheap Thrills (1217 21st St., 916/446-4103), Crossroads Trading Company (2935 Arden Way, 916/972-9900), or Prevues (2417 K St., 916/448-4556).

RECORDS
710 K St.
916/446-3973
This store actually has . . . records. There are numerous bins of vinyl, with handmade signs to help you go through the past. Records also has CDs, tapes, and used videos, but the main reason to come here is to collect oldies. It's located at the beginning of K Street Mall as it heads east from Downtown Plaza. (Central)

MIDTOWN

Midtown makes shoppers remember why they love cities and why suburban malls were originally so irresistible. Scattered about Sacramento's central grid (although predominantly along J, K, and L Streets) is a diverse collection of storefront shops, restaurants, and galleries. Admittedly, it's difficult to get much more than one focused errand done in Midtown (hence the attraction of those billion-stores-in-one malls). But when you know where you're going, find that place, and park easily right outside the front door (okay, maybe around the corner and down a block), there's an intimate satisfaction in the feeling that this is a one-of-a-kind store in your town. The best way to become acquainted with Midtown shopping is
to first take several leisurely drives down J Street so you can marvel at the variety and vitality of a real neighborhood.

THE BEAT
1700 J St.
916/446-4402
It may be a small victory, but the Beat was recently voted "Best Vinyl Record Store" in town by readers of the Sacramento *News and Review* (sorry, Tower). Not as big as the chains, the Beat competes by covering the new, the used, and the rare, with CDs as well as vinyl. (East)

HOW TACKY
2425 J St.
916/443-1379
Well, if they're going to admit it on the sign out front, how can you resist taking a look? Perhaps best described as a toy store for the politically incorrect Neanderthal, How Tacky has goofball trinkets, from lunch boxes to refrigerator photo frames. Here's the place to buy that Drag Queen Barbie you've coveted, the one with the push-up bra over manly pecs; or the white-trash Barbie with her roots showing. This is the weird, the uncool cool—how Midtown. (East)

PASHA'S, THE UNCOMMON SHOP
1055 22nd St., between J and K Sts.
916/444-5159
Pasha's may be the definitive Midtown shop—what eclectic is meant to describe. The stuff of the world trickles through this store "from faraway magic lands," as her ad says. Clothing, jewelry, art and artifacts, carpets, and uncommon kitchenware coexist in a small bazaar. (East)

RELLES FLORIST
2400 J St.
916/441-1478
This is a complete, full-service floral shop, much like what you'd expect to encounter in an FTD florist sufficiently large to handle any order. But it's worth knowing that year after year, Relles is voted best florist in the city by local reader and listener polls. They also offer green plants, silk and dried flowers, balloons, and stuffed animals. A second Relles store is on Howe Avenue. (East)

SACRAMENTO NATURAL FOODS CO-OP
1900 Alhambra Blvd.
916/455-2667
This is a full supermarket, where those who believe "you are what you eat" can buy with confidence. The Co-op has organic produce, fresh fish and poultry, a deli/juice bar, complete grocery and bulk selections, and health and body-care items. It's referred to as "consumer-owned" in their ads, but everyone is welcome. (East)

FOLSOM
*Folsom is worth visiting for many reasons, but a pure shopping trip could easily last days. Here you'll find the historic Sutter Street district of Old Town Folsom with dozens of merchants specializing in arts, crafts and gifts, many with collectible-history themes. Prominent among these shops is the **Folsom Mercantile Antique Mall** (916/985-2169) with more than 40 dealers offering everything from collectible postcards to antique scientific instruments.*

Dillard's Is on the Way

A proposed megamall is steamrolling its way toward groundbreaking in Elk Grove at Highway 99 and Grant Line Road south of Sacramento. The Lent Ranch Marketplace will be a "regional mall" (which apparently means gigantic—1.3 million square feet) and will be anchored by Dillard's, a fashion-oriented department store often described as somewhere between Macy's and Nordstrom in quality, selection, and price. Arkansas-based Dillard's is new to California and has already succeeded with a recent store-opening in Stockton, with plans to add more. And more.

The Sheepish Grin Antique Market *(916/985-0257)* carries Victorian and country furniture, railroad memorabilia and more, and the *Sutter Street Emporium* *(916/985-4647)* has collectible dolls, music boxes, and figurines. On a more contemporary note, *Clouds of Folsom* *(916/985-3411)* bills itself as the largest maker of handmade porcelain pottery in the western U.S., featuring hand-painted designs. They have a free studio tour every Saturday at 2 p.m. *The Fire & Rain* art gallery *(916/353-0943)* has unique artworks, including Raku pottery, jewelry, and sculpture, while *Snyders House of Jade* *(916/985-3269)* features antique Asian furniture and jewelry. All of this, and much more, on just several blocks of Sutter Street.

NOTABLE BOOKSTORES AND NEWSSTANDS

In an age when the new-book market is dominated by chains, Sacramento is well represented: Borders and Barnes and Noble can be found in various locations (for those who still don't use Amazon.com). But there are still small bookshops out there that provide the sheer pleasure of thumbing through aromatic pages. There are also dozens of specialty and used bookstores. What follows is only the smallest sampling.

ARGUS & CONNER BOOKS
1311 21st St.
916/443-2223, 916/444-2384 (fax)
Argus & Conner specializes in rare, collectible, and unusual books, as well as graphics, photos, and other historical printed materials. (East)

THE AVID READER
1003 L St.
916/443-7323
Across the street from the capitol and next door to Newsbeat, the Avid Reader is a new-book store with a very nice collection of Californiana. It offers the pleasure of a quiet respite amidst books while the governmental heart of the state hums just outside. (Central)

BEERS BOOKS
1431 L St.
916/443-5165
Beers evokes warm and fuzzy memories of the used bookstores on college campuses where those of us of a certain age attended. This is a big place full of new and used books, including a whole wall of old *National Geographic* magazines. There are comfortable chairs and a place to plunk down with the kids in the children's section. Book searches and special orders are available,

and even building codes can be purchased. It's next door to the Capitol Garage, if you need coffee, and around the corner from the capitol itself. (Central)

THE BOOKMINE
1015 Second St.
Old Sacramento
916/441-4609
www.bookmine.com
The Bookmine features rare books, original art, maps, prints, and graphics—a great way to become the literate tourist. They also offer a free book-search service, covering esoteric topics such as mining and geology as well as more general interests like science and medicine, western Americana, railroads, and children's literature. They'll also hunt down book sets and first editions. (Central)

CAPITOL BOOKS AND GIFT SHOP
State Capitol Basement
916/324-0313, 916/444-0317 (fax)
www.capitolbooksandgifts.com
The Capitol Books and Gift Shop specializes in California and governmental memorabilia, California history books, and other gift items. It's a small place, focused on very few topics, but provides an efficient means for taking away mementos of your capitol visit. A nice bonus: Sales benefit the disabled. (Central)

CAROL'S BOOKS
5964 South Land Park Dr.
916/428-5611
Carol's Books focuses on the works of African American writers and artists. From the outside, it's just a storefront in a nondescript strip mall, but inside, warm incense and small works of art surround shelves of books, cards, and gifts for all. (South)

NEWSBEAT
1005 L St.
916/448-2874
Newsbeat is downtown Sacramento's premier newsstand. It's across the street from the north and west entrances to the capitol building and offers an international selection of newspapers and magazines, as well as cigarettes and candy. Open daily. (Central)

TOWER BOOKS BROADWAY
1600 Broadway
916/444-6688
Tower Books Broadway, which is full of new books in rather cramped quarters, offers competitive discounts on bestsellers and has a terrific magazine and out-of-town newspaper selection. (South)

OTHER NOTABLE STORES

ANTIQUE PLAZA
11395 Folsom Blvd.,
Rancho Cordova
4401 Granite Dr., Rocklin
www.AntiquePlazaOnline.com
For a region soaked in history, it's inevitable that the past would show up so amply in furnishings for the home. The Antique Plazas are but two of a number of area antique malls where literally hundreds of dealers display their wares across tens of thousands of square feet of floor space. The Antique Plaza in Rancho Cordova is California's largest antique mall. (South)

57TH STREET ANTIQUE ROW
57th St. between J and H Sts.
Similar to the Antique Plaza, the 57th Street Antique Row has nearly 100 dealers selling goods across 45,000 square feet of space in a cluster of

adjoining shops. You'll find an auction house, free parking, and quality restaurants nearby. (East)

GREBITUS & SONS
Lyon Village, Fair Oaks Blvd.
916/487-7853
This fine jewelry and gift store produces ads in the local magazines which display those exquisite objects your mother told you not to touch. Certified gemologists and appraisers, Grebitus & Sons offer gorgeous, glittery stuff, but the eye-catching window displays feature beautiful glassware, silver, and ceramics, including decorative plates with an Asian flair. They also have a corporate gift division. A second store is located in the Downtown Plaza. (Northeast)

LIMN
501 Arden Way
916/564-2900
Owner Dan Friedlander was born and raised in Sacramento but made his first mark in San Francisco's Townsend Street design district with the original Limn, a contemporary furniture store. He wants to make his second mark here. He was recently quoted in *Sacramento* magazine as saying, "Why shouldn't people here in Sacramento have things that are modern and progressive and well designed?" To this end his store in the Del Paso arts district (which he predicts could eventually be the city's version of L.A.'s hip Melrose area) is designed to help Sac Town overcome what he calls an inferiority complex, compared to San Francisco, in its ability to appreciate fine things. This is not simply a furniture store, but what Friedlander calls "furniture theater." He combines gallery art with old and new furniture

pieces for a stagy, dramatic effect that he knows will not produce instant sales, but rather will require time and multiple visits before customers are comfortable with the international flavor of modern furniture in an art gallery setting. Architecture, interior design, and landscaped courtyards all meet for effect—with, for example, antique pieces from Japan and India mixing with the linear, clean lines of a sofa from Italy. (North)

PEET'S COFFEE
AND TEA
Lyon Village, Fair Oaks Blvd.
916/485-7887
With apologies to hometown coffee vendors who dare to stand up to the corporate java giants (La Bou and Java City are great places), Peet's just flat out has the best-tasting coffee. An intruder from the Bay Area, where Peet's shops are on every corner, this is the only Sacramento-region store where you can buy Major Dickason's blend, which when brewed will make you stand up and salute at 6:30 a.m. They'll grind it for you, of course, if need be, and they also have an outstanding selection of loose leaf teas. There's always an offer of a complimentary cup of what's brewing that day (to sip while you wait for your order to be filled), along with free samples of exotic candies, spreads, and other things to nibble, set out in dishes on the counter. You'll also find an intriguing selection of muffins and pastries in the bakery case. The polite staff will be happy to talk you through descriptions of the unfamiliar beans and leaves gathered from throughout the world. (Northeast)

THE REST STOP
3230 Folsom Blvd.
916/453-1870
This East Sacramento bike shop has enjoyed long-term success and a great reputation without selling bikes. The Rest Stop is an accessory and clothing shop, so once you've bought your bicycle elsewhere (American River Bicycles is a good place to start), you can keep it—and yourself—going by resupplying here. (East)

SHARI'S BERRIES
400 Capitol Mall
(Wells Fargo Center)
916/444-1714
www.berries.com

Sure you can call up some store or mail-order business and send flowers, a fruit basket, or, God forbid, a fruitcake. But only from Shari's can you send a gift basket of chocolate-dipped strawberries throughout the year, nationwide, and feel better about yourself. Described as "edible bouquets," they also come with party favors and catered trays. Other stores are located on Auburn Boulevard and in the Birdcage Centre. (Central)

THE TOWER ENCLAVE
Broadway at Land Park Dr.
One can easily imagine the breathless, neon billboard: "Where it all began!" But there is nothing of the

Gardening in the Ideal Climate

It's so easy to grow things here that it would be a shame to be a resident and not take advantage of the plant-friendly climate. **Capital Nursery** *(4700 Freeport Blvd., 916/455-2601; also in Elk Grove and Citrus Heights) is a large-scale garden center that sells almost anything in a pot, and if they don't have it they'll order it, as most nurseries will, from wholesalers.* **Talini's** *(5601 Folsom Blvd., 916/451-8150) has been in East Sacramento for decades and is the only locally owned full-service nursery. It's a great place to find fruit trees, especially, though they have a nice variety in a small lot that's easy to pass by. An even smaller place is* **Home Landscape and Nursery** *(6450 Freeport Blvd., 916/427-7210) where you'll get personal service and better prices on a greater variety of shade trees than you'll find in the nursery section of a home improvement center. Once you've planted things, look for finishing touches—accessories, furnishings—at Garden Elements, the Garden Gallery, Garden Gate Company, or the Gifted Gardener, where they have a special interest in indoor plants.*

sort to indicate that this is the site of the original Tower Drugstore that spawned Tower Records from its LP bins. Now, immediately adjacent to one another and fronting several intersections, are Tower Records, Tower Video, Tower Books, and the Tower Café, where customers can sit outside beneath the landmark tower itself—a beautiful art-deco ornamentation atop the recently restored Tower Theater, which screens offbeat, international, and festival movies. (The Tower Gallery is on Howe Avenue near the Sac State campus.) The café offers world cuisine, the bookstore has a terrific newsstand, and the record store (whose headquarters is across the river in West Sacramento) is more or less like any other Tower Records you'd find around the globe. But this is where it all began. (South)

MAJOR DEPARTMENT STORES

MACY'S
1701 West Arden Way
(Arden Fair Mall)
3500 El Camino Ave.
(Country Club Plaza)
414 K St. (Downtown Plaza)
6000 Sunrise Blvd., Citrus Heights
(Sunrise Mall)
This enormous chain of stores owned by Federated Department Stores is well-known throughout the country. Fashion and home accessories are the focus, with designer names and a store-within-a-store organization to aid brand loyalty. Macy's has multiple locations, and the Downtown Plaza actually has two stores, making selection there seem endless.

NORDSTROM
1651 Arden Way (Arden Fair Mall)
This fashion-oriented department store has built a legendary reputation in the West for service. The relationship Nordstrom has with its salespeople gives it a stable, knowledgeable, and helpful staff, and the clothing comes in a wide selection of the finest available off the rack.

MAJOR SHOPPING MALLS

ARDEN FAIR MALL
Arden Way at Capital City
Freeway (Business 80/U.S. 50)
This is the largest and busiest shopping center in the Sacramento area—it's what teens from all over the city mean when they say they're going to the mall. The layout is typical of suburban megamalls, with a large, mostly outdoor parking lot surrounding the two-story glass-and-metal complex. Four large department stores—Macy's, Nordstrom, Sears, and JCPenney—cover traditional merchandise, while another 161 name-brand shops fill in the smaller niches. Highlights include Godiva Chocolates, FAO Schwartz, and Abercrombie and Fitch. There are 15 shoe stores, 14 jewelry stores, 21 women's apparel shops, and seven children's clothing stores. Fourteen fast-food outlets and three sit-down restaurants are spread throughout. Immediately adjacent is the Marketplace, which is full of trendy fashion franchises, small restaurants, and a huge Virgin Records; and a multiplex theater. In a word, it's big. During the Christmas season, shoppers must be shuttled in from Cal Expo. The mall promotes it-

self as "the ultimate walk-in closet." (Northeast)

DOWNTOWN PLAZA
Fourth and K Sts.

Downtown Plaza is a commonsense name to which its owners have oddly tacked on "Westfield Shoppingtown." Built in the '70s and renovated in the '90s, this two-level complex covers nearly six square blocks of the most vibrant part of Downtown (indeed, its construction rescued downtown retail), and is looking to expand even more. Though rather forbidding at street level, inside it has an open-air design of metal and glass which gives a sunlit, modern feel to the walkways within. Conceptually it's divided into "rooms" called the Piazza (a spot for live entertainment), the Fifth Street Market (which has an industrial-feel upper level), a courtyard Rotunda under a tall dome, and the Garden Court (where an outdoor patio effect is captured with wood furniture, tile fountains, and planters filled with small trees and flower designs). Apparel stores include Macy's, J. Crew, Banana Republic, and Ann Taylor. Downtown Plaza has a lot to offer kids: Kay-Bee Toys, the Disney Store, Warner Brothers Studio Store, the Gamekeeper, the Great Train Store, and Suncoast Video. The mall also houses the outstanding Morton's Steakhouse, as well as less-formal dining spots such as River City Brewing Company and the Hard Rock Café. Century Theatres has a multiplex here. (Central)

FLORIN MALL
Florin Rd. between Stockton Blvd. and Hwy. 99

This is the Rodney Dangerfield of area malls, looking for respect. South Sacramento has struggled to maintain its retail base, but there is new commitment to refurbishing retail along the Florin Road and nearby Stockton Boulevard corridors, and the Florin Mall stands opposed to the glitter north of the river. Sears is the stalwart anchor here, and JCPenney

Arden Fair Mall

How Not to Get Lost Underground

As the architectural complexity above suggests, underground parking for the Downtown Plaza is a labyrinth. Parking is plentiful and easy to enter, but since the mall covers a number of city blocks, you need to remember where you poked your head up when, gopher-like, you emerged from the subterranean garage. Make a mental note of what store you were near and re-enter the garage at that same point, since the levels beneath the Piazza are marked identically to the levels beneath, say, the Macy's at the other end, and you cannot get from one garage to the other while underground. Should you get lost, security phones are everywhere and courteous guides will arrive to take you to your car.

has opened an outlet store as well, one of the few of its kind anywhere. While the upscale stores of outer suburbia may not be present, there's solid shopping available here, especially for the young, with 85 stores full of bargains. Kay-Bee Toys, Radio Shack, Good Guys, B. Dalton, Millers Outpost, Foot Locker, Sam Goody, and Sunglass Hut are just a few of the dozens of national franchises. The eclectic are here, too, such as the Culture Collection, which offers ethnic gifts and cards from around the globe. (South)

PAVILIONS
Fair Oaks Blvd.
and Howe Ave.

The Pavilions bills itself as "Sacramento's fashion specialty center," and it's right on the mark. Upper-end clothing dominates the center, with both one-of-a-kind stores and branches of names like Ralph Lau-

ren, Talbots, and Laura Ashley. Niko is considered the area's premier place for kids' clothing, while stores like Julius and Daitaro go for adult elegance. Relax at Pavilions Salon Spa, buy art at Ventana Art Gallery, dine at Mace's or Ristorante Piatti, or grow wise at Borders Books/Music/Café. David Berkley Fine Wines and Specialty Foods is a deli taken to another level, offering wines, quality meats, bakery items, candies, coffees and teas, and specialty foods such as casseroles and brunches that can be taken home and reheated. Circa Antiques of the Future will custom build furniture of your design, and the Williams-Sonoma selection of gourmet kitchenware has been so successful it's doubled in size. There's far more, and the center is in the midst of the Fair Oaks Boulevard "Gourmet Gulch" of shoulder-to-shoulder fine restaurants. (Northeast)

TOWN AND COUNTRY VILLAGE
Fulton Ave. at Marconi Ave.

Town and Country Village is a ranch-style, outdoor forerunner of suburban shopping. Its overall image is dominated by William Glen, which was voted "Best Place to Buy a Special Gift" by readers of *Sacramento* magazine. William Glen has 12 different departments to explore and overflows with home accessories. Fine china, flatware, crystal gourmet cookware—you can shop until you can't stand it anymore, then fall into a chair at the in-store café or coffee bar. There's also a year-round Christmas store, and, during the holiday season, more than 50 lighted miniature villages are displayed throughout the shopping center. The Trader Joe's offers gourmet foods at low cost, including wine prices that put most places to shame. You'll find fine jewelry at J.D. Bray's, formal wear at Bonney & Gordon, a terrific selection of furnishings for your home office at Office @ Home, a Pendleton Shop, casual clothing and jewelry for women at Irresistible Put-Ons, up-scale toys at Carousel Toy and Party, and a full-service salon at Morgan Taylor's. If your credit card is melting, cool it off at the Sacramento Brewing Company. (Northeast)

FACTORY OUTLET CENTERS

FACTORY STORES AT VACAVILLE
I-80 at Nut Tree Rd. (from the east, exit Monte Vista Ave.; from the west, exit I-505/Orange Dr.)
Vacaville

The factory outlet at Vacaville is flat out the biggest outlet center within driving distance. More or less across the highway from the Nut Tree Restaurant (a halfway stopping point between Sacramento and San Francisco, now closed), these factory stores along Interstate 80 offer virtually everything made, if you're willing to drive between 45 minutes to an hour from Sacramento to get there. Make sure you're actually at the Factory Stores because this area has become a retail megalopolis with several other malls jammed all around the outlets. There are more than 130 outlet stores selling apparel, linens, footware, housewares, toys, and more, all from 20 to 70 percent off. Reebok, Mikasa, Nine West, Big Dog, Black & Decker, Bugle Boy, Corning Revere, Danskin, Farberware, Foot Locker, Gap, Harry and David, L'eggs/Hanes/Bali/Playtex, Lenox, Levi's, Nike, Oneida, Oshkosh B'-Gosh, Royal Doulton, Stroud's, Vans—the list is mind-boggling and goes on and on. There's a food court to replenish your depleted shopping reserves. (West)

FOLSOM PREMIUM OUTLETS
Exit Folsom Blvd. north
from U.S. 50, Folsom

This is not the biggest outlet center

TRIVIA

When it opened in 1945, the Town and Country Village truly was out in the country. It was a harbinger of things to come—California's first suburban shopping center.

in the area, but it's the nearest to Downtown and has a wide, clothing-oriented selection. The outlet looks like a small, prefab village, with sidewalks winding around brand-new stucco-faced stores, each of which offers anywhere from 25 to 65 percent off full retail price. Saks Fifth Avenue, DKNY/Donna Karan, G.H. Bass, Gap, London Fog, Nike, Nine West, Waterford Wedgwood, and Zales Jewelers are just the tip of this 70-outlet iceberg. (West)

NAPA PREMIUM OUTLETS
I-80 to Hwy. 12 west,
then Hwy. 29 north into Napa
(west side of Hwy. 29)
These outlets are focused upon a young, upscale person's wardrobe (Tommy Hilfiger, Nautica, J.Crew, Cole-Haan, Big Dog, Esprit, Calvin Klein, and others), but still provide for all (Ann Taylor, Oshkosh B'Gosh, Maidenform). The distance from Sacramento almost warrants day-trip status, but the outlets are reachable and worth an occasional ride into the wine country. (West)

10

SPORTS AND RECREATION

In the Sacramento region, people are more apt to participate in their favorite sports than just watch them. By one accounting, there are more players registered in adult softball leagues here than in any other city in the country. Not that Sacramentans wouldn't spectate with the best of fans anywhere, it's simply that there's only one truly big-time team: basketball's Sacramento Kings. With apologies to the WNBA Monarchs, only the Kings are part of what gives a city that major league aura, that shape-shifting image of importance that cities across the nation try so hard to hold on to as sports franchises flit about in search of tax deals. While no determined couch potato need suffer in this era of cable and satellites, a positive aspect of having fewer local major league distractions is that no matter what your recreational interests, chances are there's an organization of like-minded enthusiasts here who will gladly welcome you. The immediate area is blessed with clean rivers and lakes for fishing, swimming, and boating; benign weather most of the time; and a terrain that encourages biking and skating. There's also a full range of western America's topography—from ocean beaches to alpine ski runs—within a two-hours' drive from home. But are people here still good fans? They were loyal enough to the Kings to fill Arco Arena year after fruitless year—497 sellouts during 14 straight losing seasons—until more than a decade of failure finally eroded attendance in the late '90s. It took a loan from the city to keep the Kings from moving away. But that was then. The Kings are now a premier team, and on game night Sactown's in the house—Arco Arena *rocks.*

PROFESSIONAL SPORTS

Baseball

THE SACRAMENTO RIVER CATS
837 Riske Ln. at South River Rd.
West Sacramento
916/447-HITS
www.rivercats.com
The San Francisco Giants and Oakland A's are easily accessible to Sacramento fans, each team's stadium being roughly an hour and a half away (see their box office information below). Both teams receive extensive TV game coverage and reportage in the *Sacramento Bee.* But now Sacramento has its own team, albeit minor league. The River Cats are the Oakland A's Pacific Coast League Triple-A entry, and in 1999 they were the Minor League World Series champions. They achieved this during their last season in British Columbia as the Vancouver Canadians. Their inaugural season in 2000 meant the return of PCL baseball to Sacramento for the first time in 40 years (since the Solons left for Hawaii). The Raley's supermarket chain has lent its name to the brand new, 10,400-seat Raley Field, which is directly across the river at the southwest corner of Tower Bridge in West Sacramento. It's within walking distance from Downtown and

---

TRIVIA

After less than two months of public sales, the Sacramento River Cats became the hottest-selling franchise in the 16-member Pacific Coast League by passing the 4,500 mark in season tickets.

Old Sac, and sluggers hit outfield drives in the direction of Tower Bridge, the Money Store pyramid, and, across the river, the city skyline. (West)

OAKLAND A'S
Network Associates Coliseum
7677 Oakport, Ste. 200
Oakland
510/638-0500, 510/562-1633 (fax)

SAN FRANCISCO GIANTS
Pacific Bell Park
King and Third Sts.
San Francisco
800/5-GIANTS, 415/972-BALL
415/467-8000
www.sfgiants.com

Basketball

SACRAMENTO KINGS
Arco Arena
One Sports Pkwy.
916/928-6900 (box office),
916/649-TIXS (tickets),
916/928-3650 (season tickets)
www.nba.com/kings
Joe and Gavin Maloof inherited ownership of the Houston Rockets from their father, but had to sell the team soon after. When asked recently how soon they regretted the decision to sell, Joe Maloof replied, "The following hour. You talk about seller's remorse. This family's been grieving 17 years." They waited that long to own another franchise, and when they took control of the Kings in 1999 there was widespread concern that they intended to take their new team to Las Vegas. Nothing could be further from the truth. The entire Maloof family has bought or built new homes in Sacramento, and their total commitment to producing a top team right here has already

reaped rewards. It's a potential embarrassment to be called "America's Team" (as they were frequently called during the 1999–2000 season), but the young Kings were playing some of the most exciting hoops in the NBA. Stars like Chris Webber, who, it once seemed, would only be happy in New York or L.A., have found that Sacramento is a nice place to live—and win. (North)

SACRAMENTO MONARCHS
Arco Arena
One Sports Pkwy.
916/928-6900 (box office),
916/649-TIXS (tickets),
916/928-3650 (season tickets)

Jason Williams of the Sacramento Kings

© NBA Photos

www.wnba.com
Along with the Kings, the Maloofs bought what seemed like every professional sports franchise in town. The Monarchs are benefiting from the intense interest in the Kings, as the Maloofs seem committed to shoring up the facilities at Arco for both teams and giving whatever financial support is necessary to build a WNBA winner. In a bow to the role of happenstance in sport, the Monarchs were one knee ligament away from making a major statement in the '99 playoffs when league MVP Yolanda Griffith went down at the end of the regular season. (North)

Indoor Soccer

SACRAMENTO KNIGHTS
Arco Arena
One Sports Pkwy.
916/928-6900 (box office),
916/649-TIXS (tickets),
916/928-3650 (season tickets)
www.sacknights.com
Quick: who's the first team to raise a championship banner at Arco Arena? It's not the Kings or the Monarchs, but a third Maloof franchise—indoor soccer's Knights. The 1999 World Indoor Soccer League champion accomplished this feat using 13 players on its roster who have ties to the local community, creating a special bond with the

In Pursuit of Beer

Before the River Cats, Sacramento had another go at minor league baseball when the Steelheads, an unaffiliated Western League team, played for one season on the City College campus. The Land Park neighborhood's resistance to the sale of beer at games was among the reasons the Steelheads picked up and moved down Interstate 80 to Vacaville. They are now, coincidentally, nearer to the Anheuser-Busch brewery in Fairfield.

already loyal fans and the potential fan base of 60,000 kids and 20,000 adults who play in area leagues. (North)

Other Pro Sports

CAPITOL RACING
Cal Expo Harness Racing
916/263-7894
www.capitolracing.com
The State Fairgrounds along Cal Expo Boulevard is the site of the harness-racing scene. (Northeast)

SACRAMENTO CAPITALS
Gold River Racquet Club
2201 Gold Rush Dr.
Gold River
916/638-4001
www.saccapitals.com
And the oldest, most successful Sacramento sports franchise is . . . the Capitals? Sactown's entry in World Team tennis, the league commissioned by Billie Jean King for the last 30 years, was the champion in the '97, '98, and '99 seasons and recently featured Lindsay Davenport as a team member. It's a country-club atmosphere, but exciting stuff nevertheless. (South)

SACRAMENTO RACEWAY PARK
5305 Excelsior Rd.
916/363-2653 (drag-race info),
916/363-2645 (oval track/motocross info)
A local bit of color takes place on Wednesday nights when the Raceway hosts one long amateur hour. For six dollars at the gate, and another six dollars to race, anybody can show up with their own car and push for their personal-best time around the quarter-mile track. And just about anybody does, from custom jobs that burn nitrous oxide to minivans. After time trials, there are head-to-head competitions handicapped with head starts for slower vehicles. The idea is to cut down on street racing, and management (with cooperation from the Highway Patrol) has been helping keep speed freaks out of trouble for 30 years. (South)

AMATEUR SPORTS

Adults and kids have a full selection of leagues for virtually any sport they want to participate in. Sacramento has produced more than its share of Major League baseball players (Dusty Baker and Greg Vaughn are just two examples), perhaps because amateur baseball is an almost year-round sport here. Youth football, soccer, and basketball associations continue to proliferate, and affordable city-owned golf courses and youth golfing programs encourage kids from all neighborhoods to get involved. For spectators, the local universities and community colleges provide ample viewing, though at a smaller-school level. If you're new to the area and want to get yourself or your kids started in league play in almost any sport, check out www.cityofsacramento .org/recreation. There will be links on this page for programs and events, classes, centers, sports, trips, aquatics, and Camp Sacramento, which lead to further links listing dozens and dozens of organizations for sports and recreational participation.

College Sports

The Sac State Hornets and UC Davis Aggies are Division I-AA and Division II schools, respectively. Their programs are highly competitive and, from time to time, nationally prominent, as both schools field teams across the spectrum of men's and women's intercollegiate sports.

CALIFORNIA STATE UNIVERSITY, SACRAMENTO
6000 J St.
916/278-4323
1999 marked a turning point for the CSUS football program. For the first time since moving up to Division I-AA status, a pair of Hornet football players were named to an All-America first team, as both running back Charles Roberts and offensive lineman Jon Osterhout were selected to the Sports Network All-America squad. For the second year in a row, Roberts was selected to the Associated Press All-America squad, joined by Osterhout, a second-team selection the previous year. Roberts was also named Big Sky Conference Offensive MVP as he rewrote the division record books for total yardage. Recruitment efforts have improved dramatically, as success breeds success.

The Hornet track stadium underwent a $1 million improvement as

On the Way

Yuba County, north of the city, will host a new raceway complex in 2001 next to a new SFX Presents (the old Bill Graham Presents) concert venue. Tentatively referred to as the Yuba County Motorplex, the track's eventual name has been in dispute, as area residents don't want to be poor relations to Sacramento. But the track will be home for up to six racing events per year, including Indianapolis 500–style races.

Hughes Stadium at Sacramento City College was the nation's first sports stadium associated with a junior college.

Sacramento State prepared to host the 2000 U.S. Track and Field Olympic Trials. In addition, the CSUS rowing squad's home base—located at Lake Natoma in Rancho Cordova—also underwent major construction, and CSUS now boasts one of the most impressive athletic complexes, along with what is already considered one of the best race courses, in the nation. In 1997 Sacramento State hosted the first-ever NCAA women's rowing championship, and the women's rowing team regularly travels up and down the Pacific Coast, including taking on Pac-10 opponents.

The baseball team competes in the Big West Conference, primarily against other Cal State campuses. The conference regularly produces Major League prospects. The gymnastics squad in 1999 posted the highest scores in school history and earned its first-ever berth in the NCAA Region 1 Championships. The Hornets became just one of three California schools—joining UCLA and Stanford—to earn a spot in the NCAA postseason. Things will only get better as the program funds more scholarships and recruits more top gymnasts than ever. (East)

UNIVERSITY OF CALIFORNIA, DAVIS
530/752-1915 (box office),
530/752-3505 (information)
The UCD Aggies have had enormous recent success within their Division II realm. Their men's basketball team was the national champion in 1998, and was ranked in the national Top 10 well into the 2000 season. They've recently joined a new conference, the newly expanded California Collegiate Athletic Association, arguably the best Division II conference in the nation. Their football team has gone into the postseason national playoffs for several years running.

UC Davis finished second out of the more than 250 NCAA Division II schools for the Sears Directors' Cup in 1997–98, which honors the best all-around Division II athletic program in the nation and is based on a points system that considers all

Paintball

If you have a powerful urge to shoot goopy stuff at other human beings, then paintball is your game. Try Paintball Sam's Paintball Park (916/344-9566) for an outdoor experience, or Paint the Way (916/366-9149) for an indoor field with leagues and a pro shop.

sports together and looks at gender equity as a factor. The Aggies won the first two Sears Directors' Cups ever given at the Division II level. In addition, UC Davis began offering athletic grants-in-aid in fall 1998 for the first time in the 86-year history of athletics at the school. Davis is consistently among the national leaders in the number of its athletes honored as part of the Academic All-America program, and is the top Division II school in the nation in the number of recipients of NCAA Postgraduate Scholarships. It's fun to cheer for the brains that go with the brawn. UC Davis fields 12 varsity teams for women and 11 for men. (West)

Community Colleges

Together, three campuses—Sacramento City College, American River College, and Cosumnes River College—make up the county's Los Rios Community College District. These two-year associate-degree schools are active in a wide range of athletic events and compete against one another, as well as against regional CCs such as Delta, Sierra, and Yuba Colleges in the Bay Valley Conference. Sacramento City College was the state champion among all California community colleges in baseball for 1998 and '99, a feat matched by Sierra College's women's basketball team in 1999. These colleges regularly send their "Juco" athletes on to four-year university programs, typically Cal State and UC campuses.

Hockey

Hockey on ice is hard to come by in Sacramento, with the exception of Skatetown in Roseville, the facility which both the Cal State and UC Davis club-level teams use as their home ice. Hockey on wheels is a little easier to find, with kid and adult in-line leagues at several locations, including the new Laguna Skates (see chapter 7, Kids' Stuff).

Lacrosse

A conundrum: which came first, the game or the pub? The answer is probably "Who cares?"—the Bonn-Lair pub (3651 J St., 916/455-7155) lends its name to the club team and hosts it after games. For Easterners who miss their mayhem of choice, the BonnLair team has lasted for over 20 years, attracting players

If you or your children have a disability and want to participate in a wide choice of recreation, call City Parks and Recreation (916/277-6060) and ask about "Access Leisure" programs. Baseball, soccer, wheelchair basketball and soccer, adaptive golf, track and field, and snow skiing are all available. Even more programs are listed in the "Access Leisure Ink" newsletter, which Annie Desalernos (916/277-2340) will be happy to send you. Special events, trips, social programs, teen sports, and Special Olympics are all nearby.

from throughout Northern California. Home games are played on campus at Sac State, near Carlson Drive and J Street. (East)

RECREATION

Backpacking/Hiking/Birding

There are dozens of trails available for hiking within a few minutes' drive of downtown, or without driving at all. Because of the flat terrain, kids can go almost anywhere adults can. There are many books that cover the trails of Central and Northern California, and these will all point out the many opportunities Sacramentans have to stay in direct touch with their own natural world. Without leaving the city, though, there is an entire book's worth of trails to explore in the American River Parkway alone. Fortunately, that book's been written. *Biking and Hiking the American River Parkway,* published by the American River Natural History Association, describes these very special 23 miles of preserved nature. "[The] Parkway is abundant with ever-changing plants and creatures: towering oaks, colorful wildflowers, migrating chinook salmon, waterfowl and song birds, black-tailed deer, pipevine swallowtail butterflies, and even an occasional coyote, mountain lion, or bald eagle. It is a work of art in progress. . . ." (See chapter 8, Parks, Gardens, and

© Tom Myers 1996

Bike racers on White Rock Road

Recreation Areas for more information.)

Bicycling

The college town of Davis boasts of being "bike capital of the world," with more bikes per capita than any other city. Even their schools are designed to be reached by bike trails that rarely cross vehicle traffic. On a wider scale, the entire Sacramento Valley is bike crazy—and always has been. The spectacular Jedediah Smith National Recreation Trail, more commonly referred to as the American River Parkway Bike Trail, existed in vestigial form in the nineteenth century, when wagon and stagecoach drivers took such a liking to the gravel roadway that they

TRIVIA

UC Davis is home to the Cal Aggie Cycling Team. They were the '98 Western Collegiate Cycling Conference champions and the '94 National Collegiate Road champions.

almost destroyed it with overuse (see chapter 8, Parks, Gardens, and Recreation Areas.) The flat Sacramento Valley floor lends itself to rides of great distance, and the weather allows biking all year, although December to February can be cold and wet, and the heat of day must be avoided from July to September. Foothill country is a short drive away for mountain bikers and road racers seeking near-vertical challenges. The lone rider will find bike routes throughout the city, whether atop the levees, along city streets (see chapter 2, Getting Around), or through parks. Kids should be extremely cautious near street traffic, as they would in any urban/suburban setting. For those who like to ride in groups, there's plenty of company.

DAVIS BIKE CLUB
610 Third St.
Davis
530/756-0186
dbc-owner@cycling.org
These are serious people, dedicated to racing, touring, and ultra-distance cycling. If you don't know what a double-century tour is, don't go there. (Okay, a "century" is equivalent to 100 miles.) They consider their own Davis Double Century event to be the most popular of its kind in California. Call to learn about their many other sponsored races and group tours.

OPHIR MILAN WOMEN'S CYCLING CLUB
916/361-1003
Buy a club jersey, pay a $15 membership fee, and you're in. Besides riding together, members participate in safety fairs and other athletic events as monitors and marshals. A Saturday Folsom-to-Auburn ride is held throughout the winter, and Sunday mountain-biking rides are planned.

SACRAMENTO BIKE HIKERS
916/453-1870
www.bikehikers.com
The Bike Hikers, founded in 1968, is the oldest continually active cycling club in the Sacramento area. The club's focus is on touring and recreational cycling.

SACRAMENTO SINGLETRACK SCORCHERS (SASS)
P.O.Box 188553
Sacramento
www.mother.com/~kson/sass.htm
This is the Sacramento area's first all-women's mountain-bicycling club. They welcome riders of all skill levels to share in biking the many off-road mountain trails in or near the Sacramento Valley.

SACRAMENTO WHEELMEN
P.O. Box 19817
Sacramento
916/446-5418
www.sacwheelmen.org

A cyclist could experience years of enjoyment without ever leaving the 32-mile American River Parkway Bike Trail. But for the off-road rider who needs the clacking of his or her molars to feel free, the Salmon Falls Trail in the American River Canyon along the South Fork is a place to start. The 16-mile, singletrack, out-and-back trail changes elevation just enough to be fun as it follows the north bank of the river to Folsom Lake. Take U.S. 50 to El Dorado Hills Road and go north until it becomes Salmon Falls Road. The trailhead is just after the road crosses the canyon, where you can park for $2. (Northeast)

This nonprofit organization is devoted to cycling and related activities. They schedule rides every weekend, as well as other ride series. The majority of trips are on the road, but there are mountain-bike rides and self-contained tours as well. Nonmembers and guests are welcome at all events and meetings.

Boating/Houseboats

When the Sacramento and American Rivers were "discovered" by Europeans early in the nineteenth century, what would come to be known as the Sacramento Delta was possibly the last undeveloped alluvial delta on earth. It is still a world unto itself, having more in common with rural Louisiana than with nearby San Francisco (see chapter 13, Day Trips, for a fuller accounting). Between the two rivers and the sloughs that run alongside them on their way to the ocean, there are thousands of miles of waterways, and their development turned out to be more recreational than commercial. Motorboats are, not surprisingly, the craft of choice, allowing waterskiers, anglers, houseboaters,

and personal watercraft free run of the endless water, whether going up- or downstream, with or against the tide that influences the waters even this far inland. Below are places to rent or put in your own watercraft.

DISCOVERY PARK
American River Pkwy., west end
916/875-6961
Discovery Park contains a six-lane launching area and a small-craft launch on the river. (See also chapter 8, Parks, Gardens, and Recreation Areas.) (North)

FOREVER RESORTS HOUSEBOAT RENTALS
11530 West Eight Mile Rd.
Stockton (The Delta)
800/255-5561, 602/968-5449 (fax)
Forever Resorts rents luxury houseboats at the King Island Marina in Stockton for three, four, and seven nights. (South)

HOGBACK ISLAND
FISHING ACCESS
Grand Island Rd. along Steamboat Slough (The Delta)
916/875-6672

Hogback Island Fishing Access has a two-lane boat launch and a picnic area. (South)

OLD SACRAMENTO DOCKS
Between the Tower and I St. Bridges
916/264-7031
The Old Sacramento Docks consist of 200 feet of dock space requiring no reservations. (Central)

PARADISE POINT MARINA
8095 Rio Blanco Rd.
Stockton
800/752-9669, 209/952-1000
Paradise Point Marina rents houseboats as well as ski, patio, and fishing boats. They also offer Sea-Doo sales and rentals, dry storage, and full-service boat repair. (South)

SACRAMENTO MARINA
Downtown Riverfront
916/264-5712
The Sacramento Marina has 553 berths in Miller Park just south of Old Sacramento and is a full-service marina. Barry Paulsen's Boat Center (916/447-BOAT), located at the marina, has bow rider ski boats, deck boats, and fishing boats for rent. (Central)

Fishing

Here's a fishing report from the *Sacramento Bee* during an off-

season January, a week judged as "terrible": "The rain may spur the sturgeon in the Rio Vista area. One angler caught a 30-pounder on ghost shrimp. The Port of Sacramento is yielding some stripers. . . . The American River at Watt Avenue is seeing several fishermen trying for steelhead. . . . Boaters drifting minnows behind Cal Expo are picking up a few stripers. The Sacramento River near Miller Park produced a 41-pound salmon." One can only speculate about a "good" week. Fishing is everywhere—along the riverbanks, the sloughs of the Delta, in nearby lakes—and, if you make a day trip out of it,

For more on fishing in the region visit the Department of Fish and Game's Web site, www.dfg.ca.gov/ifd/index.html.

Hobbies

Rocketry may not involve a lot of exercise, but it's an outdoor activity and involves things that might blow up. The Sacramento Area Rocketry Group/SARG (916/965-6707) is a section of the National Association of Rocketry (NAR), which is dedicated to the promotion of safe and fun activities for young people of all ages through the sport and hobby of model rocketry. All launches conform to the NAR Safety Code, which, for almost 40 years, has allowed millions of launches without any serious injury. SARG also supports youth organizations, such as the Boy Scouts of America and the Discovery Museum, through education programs. They hold three different types of events: club launches/meetings; demonstration launches/static displays for youth groups and nonprofit organizations; and monthly building sessions where beginning and experienced rocketeers alike share ideas on rocket construction and design.

throughout Northern California in such accessible spots as Trinity and Shasta Lakes, Lake Oroville, Clear Lake, Lake Berryessa, Folsom Lake, and Lake Tahoe (see chapter 7, Kids' Stuff, for tips on how to get the youngsters started). Then there's the Pacific Ocean, two to three hours away.

Fitness Centers

Sacramento has dozens of health clubs, including nationally prominent chains such as Gold's Gym and 24-Hour Fitness. Two downtown places to check out are Midtown Athletic Club (916/441-2977) and the Capital Athletic Club (916/442-3927), which are both chock-full of state-of-the-art equipment and enjoy a certain chichi reputation as the "in" clubs. Just want to

sweat and grunt? Or try a place with "No Machines. No Walkmans. No Mirrors. No Dancing. No Whiners. No Quitters. NO EXCUSES, JUST RESULTS"? Then Basic Training Boot Camp Fitness Program (916/362-1704) at the converted Mather Air Force Base is for you.

Golf Courses

The Sacramento golf scene is a rich one. In fact, developers have been so eager to build new courses that they may have outpaced the available number of golfers. Golf is so hot that in 1999 alone four new courses were added within a 45-minute drive of downtown, and in 2000 three more opened—all this after 12 new courses had already debuted during the previous four years. One result of this overbuilding is a constant stream of discounts and coupon offers as clubs vie for business in a market where many courses have had up to 15 percent fewer rounds being played. Courses are generally lush but with few surface features (unless you travel into the foothills), and are lined with towering evergreen trees to make up for the flat valley floor. During the winter, players are limited more by available light than by temperature—starters will only delay your early-morning play if the occasional frost makes the greens vulnerable to footprint damage. Otherwise, golf is a year-round activity.

Here are a few nearby public courses to try, among the more than 50 choices in the area:

ANCIL HOFFMAN
6700 Tarshes Dr.
Carmichael
916/575-GOLF
County-owned and recently upgraded, the 18-hole championship layout at Ancil Hoffman also has a grass driving range, PGA instructors, pro shop, bar, and restaurant.

Golf for the Disabled

County-owned Cherry Island Golf Course, in the Elverta area of North Sacramento, has added an adaptive golf cart to its course amenities. The four-wheeler loads the bag on the front, and the driver can swivel the seat off the back end to position him- or herself next to the ball without having to dismount. One of the few in the nation to have this state-of-the-art cart, its purchase is part of a program to expand recreational activities for the disabled. Golfers learn to use the Golf Express cart in a free, two-hour course, then may rent it at $11 for 18 holes. Call 916/991-7293.

Bartley W. Cavanaugh Golf Course

It's listed in *Golf Digest* as one of the top 75 public courses in the country. (Northeast)

BARTLEY W. CAVANAUGH
8301 Freeport Blvd.
916/665-2020
www.birdie.com/bartcavn
Bartley W. Cavanaugh, the newest city-owned course, is links-styled, with 18 holes at championship-length. The fairways roll gently near the Sacramento River. A full-service restaurant and a pro shop are also on the premises. (South)

BING MALONEY
6801 Freeport Blvd.
916/428-9401
Bing Maloney has 27 holes, including a par-3 Executive nine, an easy and inexpensive way to get in a quick bit of golf, work on your irons, and give kids a feel for the game. You'll also find a lighted driving range, practice areas, and a full-service restaurant. (South)

CHERRY ISLAND
2360 Elverta Rd.
Elverta

The City of Sacramento (as Capital City Golf) runs six courses—Bartley Cavanaugh, Bing Maloney 18, Bing Maloney Executive 9, Alister MacKenzie and Arcade Creek at Haggin Oaks, and William Land 9—that all offer inexpensive fees and easy accessibility. The Capital City Club gives huge discounts after a one-time membership fee, and it's open to all. They also offer a one-stop phone number for reservations at all six courses, 916/264-TIME.

916/575-GOLF
Large oak trees and four lakes set the Cherry Island course apart in natural beauty and challenging holes. Like Ancil Hoffman (see above), Cherry Island is county-owned, with a grass driving range, PGA instructors, pro shop, bar, and restaurant. (North)

HAGGIN OAKS GOLF COMPLEX
Alister MacKenzie/Arcade Creek
3645 Fulton Ave.
916/481-4506
www.hagginoaks.com
These two championship courses offer 36 holes, a lighted driving range, an excellent learning and fitting center, a café, lessons, tournaments, and the most complete pro shop around. The Alister MacKenzie course is the namesake of its famed Scottish course designer, who built some of the finest courses in the world. The course was recently renovated to return it to MacKenzie's original vision, including relocating greens to their historical settings. (Northeast)

TEAL BEND
7200 Garden Hwy.
916/922-5209
www.tealbend.com
Teal Bend is considered one of the premier public courses in town. They invite you to experience "your country club for a day" and offer lessons, a pro shop, and a restaurant. (North)

TWELVE BRIDGES
3070 Twelve Bridges Dr.
Lincoln
888/893-5832, 916/645-6730
www.twelvebridges.com
Judged *Sacramento* magazine's "Best Local Golf Course" in a readers poll, the tour-quality Twelve Bridges course includes a pro shop and Chadwick's Bar and Grill. (Northeast)

SAY-Golf Association
(Sacramento Area Youth Golf)

This association's goal is "to introduce even more people from all walks of life to the great game of golf." Inner city, school, and disabled (deaf, blind, and physically challenged) programs bring kids from all over the city to SAY-Golf teaching centers, where lessons and greens fees are kept affordable, to move the game away from a country-club brand of exclusion. Junior clubs and camps at courses throughout the Sacramento area enable kids to learn the sport, compete in tournaments, and even receive college scholarships. Call 916/455-7888.

To compare courses, ratings, and fees, go to www.citygolf.org for a site named GolfSacramento.

WILDHAWK
7713 Vineyard Rd.
916/688-GOLF
www.wildhawkgolf.com
One of the county's newest public courses, Wildhawk is an upscale and somewhat more expensive outing with a dress code. (South)

WILLIAM LAND
1701 Sutterville Rd.
916/455-5014
Comprising most of William Land Park, this nine-hole course is surprisingly beautiful and fun to play. It's handily located right in the middle of the city. Al Geiberger of PGA fame spent his youth on this course. They offer practice chipping and putting areas, a teaching center, and newly remodeled coffee and pro shops. (South)

Horse Stables

In one recent estimate, which should be adjusted downward almost daily, 59 percent of the land in Sacramento County was still open and rural. Discovered by Europeans on horseback, the Sacramento Valley is still hospitable to trail rides. A

Something Different

Snowshoes. That's wooden tennis rackets on your feet, right? Not anymore, as technology has affected even this mode of transportation. Today's snowshoes are made mostly with lightweight metal tube frames. Solid or webbed decking keeps you above the surface, while metal cleats dig in for traction. These devices are much easier to get used to than their historical counterparts, and snowshoe sales tripled between the 1999 and 2000 seasons. Some makers even make compatible bindings so snowboarders can 'shoe up the hill and board down. Check any ski resort, as most have snowshoe trails, or try Backcountry Tracks (888/687-2257, info@backcountrytracks.com) for guided tours. The California State Parks Service (530/525-7372) will help you find the backcountry area nearest you and can offer advice on avalanche safety.

quick glance at the Yellow Pages will reveal dozens of stables offering hundreds, even thousands of acres of riding area and paths, including the American River Parkway. Many stables offer boarding, lessons, and training (for the horses, not your kids). Here are two places to try:

GIBSON RANCH
8556 Gibson Ranch Rd.
Elverta
916/991-7592
A county park (see chapter 7, Kids' Stuff; and chapter 8, Parks, Gardens, and Recreation Areas), Gibson Ranch offers horse rentals, lessons, secure trails, and party packages including ponies brought to your location. (North)

SHADOW GLEN RIDING STABLES
4854 Main Ave.
Orangevale
916/989-1826
Shadow Glen boasts of over 10,000 acres of scenic trail rides for groups and individuals. Ride hourly or by the day, take riding lessons at all levels of skill (or no skill at all), or sign your kids up for a summer camp. Guided tours are available, along with overnight camp trips, a boarding service, and lessons in western trail riding. The stables are affiliated with the Folsom Lake State Recreation Area. (Northeast)

Rafting

The popular image of rafting is a rousing, death-defying plunge through whitewater. You can do that nearby, if you like, especially on the three forks of the American River in Gold Country (see chapter 13, Day Trips). But if you do it closer to home, it's easier to keep the whole family involved, especially if you have little ones. The purpose of the Folsom Dam was not only electricity generation, but also flood control. As a result, the American River close to town is quite placid most of the time. Several outfits, such as American River Raft Rentals (916/635-6400), provide groups large or small, young or old, with all they need to float for several hours downriver to a pickup spot, from which they'll drive you back to your car. A four-person raft will cost about $32 plus a small

---

T I P

Each year brings fresh tragedy to swimmers along the Sacramento and American Rivers. The water is not swift here, except during spring runoff conditions when it's much too cold to venture into the water anyway (it is, after all, melted snow). The danger is the tempting diving platforms that bridges and other riverside structures present. Too often the water is simply too shallow to dive into. Other times, a dive which was possible one day may be deadly the next due to shifting currents and new deposits of sediment. In any case, the activity is illegal.

launch fee, shuttle fee, parking fee, and damage waiver, totaling about $40. Do bring sunscreen, sunglasses, a bag of snacks, and water shoes or sandals. Do not bring pets. (South)

Skating

Ice skating has only a toehold in the region, while in-line skating is spreading rapidly beyond street play to small amusement-park settings (see chapter 7, Kids' Stuff).

Skiing

If you stand in the middle of the city without knowing local geography, it's impossible to believe that Sacramento has anything to do with skiing. Yet if you drive northeast, before you leave the county limits you'll see the city skyline in your rearview mirror and the Sierra foothills directly before you, snowcapped during winter. The Donner/Tahoe skiing area can be reached in an hour and a half if you avoid the Friday-night crush to get there. It's definitely possible to get up to a resort and back in a day,

with plenty of playtime (see chapter 13, Day Trips, for suggested destinations). Just a few of the better known resorts are Squaw Valley, Alpine Meadows, Diamond Peak, Heavenly Valley, Kirkwood, North-Star, and—one of the first you'll reach and very kid-friendly—Boreal.

Swimming and Rowing

As mentioned above, you can contact the city by logging on to www.cityofsacramento.org/recreation and following the link to "Aquatics." There you'll find more than a dozen pools that are managed throughout the summer by the city, many of them outdoor pools at area high schools. There are also many wading pools for kids, an essential Sacramento activity when the thermometer squirts mercury out its top. Contact Parks and Recreation at 916/277-6060 or 916/448-4FUN (24-hour information).

On an entirely different level, the Cal State (CSUS) Aquatic Center (916/985-7239) at Lake Natoma is a water-world of its own. Its eight acres of land along the lake include

A Runner's Event

In 2000, the Sacramento Marathon held its 24th annual race, a flat course that meanders around William Land Park, follows the Sacramento River north to Old Sacramento, and then returns. Half-marathoners collapse at this point, while full-marathoners do it all over again. It's a USA Track and Field–certified course, with a variety of divisions, including a half-marathon division for 9- through 12-year-olds. It's usually held in early October. Call 707/678-5005 for details.

Eppie's Great Race

Self-billed as "the world's oldest triathlon," this annual charitable fund-raiser sponsored by the restaurant of the same name starts in the middle of the American River Parkway. From there, runners race six miles west to the Guy West Bridge at Sac State, bicycle to the Jim Jones bridge at Sunrise, and kayak downriver to Goethe Park, where a celebratory picnic is held. The race takes place on the second Saturday of July.

a sandy beach, grassy areas, picnic tables, volleyball courts, barbecues, a boat-launching ramp, three boating docks, and plenty of parking. The CSUS Aquatic Center has many parents, being jointly operated by several university organizations, the State Department of Boating and Waterways, and the State Department of Parks and Recreation. The center was created to provide high-quality boating and water-safety instruction and sponsors races such as the Pacific Coast Rowing Championships. Classes include sailing, sailboarding, rowing, waterskiing, kayaking, canoeing, and summer youth camps, with private lessons available.

The CSUS Aquatic Center is also the focus of competitive clubs for the region. It's the home of the CSUS Sailing Team, Water Ski Club Team, and Rowing Team, and also the Capitol Crew Rowing Team for high school–aged rowers. The center sponsors sailing regattas, rowing regattas, volleyball tournaments, and waterskiing tournaments. Recent highlights have been the State Rowing Championship, PAC 10 Rowing Championship, and Head of the American and Western Regional Rowing Championships. (South)

© Tom Myers 1998

11

PERFORMING ARTS

If the health of the local arts scene reflects a community's overall quality of life, Sacramento is hale and hearty. A description of the city's theater scene by Leland Ball (producing director of the California Musical Theatre) in a recent *Sacramento Bee* article could be applied to the region's cultural life in general: Compared to large metropolitan cities, the differences are in scale and quantity, not quality. In theatrical circles, Sacramento is known as one of the strongest one-week markets in the country. A touring company might stay in Los Angeles for a month, but its one week in Sacramento will be sold out. And though San Francisco is reachable for a night on the town, it's still far enough away that it's a distinct market, with occasional events that the arts patron has to travel to the Bay Area to see or hear. That distance has forced Sacramento cultural life to be self-reliant, and there is still more going on here than any one person will find time for. All the performing arts are well represented by professional organizations with long histories, and new venues are on the way.

THEATER

ACTOR'S THEATRE OF SACRAMENTO
1616 Del Paso Blvd.
916/484-3750
The Actor's Theatre of Sacramento's professionally trained actors perform classics, contemporary plays, and original works by local playwrights in the Building on the Boulevard at the center of the Uptown arts district. (North)

AMERICAN RIVER COLLEGE THEATRE ARTS
4700 College Oak Dr.
916/484-8124

The Theatre Arts Department at American River College not only offers a wide range of classes in all areas of theater, but also maintains a busy production schedule of four main-stage performances, faculty-directed touring and showcase productions, touring children's theater productions, a student-directed one-act play series, and an ongoing partnership with the Fair Oaks Theatre Festival. (Northeast)

BEST OF BROADWAY
916/974-6280
Best of Broadway Benefit Productions, Inc., is a nonprofit organization aiming to develop and showcase local talent in Sacramento. Volunteer talents bring a little of the Big Apple to the Big Tomato each year as they perform a musical revue of that season's Broadway highlights in song and dance. More than 200 cast members are chosen from more than 1,000 who audition. Their performances help raise charitable funds. Call ahead as locations vary.

THE B STREET THEATER/ FANTASY THEATRE
2711 B St.
916/443-5391
In 1992, brothers Tim and Buck Busfield founded a place of their own, calling their B Street venture "Sacramento's Resident New Works Theatre" and dedicating it to the development of new material. The B Street Theatre is a professional theater company that presents world-class premieres of plays by writers such as Aaron Sorkin, Joe DiPietro, and James McLure, as well as many West Coast premieres of other new works. Seating fewer than 200, the B Street stage provides an intimate experience. Tim is a well-known actor

who has worked on Broadway and in feature films and also won an Emmy for *Thirtysomething*. He often stars in, and sometimes directs, the B Street productions. Cofounder Buck Busfield has directed more than 50 of their shows and wrote 6 of them. Their Fantasy Theatre was named by *Sacramento* magazine as "the most productive and popular theater for children in Northern California." Fantasy productions are performed by professionals who travel to schools and other venues to bring theater to the kids. Both brothers have made Sacramento their home. (East)

BEYOND THE PROSCENIUM PRODUCTIONS
2030 Del Paso Blvd.
916/922-9774
Beyond the Proscenium offers experimental plays and premieres of new works. The company is committed to theater that challenges, educates, and maybe even changes the world. A fine example in the recent past is their presentation of *Angels in America*. (North)

CHAUTAUQUA PLAYHOUSE
5325 Engle Rd.
Carmichael
916/489-7529
The Chautauqua Playhouse is some of the best that community theater offers. A recent season included six productions for adults and six productions for kids, in a mix of comedy and drama that was both professionally staged and affordable. (Northeast)

DAVIS MUSICAL THEATRE COMPANY
616 Second St. (Varsity Theatre)
Davis

530/758-8058, 530/756-3682
The Davis Musical Theatre Company was California's first amateur, all-volunteer, musical theater company. For over 15 years, founders Jan and Steve Isaacson have produced 10 musicals a year at the Varsity Theatre in Davis, giving almost 100 performances annually. Six of the productions feature adult performers and four are by the Young Performers Theatre (actors aged 7 to 17), in musicals ranging from *Evita* to *Charlotte's Web.* (West)

EAGLE THEATRE (RUNAWAY STAGE PRODUCTIONS)
925 Front St.
Old Sacramento
916/207-1226
www.runawaystage.com
The Eagle is a bit of history all by itself. The existing building is a reproduction of the first theater constructed in California (the original met a quick demise in flooding). Children's weekend theater, light fare for adults, and educational programs about the theater's history now share the structure. (See chapter 7, Kids' Stuff; and chapter 5, Sights and Attractions.) (Central)

FOOTHILL THEATRE COMPANY
888/730-8587, 530/265-8587
www.foothilltheatre.org
The Sierra Shakespeare Festival is the highlight of the season at Foothill Theatre Company, but they also mount seven other productions per year. The Nevada City company maintains an international exchange program (with Russian actors) and holds a Shakespeare Camp at Lake Tahoe. (Northeast)

GARBEAU'S DINNER THEATRE
12401 Folsom Blvd.
Rancho Cordova
916/985-6361
Garbeau's offers a wide range of material, usually of lighter fare, along with a meal. Children's theater is incorporated into a special buffet on Saturday afternoons (see chapter 12, Nightlife). (South)

Eagle Theatre

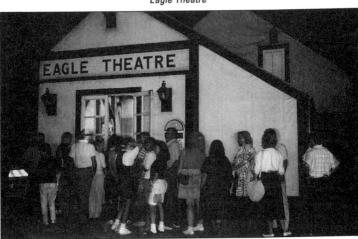

© Tom Myers

A New Home for the Impresario

Ground was broken in May 2000 for the new UC Davis Center for the Arts, scheduled for completed by fall of 2001. The $61-million facility will house a complete stage facility in its 1,800-seat main theater, and a smaller 250-seat studio theater. Rising at the southern edge of campus, the landmark center will serve as a "new front door" not only to the UCD campus, but to the town of Davis as well. UC Davis Presents (in effect, the region's impresario) has always produced about 45 events per season, making it the largest presenter of arts north of the Bay Area. But the organization has been limited by the capacity of the Sacramento Community Center Theater's calendar, where the ballet, the opera, and the philharmonic (among others) perform. But no more: the new Center for the Arts will enable UC Davis Presents to offer as many as 80 events a year by the 2001–02 season, which will expand the entire regional arts scene. The Sacramento Ballet's Ron Cunningham has already told the Sacramento Bee *that he sees it as "a spectacular opportunity to increase our activities."*

INTERACT
916/452-6174

This company's name is derived from "Interactive Asian Contemporary Theatre." In five seasons of plays in all genres, interACT has given Asian American actors a chance to realistically portray Asian American characters. Their productions have included plays by Philip Kan Gotanda, David Henry Hwang, and Wakako Yamauchi, among others. The first-rate quality of production makes interACT accessible to all audiences. While they expose concerns specific to the Asian community, they also touch the universal heart. Call ahead as locations vary.

MAGIC CIRCLE
REPERTORY THEATRE
241 Vernon St.
Roseville
530/782-1777

Each year this community theater produces three musicals and three comedies, as well as three adult-cast children's shows on Saturday afternoons. The theater also runs workshops for young actors ages 4 through 19, in three age brackets. (Northeast)

RIVER CITY THEATRE
COMPANY
8194 Belvedere Ave.
916/457-RCTC

Top Five Reasons Not to Attend the Sacramento Jazz Jubilee
by Roger Krum, Executive Director of the Sacramento Traditional Jazz Society

The Sacramento Traditional Jazz Society annually presents the Sacramento Jazz Jubilee, the world's largest traditional jazz festival (www.sacjazz.com). Each Memorial Day weekend more than 100 bands from across the United States and around the world give more than 1,000 performances on more than 40 stages, clustered in six Jubilee Jazz Centers.

The Sacramento Jazz Jubilee's slogan is "Sounds Like Fun!" And that's what it is. Still, not everybody loves the Jubilee. Here are the top five reasons not to attend:

Number 5: "I don't like Dixieland."
The focus of the Jubilee, in fact, is all of the jazz styles from the first 50 years of jazz history (approximately 1895-1945). This covers the period from the origins of jazz in New Orleans to the big band era. Still, the general public still tends to lump many, if not all, of the early jazz styles under the single category of "Dixieland." In reality, there are many different styles and sounds of traditional jazz presented at the Jubilee. In addition, several music styles related to early jazz have recently been added, such as blues, gospel, ragtime, swing, western swing, and zydeco. These "jazz cousins" add texture and variety to the Jubilee.

Number 4: "There's not enough 'trad'."
This is an interesting one. Each year we include 30 to 35 bands that most traditional jazz fans would consider to be "trad" bands.

Twice a year, River City Theatre Company, a children's-theater workshop, registers more than 150 children from the 1st through 12th grades—on a first-come, first-served basis—to perform a Broadway musical (see chapter 7, Kids' Stuff). The workshop provides young people with the opportunity to develop skills, self-confidence, and self-esteem through learning all aspects of musical theater in a positive, supportive environment. (South)

RIVER STAGE
(Cosumnes River College)
8401 Center Pkwy.
916/688-7364
www.riverstage.org
River Stage Director Frank Condon was recently awarded the Mayor and Supervisor's Lifetime Achieve-

No other traditional jazz festival in the country books this many bands in total. Therefore, in sheer numbers, the Jubilee has more trad bands than any other jazz festival in the country. Further, there are four performance sites that feature trad bands exclusively. Therefore, we offer trad fans the opportunity for a totally trad four-day weekend.

Number 3: "The Jubilee is too expensive."

Jubilee prices range from $15 to $85. Tickets for major rock concerts are in the $75 to $150 range. The top tickets for performances of plays by touring companies is approximately $75. In both instances we are talking about a single performance of approximately three hours in length. With more than 100 bands performing for four days, the Jubilee is a major bargain.

Number 2: "The Jubilee is too big and too crowded."

I recently heard, "No one goes to the Jubilee anymore because it's too crowded." What did you say, Yogi? It's true that the Jubilee is big. However, it's structured so you can make it as small or as large as you choose. Each of the six Jubilee Jazz Centers (Cal Expo, DoubleTree Hotel Sacramento, Convention Center, Old Sacramento, Radisson Hotel Sacramento, and Red Lion Hotel Sacramento) has its own character and ambience. Some people spend the entire Jubilee weekend at one Jubilee Jazz Center. Others take in all six centers during the four days of the Jubilee. Most people mix the Jubilee Jazz Centers in different combinations between these two extremes. The official Jubilee program is like a menu. The choices range from a Jubilee snack to a multiple course Jubilee gourmet feast.

Number 1: "I don't like music, people, or fun."

Have a nice time wherever you are on Memorial Day weekend. Those attending the Jubilee will be having a great time!

ment Award by the Sacramento Metropolitan Arts Council for establishing a company that has tried to represent on stage the same multicultural makeup as the city itself. Condon brings directing experience at the Odyssey and Mark Taper Theaters in Los Angeles to his provocative offerings and has recently established an annual Playwright's Festival, with staged readings of original plays by authors from across the nation. (South)

SACRAMENTO CITY ACTORS' THEATRE
3835 Freeport Blvd.
(Sacramento City College)
916/558-2228
Sacramento City Actors' Theatre features a blend of students and professionals acting together in a

variety of works, often grouped according to an annual theme in an attempt to unify classical and contemporary material. (South)

SACRAMENTO THEATRE COMPANY
1419 H St.
888/4STCTIX, 916/443-6722
The Sacramento Theatre Company produces highly professional works and is often considered the preeminent theater venue in the city. With a history going back 60 years, it has received a recent transfusion of enthusiasm with new artistic director Peggy Shannon, who put this once-struggling organization back on solid financial footing. Their season might include anything from Greek tragedy to Neil Simon to new works, with cast members drawn from equity theaters up and down the Pacific Coast. The STC is aggressively seeking a younger audience and offers a high school program to entice a new

Helping Out the Arts

Various studies have shown that arts instruction helps kids improve their schoolwork. The Sacramento Metropolitan Arts Commission (SMAC) has several programs to maintain the connection between art and students. Its Arts Education Program places artists in classrooms, funds community murals by local youths, and provides job training and educational enrichment for 75 teens in a design program every summer. In 1998 SMAC also awarded 48 arts organizations a total of $465,000. Those organizations reported an estimated attendance of one million, with revenues of $19 million—a good investment in the local economy. The Sacramento Symphony League, a 45-year-old organization dedicated to fund-raising and youth education, continues to offer music scholarships and educational concerts to schools, even after the demise of the Sacramento Symphony. Business Volunteers for the Arts (BVA) coordinates more than 100 volunteers to donate time and expertise to over 130 nonprofit arts and cultural organizations throughout the Sacramento region. Each year BVA assists an average of 60 projects, providing services valued at more than $200,000. According to BVA Board President Stephen Murrill, "If you're going to have a strong community and not just a location where a lot of people live, that includes an emphasis on arts."

generation of theatergoers. "Theater—Don't Do It Alone" offers students two for one tickets and a two for one dinner package to make theater as affordable as dinner and a movie. (Central)

SUSPECTS MURDER MYSTERY DINNER THEATRE (*DELTA KING*)
1000 Front St.
Old Sacramento
916/443-3600
It's interactive, so watch out (see chapter 12, Nightlife). (Central)

THISTLE DEW DESSERT THEATRE
1901 P St.
916/444-8209
This tiny, intimate theater recently made a Sacramento *News and Review* Editors' Choice list for favorite theater experiences, not only for its "edgy, innovative theater," but also for its repertoire of Irish dramas and comedies that "capture a century of conflict in the beleaguered Emerald Isle and explore how all that pain and confusion plays out." The theater is in a gallery setting, with art exhibits for patrons to enjoy. (East)

UC DAVIS
Department of Dramatic Art and Dance
One Shields Ave.
Davis
530/752-1915 (campus box office)
UCD students in this department study art and dance in the context of dramatic performance. In a typical year, productions are separated into two seasons. The University Theatre Season consists of established plays, world premieres, and dance productions. The Studio Season consists of smaller productions of established plays, as well as new student-written works. Occasional

presentations of experimental plays and many class-related projects are also produced. The department's unique Granada Artist-in-Residence Program is a cooperative effort with Granada Television of London, celebrated for its productions of *Brideshead Revisited* and Laurence Olivier's *Lear*. Since 1982, students under the Granada Artist-in-Residence Program have been benefiting from working closely with a group of the most distinguished directors in the English-speaking theater in every aspect of production (as actors, assistant directors, stage managers, playwrights, and designers) and also in the courses taught by these professionals, who visit from London. (West)

MUSIC AND OPERA

CALIFORNIA MUSICAL THEATRE
1419 H St.
916/557-1999
The California Musical Theatre presents two series of musicals annually. In the summer, the Music Circus uses a tent and poles to uphold its 50-year-old tradition of musical theater-in-the-round. Throughout the year they also produce a Broadway series, featuring touring professionals, at the Community Center Theater. Recent highlights included *Riverdance* and *Cabaret*. Well-connected producer Leland Ball draws on his New York theater background to bring top talent to Sacramento, not by offering more money (though the SLOA has an operating budget of $11 million), but by offering great roles. (Central)

CALIFORNIA WIND ORCHESTRA
Westminster Presbyterian Church

The Sacramento opera scene shuts down during late spring and summer. The high local pollen count devastates tenors and sopranos visiting from the East.

1300 N St.
916/489-2576
After performing for more than five seasons, the California Wind Orchestra has found a permanent place in the local culture. CWO is a 38-piece professional ensemble of woodwinds, brass, and percussion. They've performed masterworks, world premieres, and popular Broadway music, often with distinguished guest soloists. (Central)

CAMELLIA SYMPHONY ORCHESTRA
Westminster Presbyterian Church
1300 N St.
916/929-6655
Critically acclaimed locally for over 37 years, the Camellia Symphony Orchestra has gained national attention by winning seven ASCAP awards for their programming. Eugene Castillo, the first Filipino American to be appointed music director of a major American symphony orchestra, has overseen numerous Sacramento premieres, as well as a wide-ranging classical repertoire. A sample of their innovative programming is the 2000 season's world premiere of *Zodiac,* written by Han Yong as a tribute to Asian immigrants who built the railroads to California more than 150 years ago. His music, as described by Castillo, uses both non-Western instruments and Western orchestra in "an interplay whose paths reflect our own present-day culture. Sometimes they merge,

sometimes they parallel, and sometimes they move in different directions." (Central)

CAPITOL OPERA SACRAMENTO
6219 Ross Ave.
Carmichael
916/944-2149
Capitol Opera Sacramento is a non-profit, all-volunteer community opera company that produces several operas each season, recently including *Carmen* and *Madame Butterfly*. The company has performed for 10 years now and offers as many as five productions per year of high-quality operas and operettas at reasonable prices. (It was formerly known as the Voice Fitness Institute of Sacramento, acting as a resource and information center for "voice professionals" of all types including trained singers, broadcasters, and public speakers.) Each April, COS holds the Teresa Tweed/Capitol Opera Annual Scholarship Competition, awarding up to $1,000 to local voice students between the ages of 15 and 25. (Northeast)

CHAMBER MUSIC SOCIETY OF SACRAMENTO
916/443-2908
The Chamber Music Society offers six concerts a year on the CSUS campus. The programs feature small groups of varied instruments that change according to which of their wide selection of pieces is being performed. (East)

MUSIC IN THE MOUNTAINS
530/265-6124

Music in the Mountains is actually three festivals held in the towns of Grass Valley and Nevada City, which lie next to one another in the foothills northeast of Sacramento. In the fall, there's a short program of chamber and holiday chorale music; in spring, chamber music; and in summer, a full-blown festival of 19 concerts in 21 days, featuring pop, jazz, classical, and big-band music. The festival is attended by more than 10,000 people each year. (Northeast)

SACRAMENTO CHORAL SOCIETY
916/264-5181, 916/766-BASS

Donald Kendrick is the volunteer director of the Sacramento Choral Society—when he's not at his day job as professor of music and director of choral activities at California State University, Sacramento. At CSUS he has four choirs and teaches undergraduate and graduate choral conducting. He also judges competitions and works with high school choirs from all over the state. The Sacramento Choral Society is a 135-member group which, until three years ago, was known as the Sacramento Symphony Chorus. When the Sacramento Symphony went bankrupt in 1996, many of the Choral Society's members had been singing together for decades, so Kendrick helped them reorganize. As he recently told the *Sacramento Bee,* "Our mandate was to continue the tradition of providing the community with performances of the great choral-orchestral repertoire. Nobody else was doing that then." They also created a community outreach component, working with children and doing choral workshops. "The symphony," says Kendrick, "used to hire us. Now we're the presenters."

SACRAMENTO MASTER SINGERS
916/338-0300

Sacramento Master Singers is a mixed choral group of 45 performers who present as many as 10 concerts a year, including a holiday concert given at the St. Francis Church (downtown on K Street). Ralph Edward Hughes has served as conductor of the group for 13 seasons, and his leadership during this period has brought the group recognition for its high performance

Tickets

1. *All Events*
   916/783-6666
   www.alleventstickets.com

2. *Bass Tickets*
   916/766-BASS

3. *Sactix*
   916/442-2500

4. *Preferred Seating*
   Ticket Service
   916/498-1400
   www.preferredseat.com

5. *Howe Avenue Box*
   Office
   916/920-1121

Michael Morgan to the Rescue

Sacramento shares its principal conductor Michael Morgan with the Oakland East Bay Symphony, an organization that he helped rebuild. The recent calamitous end of the Sacramento Symphony caused many to doubt that an orchestra could succeed here, but the Philharmonic is well on its way to erasing those fears as Morgan seeks to unite audience, orchestra, and community in the effort to sustain this new endeavor. The UC Davis music department recently announced that it was dropping plans to form its own symphony, as the Morgan-led Sacramento Philharmonic Orchestra was succeeding so splendidly.

standards, innovative programming, and service to the community. They've presented national and area premieres, such as Benjamin Britten's *A.M.D.G.,* Arvo Pärt's *Te Deum,* Robert Levin's arrangement of Mozart's *Requiem,* and, most recently, Alfred Schnittke's *Requiem.*

SACRAMENTO OPERA ASSOCIATION
Sacramento Community Center Theater
1301 L St.
916/737-1000, 916/264-5181
www.sacopera.org
The Sacramento Opera Association has been producing high-quality operatic performances for nearly 50 years. Though limited in seasonal scope (two productions per year), the shows are full-scale in staging and talent. A typical recent season offered Verdi's *Falstaff,* and Puccini's *Tosca.* New artistic director Timm Rolek has brought fresh enthusiasm to the company and has plans to include a third annual production soon

and pool resources with the Reno-based Nevada Opera so that both companies can expand their programs. The addition of supertitles—a scrolling English translation that appears above the main stage—and a full live orchestra have made opera more accessible to patrons. In fact, the audience for opera is now the fastest growing among the performing arts. (Central)

SACRAMENTO PHILHARMONIC ORCHESTRA
Sacramento Community Center Theatre
1301 L St.
916/922-9200, 916/766-BASS
Newcomer Michael Morgan has noticed a hunger in his Sacramento audiences for good concerts, and he has fed that hunger with world-class music. He's determined to see a major orchestra succeed here. A "Meet the Maestro" program before each performance creates a bond between the orchestra and its audience in an informative and enter-

taining way. A recent season included Berlioz, Mahler, Beethoven, and Mozart, but also featured an all–Leonard Bernstein program, conducted by Morgan, who is Bernstein's former student. By the age of 42, Morgan had already been assistant conductor of the Chicago Symphony under George Solti and had guest-conducted the Vienna State Opera; the New York Philharmonic; the Berlin State Opera; the New York City Opera; the National, Baltimore, Seattle, Detroit, and Oregon Symphonies; the Los Angeles and Warsaw Philharmonics; and the Philadelphia Orchestra. And he's just getting started. (Central)

SACRAMENTO YOUTH SYMPHONY
916/388-5777
The Sacramento Youth Symphony's performers range in age from 9 to 21 and train at multiple levels. The advanced orchestra performs three classical concerts a year and recently competed in the Tuscany Music Festival. They perform an an-

nual holiday concert at Johnson High School's Bert Chapell Theatre.

UC DAVIS PRESENTS
530/757-3199 (information),
530/752-1915 (subscriptions)
www.ucdavispresents.ucdavis.edu
The motto at UC Davis Presents is "think globally, applaud locally," and they back it up with music, dance, and theater programs from around the world that cross national and cultural borders and feature world-class artists. The programs are presented on both Davis- and Sacramento-area stages throughout the year. Here is a list of just a few of the visiting acts from one recent season: Jazz at Lincoln Center, Les Ballets Africains, National Symphony Orchestra, Vienna Boys' Choir, Borromeo String Quartet, Royal Philharmonic Orchestra, Trinity Irish Dance Company, Parsons Dance Company, Australian Chamber Orchestra, Children of Uganda, Ballet Folklorico, Beau Soleil, and dozens of internationally renowned artists. You can buy tickets to individual

Sacramento Philharmonic Orchestra

© Tom Myers 1992

A New Tent for Sacramento

The Sacramento Theatre Company and the Music Circus (a summer program of the California Musical Theatre, formerly the Sacramento Light Opera Association) have shared a home on H Street between 14th and 15th Streets for years. In October 1999, the city council and the board of supervisors approved an $8 million renovation to help both facilities. Most of the new construction will go to replace the canvas-and-pole tent that the Sacramento Light Opera Association has used for 50 years in its Music Circus productions with a Teflon-coated, fiberglass structure (think Denver Airport) that should last for decades. The new tent's enclosure will enable Music Circus productions to be air-conditioned. The STC will have better seats, lighting, and sound, and the companies will share an open arts courtyard and marquee. The new venue should be ready for the 2002 season.

events and regular series tickets, or create your own series for discount savings. Call ahead as locations vary.

WOODLAND OPERA HOUSE
340 2nd St.
Woodland
916/666-9617
The Woodland Opera House does five musical productions per year, scheduled from fall to spring, with a melodrama in the summer. Originally built in 1885, the opera house burned down, along with much of Woodland, in 1892. The rebuilt, horseshoe-shaped theater is one of the last of its kind in the United States, fortified on the outside by stately brick walls and still retaining much of the original seating. Typical of nineteenth-century English music halls, the building was never, even in its earli-est days, a true opera house. Its original owners, who operated the hall as a playhouse for touring performers like Nance O'Neill, Harry Davenport, and Polish actress Madame Helen Modjeska, thought the name would class up the joint. Revamped in 1989, the Opera House is now in effect a museum, with period costumes, old performance bills, and even the old plumbing on display. Remnants of the gas lighting system are reminders of why so few of these places still exist. The building is now a state historic landmark. (West)

DANCE

DALE SCHOLL DANCE/ART
916/451-3732
The Dale Scholl company performs

a thoroughly modern repertoire, blending ballet with jazz and other modern dance forms. They frequently collaborate with local musical groups and have choreographed works to music sources as unlikely as Jimi Hendrix.

EBO OKOKAN
916/427-3876
www.cwo.com/~lucumi/ebo.html
Blending African and Cuban roots in its folkloric dance, the Ebo Okokan troupe has performed for almost 10 years in Sacramento and throughout Northern California. The troupe also provides lectures, demonstrations, and workshops.

PAMELA TROKANSKI
DANCE THEATRE
911 Third St.
Davis
530/756-3949
The PTDT has thrived in Davis as a professional contemporary dance company since 1985, offering two concert series a year in Davis while also touring Northern California.

Talks and demonstrations in area elementary schools help bring dance to audiences of all ages. PTDT also sponsors Third Stage, the area's only multigenerational dance company, with performers ranging in age from 10 to 90. In addition, they offer classes (from ballet to belly dancing) for all ages, and seniors over 65 can learn for free. (West)

RUTH ROSENBERG
DANCE ENSEMBLE
24th Street Theatre
2791 24th St.
916/457-RRDE
Ruth Rosenberg choreographs many of the works in this company's repertoire and works with Bay Area choreographers as well. Once a year (usually February) RRDE presents an "Other Visions" program, featuring the work of cutting-edge companies from the Bay Area. RRDE also offers what they say is Sacramento's only studio with a full modern dance curriculum. They train the RRDE Kids Dance troupe, as well as

The Sacramento Ballet performs The Nutcracker, *p. 216*

© Tom Myers 1999

other students. RRDE is notable for its collaborative nature, and works with local composers, poets, musicians, and artists to create innovative dance. (East)

SACRAMENTO BALLET
Community Center Theatre
1301 L St.
916/264-5181, 916/766-BASS
916/552-5800 (subscriptions)
This versatile company performs ballet classics such as *Romeo and Juliet,* as well as modern works by new choreographers, recently including director Ron Cunningham's world-premiere of *A Streetcar Named Desire.* They've also collaborated with nontraditional groups such as the Taiko Dan Drummers to create unique music and dance performances. A recurring audience favorite, entitled *Fluctuating Hemlines,* is a mixture of highly technical ballet with the fast feel of an MTV rock video. And yes, they do *The Nutcracker.* (Central)

CONCERT VENUES

ARCO ARENA
One Sports Pkwy.
916/928-6900
With a seating capacity of over 17,000 in its basketball configuration, this is the venue for arena acts. Not only do all the stars of rock, pop, and country roll through here, but so do the ice-show acts (Disney on Ice, Ice Capades, Sesame Street) and the unclassifiable big-space events like tractor pulls and wrestling. With new ownership (the Maloof family not only owns the Kings, the Monarchs, and the Knights, but Arco Arena itself), there will be upgrades in the near future to keep Arco state-of-the-art. (North)

CAL EXPO AMPHITHEATER
1600 Exposition Blvd.
916/922-9250
This outdoor venue seats about 14,000 and handles many of the acts which can't fit into the fairgrounds during the State Fair. (Northeast)

"Fusion"—It's Not Just for Restaurants

There's a cooperative air about much of the Sacramento regional arts scene. A recent aspect of this has been joint productions by various music and dance companies. The Chamber Music Society, for instance, invited the Ruth Rosenberg Dance Ensemble to perform with them; they have also collaborated with Germany's Charis Eurythmy Ensemble. In addition, the Sacramento Ballet and the Sacramento Traditional Jazz Society have performed several Duke Ellington improvisations with one another, while the Dale Scholl Dance/Art troupe has performed with Howard Hersh's Music Now group to the beat of contemporary California composers.

CREST THEATRE
1013 K St.
916/44-CREST
www.thecrest.com

This art-deco landmark, with 975 seats, is the largest main theater in the area. It's unique to Sacramento as a concert hall, filling a void of venues this size by attracting groups who can profitably play to the theater's capacity but can't yet fill Arco Arena. The Crest also hosts meetings and cultural events, and it's just two blocks from the Convention Center. (See "Movie Houses of Note" in chapter 12, Nightlife.) (Central)

K Street Mall

SACRAMENTO COMMUNITY CENTER THEATER
1301 L St.
916/264-5181

Adjacent to the Convention Center at the heart of the suddenly active Esquire Plaza and with some of the best restaurants in town within easy walking distance, the Community Center Theater is the focal point of Sacramento's performing-arts scene. With 2,452 seats, it's the largest and most formal of traditional concert venues and was built, along with the Convention Center, in the 1970s. It's well known for its excellent acoustics and serves as the home of Sacramento's opera, ballet, and philharmonic companies. (Central)

SACRAMENTO MEMORIAL AUDITORIUM
15th and J Sts.
916/264-5181

The Memorial Auditorium has hosted performing arts and events in Sacramento since 1927. It has also hosted roller derbies, basketball games, grudge wrestling matches with Hulk Hogan, and high school graduations. Judy Goldbar, administrator for the Sacramento Convention Center (which oversees the Memorial Auditorium), describes the Memorial as "an arena/performing arts house." It sits on a block donated by Sacramento city founder John Sutter Jr. and was dedicated to Sacramentans who died in war. An honor roll listing those killed in battle, from the Spanish American War through the Persian Gulf War, is displayed adjacent to the main lobby. Numerous health and fire-code violations and the need for an earthquake retrofit forced it to close in 1986. Much of the Memorial's original glory was uncovered by the renovations, and since reopening in 1996, the Memorial has not only hosted more concerts and graduations, it has also established itself as one of the city's most popular skateboard spots (see chapter 5, Sights and Attractions). (Central)

© Tom Myers

12

NIGHTLIFE

As already mentioned, Sacramento is more of a big town than a metropolis. That's both the good news and the bad news when it comes to local nightlife, and it affects live music presentations in particular. At one extreme of the concert venues there's Arco Arena (big enough to host the Rolling Stones); at the other, innumerable neighborhood holes-in-the-wall, which host the vast majority of live music. This makes Sacramento a great place to catch local bands who are just making names for themselves (like Oleander, the Chrome Addicts, and the Deftones), but it also makes it hard to see anything in between these cutting-edge garage bands on their way to national prominence and the gigantism of an Arco-level act.

That suits the local jazz and blues fans just fine. Restaurants, clubs, pubs, and hotel lounges keep Sacramento a lively center for these more intimate genres. And beyond live music, anyone looking for a night out of deejay-driven pop dancing, ballroom or swing dancing, cover-band entertainment, karaoke, or hooking their thumbs through their belt loops for a hoot in a cowboy and cowgirl line dance will find places to go throughout the region. The dance scene has to be checked out club by club, as there are almost no places that specialize in just one taste. A club that features industrial rock on Thursday is just as likely to have a deejay spinning Latin-beat dance tracks on Friday, reggae on Saturday, and live blues or jazz on Sunday. Most establishments, then, do most music. It's best to check the Friday *Bee* or the weekly *News and Review* to get the plan for the week.

CLUBS, BARS, AND MUSIC HALLS

ANDIAMO!
3145 Folsom Blvd.
916/456-0504

Besides being a quality restaurant (featuring Northern Italian food), Andiamo! has a classy atmosphere and is widely considered a great date place—to bring one or find one. Though it was originally a jazz spot, the live music acts now include alternative and swing-band groups. The dance crowd tends toward the young and hip, making Andiamo! a place to be seen. (East)

A SHOT OF CLASS
1020 11th St.
916/447-5340

This is an elegant restaurant, first. But on Friday and Saturday nights, A Shot of Class also becomes several ballrooms for big-band dancing to swing and Latin sounds. This downtown nightspot just off the K Street Mall was once a department store. The interior design has preserved the art-deco sweep of the large space, giving you a chance to live, for a few hours at least, inside a supper club straight out of a '30s Hollywood studio movie, only in subdued color. On weekend nights, this is one of the few places in town where you'll want to be (and are expected to be) dressed up a little. (Central)

BACK DOOR LOUNGE
1112 Firehouse Alley
Old Sacramento
916/442-5751

Las Vegas comes to Sacramento. Sit in black leather booths beneath gold and red velvet wallpaper, listening to the original Brat Pack, as you imagine yourself on the Strip in decades past. The Back Door Lounge is a place to sip martinis or anything on the rocks and catch the spirit of romance from another era. If Sinatra came to town, he'd sit in at the Back Door. But then Elvis would, too. They have live music, as well as Vegas tunes, for dancing. Go casual or dressy. (Central)

THE BALLROOM
6009 Folsom Blvd.
916/737-7929

The Ballroom claims to have Sacramento's largest dance facility, and who can argue with 8,000 square feet? The Let's Dance Ballroom Club will occasionally hold public dances here, which might begin with a tango lesson, then move on to "ballroom smooth," Latin rhythm, swing, salsa, night club two-step, and "the hustle." For more info on this nonprofit group dedicated to the cultural, social, and educational aspects of ballroom dancing, call Roger Zabkie at 916/965-6929. (East)

BIGSHOTS
1000 Melody Ln.
Roseville
916/773-6275
www.bigshotsroseville.com

A showcase of some of the best music in town, Bigshots has recently been involved in grinding arguments with residential neighbors over noise levels, traffic, and the usual not-in-my-backyard stuff. This is because Bigshots is a rarity in the region—a live music venue that can handle an audience of 300 to 400, making it the one stop in Sacramento for touring acts that have outgrown bars but can't yet fill the Crest Theater or Arco Arena. A converted pool hall, Bigshots strives for all-age shows and has no alcohol on the scene—just darts, video games, and some food, including pizza. (Northeast)

THE BLUE CUE
1004 J St.
916/442-7208
Part of the Paragary restaurant empire, the Blue Cue is an upscale billiard lounge boasting custom pool tables, shuffleboard, and a popular bar with a huge selection of spirits for the young professionals who crowd the place. (East)

THE BOARDWALK
9426 Greenback Ln.
Orangevale
916/988-9247
www.boardwalkrocks.com
A bit of a drive up the freeway, the Boardwalk has undergone a recent management change that will increase the number of nights devoted to live country sounds. But on any given weekend they might present heavy metal, alternative rock, or a classic act like Blue Oyster Cult. The variety of artists creates an interesting mix of clientele, mostly 20-somethings, but also those proud to be called punks and rockers with a little gray showing. All shows are for the 18-and-over audience. (Northeast)

BOJANGLES
7042 Folsom Blvd.
916/386-0390
This eclectic club is at the south edge of the Sac State campus. Separate rooms include a small dance floor, a bar, a game room, and an eating area. Outside is a large courtyard with a fire pit. BoJangles may be small but its diverse theme

nights attract an equally diverse crowd, including frequent visits from the gay and lesbian community and from alternative-music fans. Depending on which night you pick, BoJangles favors '80s tunes, industrial-gothic sounds, and even a fetish night, which will not be explained here. Well, okay: On Thursdays the Biomech Industrial Dance Club takes over a room at BoJangles for what their logo calls "Better Living through Self Destruction." The last Saturday of each month is their "Biomech Fetish Night," which features heavier music and "lots of wild and weird stuff for the freak at heart." Dressing up and participating are encouraged. There, you've been warned. Dressing up will not be explained either, except that it involves peculiar materials. If you do dress up, there's a reward, as posted on their Web site: "$5 if you look the part (Halloween costumes, leather, vinyl, pvc, velvet, rubber, metal, corsets, creative costumes, uniforms, drag, etc.), $6 if you have a clue (plain all-black clothing), $8 for Young Republicans. You get into it, you benefit. Get it?" Yes. (East)

CANTINO
DEL CABO
139 G St.
Davis
530/756-2226
As you would expect, the crowds at Cantina del Cabo tend to be predominantly UC Davis students, but nobody's excluded here. If you're not a student, however, go with a group, since mingling will be a little harder than in downtown. The Cantina features live music most Thursdays, Fridays, and Saturdays. A huge selection of beers and ales will keep you busy. (West)

Though it's part of the truly hip bar scene, Cheaters is but one of a number of closely spaced clubs that can be visited in one night. This is the crossroads where Midtown becomes East Sacramento, the meeting place of young professionals and college imbibers. In close proximity to Cheaters are the Limelight, the Monkey Bar, the Raven, and Andiamo!

CAPITOL GARAGE
COFFEE COMPANY/CABARET
1427 L St.
916/444-3633
This is a great little café (see chapter 4, Where to Eat), but it's also the spot for an intimate, close-up encounter with the best alternative groups that come through town. It's right around the corner from the capitol, with low-cost admission and balcony seating. Open mike is on Tuesday nights. (Central)

CHEATERS SPORTS BAR
3221 Folsom Blvd.
916/736-0563
For those who like to reminisce, this was once the Ben Parino Club, a cozy neighborhood bar. A new, ambitious management came in and took over the store space of its neighbors. The expansion and remodeling created a huge sports bar with state-of-the-art televisions, a kitchen, and lots of room to sidle up next to the taps. The patrons include Ben's old regulars and the local college crowd. (East)

CLASSIC JUKEBOX
8200 Sierra College Blvd.
Roseville
916/791-2131
Those who still feel the beat and just want to have fun dancing to it can come to the Classic Jukebox and feel okay about not having purple tips to their hair spikes (or even hair spikes). (Northeast)

CLUB BRANNAN'S
1117 11th St.
916/558-8089
There are two floors to dance on, and on any given night you can choose just one or mix them up—hip-hop with salsa with rhythm and blues. A little more upscale and metropolitan than most clubs in town, Club Brannan's is also a little dressier. There are occasional celebrity spottings, including of members of the NBA Kings and the local music industry. Salsa-dancing lessons are available. (Central)

CLUB LA COSTA
7218 Franklin Blvd.
916/424-9608
Club La Costa is a bar and a restaurant where you can also dance to live music Friday and Saturday nights. You'll hear every shade of Latin music, from romantic to salsa. (South)

CLUB 2 ME
4738 J St.
916/451-6834
Club 2 Me is considered by some locals to be the ultimate pub—good

beer, good pool, and good times. Its proximity to both Sac State and old residential neighborhoods means it brings in everybody, from frat boys (who might refer to "Club Do-Me") to serious imbibers two generations ahead of them. It's a tiny place, so just look for the shamrocks out front. (East)

COUNTRY CLUB LANES
2600 Watt Ave.
916/483-5105
Country Club Lanes—with Glo-bowling and 48 lanes—is much more than a bowling alley. It's open 24 hours, which leaves you all the more time to try billiards, the high-tech video arcade, and Lazer Tag, and then belly up to the full-service bar. The nightclub showcases live bands. (Northeast)

CROCODILES—RADISSON HOTEL
500 Leisure Ln.
916/922-2020
The resort theme at this Radisson Hotel locates Crocodiles on the lakefront side, which gives you an out-of-the-city experience even as the high-tech audio-visual equipment enhances the dancing. Appetizers keep you hopping. Nightly. (North)

THE DAVIS GRADUATE
805 Russell Blvd.
Davis
530/758-4723
There's no live music at the Davis Graduate, but who cares: Deejay-driven theme nights have something for everybody. During the day the place has a sports-bar feel (games on 22 screens, no less), including a restaurant and salad bar. The nights cover country (Monday), salsa for 18 and over (Tuesday and Thursday),

college party night for 18 and over (Wednesday), and college party night for 21 and over (Friday). On weekends they have dancing for all ages, with the drinking barrier handled in different areas of the club. (West)

DELTA LOUNGE—
DELTA KING HOTEL
1000 Front St.
Old Sacramento
916/441-4440
Just as it figured in the Where to Eat and Where to Stay chapters earlier in this book, the *Delta King* has riverfront ambience, which makes a night in the lounge a special time. The riverboat setting gives off quiet class while you sample the appetizers and specialty drinks, listen to the piano music, and enjoy the view. (Central)

THE DISTILLERY
2107 L St.
916/443-8815
The Distillery offers the ambience of a bar and restaurant that's been around for over 35 years. Here you get the unusual combination of a young crowd and a prime-rib spot. Wednesday nights they have an open mike, while Thursday through Saturday nights they feature live acts performing rock or hip hop and plenty of dancing. Check local listings for occasional Songwriters Nights. (East)

815 L STREET
815 L St.
916/443-8155
A huge mahogany bar gives 815 L the feeling of an old-time, downtown club. The wooden booths and stained-glass lamps cap the atmosphere. There are lots of drink specials and there's plenty of room to

Cover Bands

In a recent Bee article, Bary Burns, president of the American Culture Association, was quoted regarding nostalgia: "It's the desire for repetition and familiarity and predictability, taking comfort in what one already knows and being able to relive past experiences." Lest that sound too dreary and downright retro, remember that the Beatles and Stones and the big bands of the '40s were also cover bands in the beginning. Whatever the motivation, and whatever the crowd (it's the young as well as the boomers who are feeling the disco groove), cover bands have become huge in the live-music scene. There's a lot of silly humor in it (the Cheeseballs, favorites from the Bay Area, feature Bruce Stringcheese and Ricky Ricotta), but there's solid musicianship as well. Cover bands may be driving out new acts, or they may be saving the small clubs financially so they can afford to showcase new acts. Either way, it's a growing trend. Oh baby, do you wanna dance?

move, as the action is spread over three dance floors. Deejay-driven house music of all flavors makes you party. (Central)

FACES
2000 K St.
916/448-7798
Often voted best dance club as well as best gay bar in local newspaper and magazine reader polls, Faces attracts everyone across the young-human spectrum. It has several bars and dance floors, including a video dance room, where you'll move to anything from techno to country. Happy hour includes drink specials, there's a low cover charge, and the parking is free. Gay or straight, this place gets votes for best dancing in town. (East)

FANNY ANN'S SALOON
1023 Second St.
Old Sacramento
916/441-0505
Fanny Ann's Saloon is a Wild West bar full of weird memorabilia, with Old Sacramento adding to its ambience. This may not be history—the saloon is from the 1970s, not the 1850s—but the place is full of quirky fun, from deliberately mislabeled restrooms (no need to be a grown-up here) to the traditional shot-and-a-beer during happy hour. Get a burger, too, while you dance Thursday through Saturday nights to deejay-spun music. (Central)

FOX AND GOOSE
1001 R St.
916/443-8825

Near the political and business centers of Downtown, this classic English-style pub serves a great breakfast (see chapter 4, Where to Eat). It also provides a showcase for local music acts, featuring traditional Celtic folkies but also covering everything from bluegrass to modern rock tastes as well. Open mike night on Mondays. (Central)

THE G ST. PUB
228 G St.
Davis
530/758-3154

The G St. Pub is the old Davis Saloon. It now offers a complete pub experience, with a bar serving nightly drink specials, live music (including jazz), a grill, pool tables, and darts. (West)

HARD ROCK CAFÉ
7th and K Sts. (Downtown Plaza)
916/441-5591

The Hard Rock serves food and drinks in a rock-and-roll ambience. It's also in an ideal location, at the meeting place of the Downtown Plaza and the K Street Mall. The plan for putting on live acts hasn't worked out recently, but this is still a great place to get an informal meal and a brew. (Central)

HARLOW'S
2798 J St.
916/441-4693
www.harlows.com

Long one of the town's favorite nightspots (voted best nightclub in a recent poll by *Sacramento* magazine), Harlow's recently underwent a complete remodeling. It retained the art deco and moderne decor, which enabled it to become not only a fine restaurant and lounge, but a live-music showplace for local and na-

tional acts as well. This eclectic mix is representative of the city as a whole—dance-party music one night, then reggae, then swing or Motown to fill out the week. The restaurant is open for dinner Tuesday through Sunday until 9:30 p.m.; the club rocks until 2 a.m. The Momo Lounge is Harlow's upstairs cigar lounge, open Tuesday through Saturday for those of that peculiar persuasion. (East)

HOT AND SPICY
117 J St.
Old Sacramento
916/443-5051

At Hot and Spicy, you can pump up the burn with Cajun cuisine and then hit the dance floor. They have deejay dancing every Sunday, Tuesday, and Wednesday (cover charge); live reggae every Thursday (cover); and live classic rock and rhythm and blues Friday and Saturday (no cover). (Central)

IN CAHOOTS
1696 Arden Way
916/922-6446
www.incahootssacramento.com

In Cahoots is one of the few places in town that has one theme and one theme only—country! Learn to dance the two-step and western swing here, with free lessons given nightly (at 6:30 and 7:30) so you'll be ready when the fancy hoofers show their high-falutin' faces later on. All ages appear in the big warehouse-like building (they claim the second-largest dance floor in the county), complete with several bars and pool tables. The line dancing is a great way to meet someone new, as it doesn't require a partner to participate. They offer karaoke on Sunday nights. (Northeast)

JAZZMEN'S ART OF PASTA
1107 Front St.
Old Sacramento
916/441-6726

A full-service restaurant and bar, this is also a cool spot to catch jazz, blues, and cabaret acts. Jazzmen's offers indoor or courtyard dining with an Italian theme to get you in the mood. (Central)

THE LIMELIGHT
1014 Alhambra Blvd.
916/446-2236

The Limelight is not a dance club. You're more likely to find students playing darts and pool here as they nurse their beers. They'll serve you breakfast any day of the week (though Monday through Friday the place doesn't open until 11:30 a.m.), as well as lunch and dinner. They also have pizza specials and Kings games on big-screen TVs. As a popular stop on a circuit of Mid-town establishments within walking distance of one another, it has a clubby, insider's feel. (East)

LOS NOPALES
106 J St.
Old Sacramento
916/443-6376

Los Nopales is a full-time Mexican restaurant, but the place comes alive weekend nights with live salsa music. The atmosphere—in a hollowed-out Old Sac brick building that feels like an enclosed patio—is great, and the food is simple, inexpensive, but very tasty (try the calamari salad, a cold dish with hot spice). (Central)

MARILYN'S
1177 K St.
916/446-4361

Marilyn's is a full-service bar only a block away from the Convention Center, the Hyatt, the IMAX, and the Community Center Theater. With this ideal location, Marilyn's is becoming a favorite live-music stop for adults who haven't lost it yet. Open late (until 2 a.m.) nightly. (Central)

THE MONKEY BAR
2730 Capitol Ave.
916/442-8490

Yet another Paragary establishment (it's part of Café Bernardo—see chapter 4, Where to Eat), the always-crowded Monkey Bar appeals to the fashionably trendy over a wide age range. There's no dancing, no billiards, no spittin'—but it's a great place to be on the look for others on the look. Attire varies from casual to dressy. (East)

MUSICQUARIUM
2601 Del Paso Blvd.
916/484-4111

Located in the reborn arts district of North Sacramento, the Musicquarium's eclectic offerings carve a distinct profile among city venues. The entertainment club is new and tries to provide a comfortable, upbeat, and positive atmosphere for all ages. The bar is nonalcoholic, and the acts might perform anything from live music to dance to poetry to video presented with a theatrical flair in the sound and lighting systems. Check ahead for the day's artists—the music could be alternative, jazz, Christian rock, gospel, blues, or cover bands doing the oldies. (North)

OLD IRONSIDES
1901 10th St.
916/443-9751

They'll serve you lunch at Old Ironsides Monday through Friday or

Jazz—at the Elks Club?

The Sacramento Traditional Jazz Society in West Sac was organized over 30 years ago to preserve and promote traditional jazz music, and it's the sponsor of the Sacramento Jazz Jubilee held every Memorial Day weekend in Old Sac. On the second Sunday afternoon of each month, they also have a jazz session at the Elks Lodge, located at Riverside Boulevard and Florin in the Pocket neighborhood. Call 916/372-5277 for details. (South)

rock you every night. Though it's been family-owned since 1934, the demographics are nevertheless up-to-date in this old brick neighborhood bar that was a speakeasy during Prohibition. In fact, it's the oldest continuously operating bar in the city, with roots in the nineteenth century. The place still oozes atmosphere and boasts a central stage that lets you get close to the bands, which are often top-flight alternative acts. There are occasional comedy shows and special dancing nights for all ages, including kids. (Central)

ON BROADWAY
1827 Broadway
916/446-5251
Modern versions of rhythm and blues, plus what some call "old school" R&B (late '70s to early '80s), are attracting a young adult crowd to On Broadway. Atypically (for Sacramento), there's a dress code: no jeans or athletic wear of any kind. The club has deejayed dancing and two bars, and it's in the Tower neighborhood. Check the weekly calendars because this is also considered

one of the best jazz venues in town. (South)

THE PALMS
726 Drummond Way
Davis
530/756-9901
According to their ad, the Palms is "Your Cultural Oasis!" They're heavy on the live blues acts here. Though it's just a little place, it has a history of playing big (or soon-to-be-big) acts. (West)

POWER HOUSE PUB
614 Sutter St.
Folsom
916/355-8586
The Power House Pub calls itself "the Music Box of Folsom" and features local musicians. They have lots of games on TV for the sports-bar crowd, as well as karaoke on Tuesdays. (Northeast)

THE PRESS CLUB
2030 P St.
916/444-7914
This neighborhood joint is your prototypical Sacramento club. The Press Club has hosted a number of

alternative groups on their way up to the big time (like Matchbox 20 and Everclear), but also makes room for every type of popular music—from blues, jazz, swing, ska, and hard rock to heavy metal and industrial. The young crowd includes college students who also enjoy darts, video games, pinball, and billiards. The neighborhood's a little down, but the energy inside is way up. (East)

THE RAGE
1890 Arden Way
916/929-0232

The Rage seeks the cutting edge for nearly every dance type that young crowds might want. Six nights a week, the deejays (who are the real stars here) mix it up on three turntables, using a top-of-the-line sound system. The video screens, mirrored walls, new bar areas, and a recently added Chat Room make the Rage both a hot dance venue and an intimate place for a dating experience. Tuesday it's "Pure House Music;" Wednesday, College Night/Top 40 Dance; and Thursday, Top 40/European Dance Music. On Fridays the Rage plays the best of the '70s, '80s, and '90s (not necessarily a contradiction in terms), with a special emphasis on the disco beat. Saturdays feature "Way Bitchen '80s," and on Sunday "The Asylum" blends the best of alternative, progressive, gothic, and industrial music. (Northeast)

THE RAVEN
3246 J St.
916/442-9780

A downtown nightspot for more than 50 years, The Raven mixes the young and hip with neighborhood old-timers, and everybody seems to get along in the warm, happy atmos-

phere. The jukebox dance tunes are a mix as well: Frank Sinatra shares time with country and every flavor of new and old rock. The Raven shows plenty of sports on the tube, and there's a free parking lot (plus street parking). (East)

R.J. GRIN'S—DOUBLETREE HOTEL
2001 Point West Way
916/929-8855

At R.J. Grin's you can eat pizza, play shuffleboard or pool, and dance to the deejayed music until your head spins—the better to see all eight TVs showing sports. Monday through Friday you can swine out with the all-you-can-eat, pizza-and-wings special during happy hour. Wednesday features karaoke. Thursday's Pint Night is your chance to get bloated. And Friday and Saturday you can dance to music from the '60s through the '90s (and now the '00s). On Sunday perhaps you'll meet another single as you share hors d'oeuvres. (Northeast)

THE ROADHOUSE
1556 Bell Ave.
916/929-3957

Just east of Cal Expo, The Road-house specializes in live, bring-your-ax-and-sit-in blues jams. They have a large dance floor, several pool tables, a separate area for the bar, and a nice patio out back. (Northeast)

RYDE HOTEL
14340 Hwy. 160
Ryde (in the Delta)
888/717-RYDE, 916/776-1318,
916/776-1195 (fax)
www.rydehotel.com

This former speakeasy has kept its art-deco ambience (see chapter 5, Where to Stay), and offers dinner and dancing on Saturday nights. Eat, drink, be merry, and stay the night in a setting that will transport you to another time. (South)

SAVANNA'S—
SACRAMENTO INN HOTEL
1401 Arden Way
916/922-8041
Not just a hotel bar and restaurant, Savanna's is one of the best places in town to take in "old school" R&B. In fact, that's all they do, all three weekend nights, so they get it right. The deejay-run shows feature the rhythms of the late '70s to early '80s. Think Marvin Gaye, Rick James, Michael Jackson, Sly and the Family Stone, and then get out and dance. (Northeast)

STONEY INN
1320 Del Paso Blvd.
916/927-6023
This ain't your dad's dinner theater. Just go have dinner with a show at the Stoney Inn and enjoy the live music that rocks Thursday through Sunday. It's in the renewed arts district. (North)

THE TORCH CLUB
15th and I Sts.
916/443-2797
As of this writing, this venerable landmark for live music was in the process of moving several blocks from its former location of 60 years.

The Torch Club is a classic blues bar with bartenders from Central Casting. Here's hoping the new location catches the same atmosphere. (East)

WILD SADDLE SALOON
7942 Arcadia
Citrus Heights
916/721-5500
The Wild Saddle Saloon features special drinks with bull rides (bring a designated rider). There's a dance floor, too, if you're not too sore. (Northeast)

COMEDY CLUBS

LAUGHS UNLIMITED
1207 Front St.
Old Sacramento
916/446-8128, 916/446-3148 (fax)
There's a cash cover charge at Laughs Unlimited, but no required bar tab, so you get high-value laughs. A lot of familiar faces have performed at this Old Sac brick storefront club, since Los Angeles is accessible as a source of talent without emptying the cash register for travel expenses. Many top-level comedians have enjoyed trying out new material away from Hollywood's glare. They have food, drinks, desserts, and, from time to time, an open-mike night. Get up there, if you've lost all pride. (Central)

Blues got you down? Need some blues to get you up again? The Sacramento Blues Society provides a hotline that lists any and all blues bands playing around town at any given time. Call 916/556-5007.

PUNCH LINE SACRAMENTO
2100 Arden Way
916/925-5500
Located in the Howe Bout Arden Center just east of the Arden Fair Mall, this local franchise of the national chain brings in high-caliber comedians as well as local talent. Punch Line Sacramento is also a full-service bar and restaurant, with comedy and calories nightly, Wednesday through Sunday. (Northeast)

DINNER THEATER

GARBEAU'S DINNER THEATRE
12401 Folsom Blvd.
Rancho Cordova
916/985-6361
Garbeau's Dinner Theatre is located in the old Nimbus Winery Building. Diners are seated at six, with the curtain going up at eight. They offer light theatrical fare, including hit musicals, comedies, and mysteries, as well as concerts. The theater can host group events up to 250. Here also is Garbeau's Family Theatre, which features "live theatre by adults for children of all ages." The offerings lean toward fairy tales, but often with a humorous twist—*Snow White and the Seven Monsters,* for example. They have Saturday matinees, with an all-you-can-eat kids' buffet one hour before show time. (South)

SUSPECTS MURDER MYSTERY DINNER THEATER
1000 Front St.
Old Sacramento
916/444-5464
This is yet another showcase aboard the *Delta King* paddle wheeler permanently moored at the riverfront. At the Suspects Theater, interactive mysteries get the audience involved while they dine. Warning: You too could end up the murderer—or even the victim. Enjoy the ambience of the riverboat's restored grandeur, along with first-class food. The theater/dinner can be combined with a hotel package for a memorable weekend. (Central)

MOVIE HOUSES OF NOTE

In the 1970s, Sacramento lost one of its landmarks—the beautiful Alhambra Theater movie palace—to the developer's wrecking ball. That was a shame, but it was a shame not soon forgotten, as some of the other old theaters received that much more attention and were saved, restored, and given new life. They are all within a long walk of one another, and while this hasn't created a "cinema district," it has brought a special moviegoing experience to Downtown.

THE CREST THEATER
1013 K St.
916/44-CREST
www.thecrest.com
What began its life as a vaudeville house in 1912 was converted to a silent movie theater in 1918, and then became the Crest Theater after it was remodeled in 1949. It still displays the swirling art-deco embellishments of its heyday and, with 975 seats, has the largest main theater in the area. The lobby and the main theater itself display huge arabesques of gilded ornamentation, with sweeping vine-and-leaf patterns newly restored. Even though the Crest now offers three screens, this was not done at the expense

of the main theater. Two additional screens were added in a downstairs area when a fire in next-door businesses made expansion feasible. The Crest exclusively offers independent films, all personally picked by the local owner, Sid Heberger, who operates the Crest with her husband, Bill. The large main theater doubles as a concert hall, filling the void of medium-sized venues and attracting groups who can profitably play to the theater's capacity but can't yet fill Arco Arena. Located just two blocks from the convention center, the Crest also hosts meetings and cultural events. (Central)

ESQUIRE IMAX THEATER
1211 K St.
916/446-2333
The IMAX movie experience has been part of the revitalization of the Esquire Plaza area. Along with the opening of Esquire Grill and the relocation of both Gallagher's Restaurant and The Broiler Steakhouse, the IMAX has joined the Hyatt Regency, the Convention Center, and the Community Center Theater, creating a densely cultural neighborhood at the east end of the K Street Mall. Inside the theater, projectors use the latest high technology to blast light through the biggest film format in the industry and create images on a screen six stories high (often in convincing 3D), while 12,000 watts of "surround sound" rumble through the moviegoer's brain. Outside, the building itself appeals to fans of its 1940 architecture, but its preserved Streamline Moderne façade is all that's left of the old Esquire Theater. (Central)

THE TOWER THEATER
16th and Broadway
916/442-4700
The Tower Theater is the flagship of the Tower enclave—stores that together take up several city blocks. Indeed, it's the theater's tower that gives the stores their identity and serves as virtually the only visible landmark of Sacramento's south side. Built by the same architect who built the Esquire (and in the same year), the beautiful white, neon-trimmed moderne spire stands above the carefully gardened outdoor seating of the adjacent Tower Café and can be seen for many blocks, especially by travelers zipping through town via the Capital City Freeway. If you look up from your meal at the café, you'll see the original neon sign for Tower Records, an international business that was founded by Russ Solomon in a section of his dad's pharmacy (the sign still advertises "records, cosmetics, films"). Inside are three screens (the largest theater seats 410) for the foreign and art films booked by the theater's parent company in New York, which means some films reach Sacramento that one might not expect, broadening the horizons of a local audience otherwise limited to multiplexes. (South)

© Tom Myers 1997

13

Day Trip: Gold Country

Distance from Sacramento: 30–50 miles.
Where would you place this vintner? His award-winning merlot has been served at the White House and his zinfandel was once specially bottled for Queen Elizabeth. His tasting room is in a stone winery that was built in the 1860s by the Italian immigrant Giovanni Napoleon Lombardo in the middle of what was then California's most renowned wine country. Is this Napa? Sonoma? No. Greg Boeger's Boeger's Winery is in the Mother Lode, otherwise known as Gold Country, an area that remains (until word gets out) almost unknown as "The Other Wine Country." At the time of the Gold Rush, growers in El Dorado County alone had already planted over 5,000 acres of vineyards. A century later, that figure had dropped to 11 acres, a reduction caused by Prohibition, insect infestations, a changing economy, and region-wide disinterest. But today, Mother Lode wineries stretch along the Sierra foothills from Calaveras to Yuba Counties, with the greatest concentration less than an hour's drive from Sacramento in El Dorado and Amador Counties. Between them, these two counties have 40 wineries with tasting rooms.

Napa Valley is surprisingly close as well (as close to Sacramento as it is to San Francisco) and affords an easy day trip for wine tasting or a trip aboard the restored, luxurious **Napa Valley Wine Train,** (800/427-4124) complete with gourmet meals. But Gold Country beckons with a less commercialized, more personal experience than you'll find in Napa and Sonoma, and it has a rapidly growing reputation for equally high-quality wines. A typical treat in Amador County is the **Fitzpatrick Winery and Lodge,** (530/620-3248) where the owner serves wood-fired pizzas on Friday nights and an

SACRAMENTO REGION

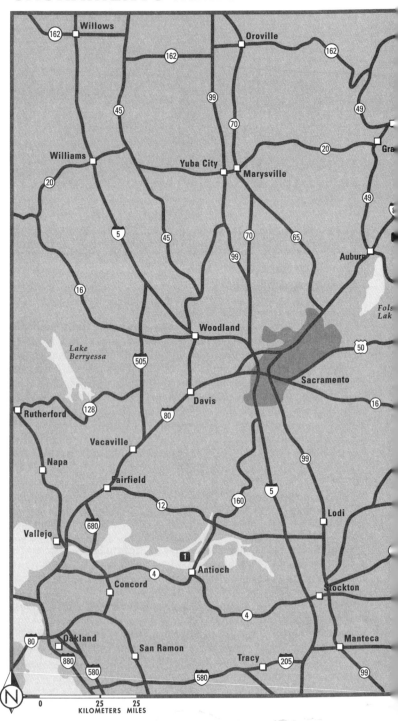

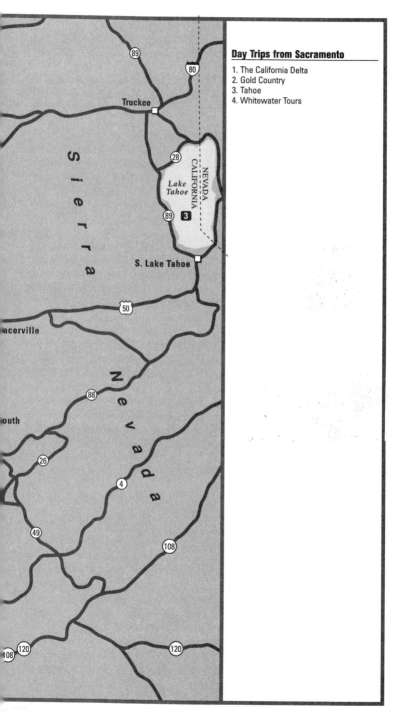

Day Trips from Sacramento

1. The California Delta
2. Gold Country
3. Tahoe
4. Whitewater Tours

Truckee

Sierra

89

80

28

NEVADA
CALIFORNIA

Lake
Tahoe

89 **3**

S. Lake Tahoe

50

acerville

Nevada

88

outh

26

4

49

108

108 120

120

Irish ploughman's lunch on weekends to guests who come to try his organic cabernet sauvignon.

Beyond wineries, Gold Country is a living, working museum, where the life of the 49ers is not so hard to imagine. Abandoned mines and cemeteries, mining towns like **Nevada City** that prosper to this day, and small camps immortalized by Mark Twain and Bret Harte are all easy to find along Highway 49, where art galleries, antique shops, historic inns, and small museums keep yesterday and today hand in hand. Christmas-tree farms, **Apple Hill** orchards, camping, hiking, fishing, and biking are all here—and more.

Getting there from Sacramento: Head east out of Sacramento on U.S. 50 to Highway 49 at Placerville. Head south on Highway 49 toward Plymouth and Fiddletown for the majority of the Amador wineries, or go southeast on Cedar Ravine Road toward a cluster of El Dorado wineries near Somerset and Fair Play.

Day Trip: The California Delta

Distance from Sacramento: 10–30 miles.
The Delta had its modern origins when disillusioned gold miners returned empty-handed from the foothills and saw a different kind of wealth in the rich peat soil of the alluvial plain where the Sacramento and San Joaquin Rivers join and meander toward the San Francisco Bay. Handmade levees were constructed, largely by Chinese workers, who proved the area could be farmed. These levees were good for soil reclamation, but inadequate for flood prevention until giant clamshell diggers, invented in the 1870s, took bites out of the riverbed's hard clay and lined the banks with the "slickens." Today's Delta is still covered with vast orchards and other crops, but it's the water—in its proper place—that draws visitors.

One of the unanticipated results of levee-building was the deepening of the water channels as the mud was removed from the river bottom. This created a maze of pleasure-boating routes—roughly 1,000 miles of navigable water for all kinds of "messing around," as locals term it. The plentiful marinas are home to thousands of pleasure craft kept here by owners from the entire San Francisco Bay area. They use this quiet, secluded, otherworldly setting in every watery way.

Fishing
There are many free angling seminars held each year throughout the Delta, taught by knowledgeable guides. Charters are available with these Delta guides, who will not only help you catch the fish but also teach you all about the process. Most area bait shops will give you good advice on the tackle and bait you need, and advise you when and where to drop a line. There are numerous sites for bank fishing as well, including two public piers in **Antioch,** as well as parks with fishing access. A number of marinas rent small boats. Striped bass ("stripers") are the favorite fish here, running from 2 pounds to over 50 pounds, but an 8- to 20-pounder is more typical. You can troll for them with jigs and lures or use bait such as sardines.

Amador County vineyards

Sturgeon are gigantic, prehistoric fish. How big? There's a regulation which states that you must return the one you've caught if it's *over* six feet long. Delta legends include hauling 1,000-pound sturgeons out of sloughs with mule teams.

It's relatively easy to catch 20 or 30 catfish on one evening's outing, with many tipping the scales at 8 to 10 pounds. The Delta is also becoming well known for its excellent black bass. Bass tournaments are held each year, with as many as 600 anglers competing for cash and merchandise awards worth over $75,000 for one event. All practice catch-and-release. Salmon, shad, and crawdads are caught in abundance, and fly-fishing has become popular in the Delta, especially for stripers and largemouth bass.

Swimming

There are a few sandy beaches in the California Delta. Some exist only at low tides (remember you're connected to the ocean here, through the Bay). Some resorts have private beaches (**B&W Resort, Snug Harbor, Lost Isle,** and **Orwood Resort,** among others) and a few have swimming pools (such as **Delta Bay Marina** and **Sugar Barge Marina**). Most boaters swim or float on their rafts and tubes off the stern of the anchored boat—never when the engine is running. Anchorages with sandy beaches are considered premium, and waterskiers often will rise early in the morning to commandeer a sandy ski beach for the day. There are almost no restrictions on anchoring out, although it would be unwise to anchor in the middle of a narrow channel or in the middle of a heavily trafficked waterway.

Boating

There are dozens of yacht clubs, boat clubs, and waterskiing clubs in the Delta area. Some of them have clubhouses, and some waterskiing clubs

Ten California Delta Historical Notes and Oddities

by Hal Schell, webmaster and member of the California Delta Chamber and Visitors Bureau

1. **Ferry Rides.** It is easy to take free rides on Delta ferries that differ little from ferries used 100 years ago. Heading west on Hwy. 12, turn right immediately after crossing the Rio Vista bridge, following signs to the Ryer Island Ferry. After crossing this ferry, turn right and in a few miles you will arrive at the J-Mack Ferry which will transport you across Steamboat Slough.

2. **County Park.** Sacramento County's Hogback Park is a beautiful little tree-shaded park on Steamboat Slough. But the name "Hog's Back" used to strike fear into the heart of paddle wheeler captains. This was the site of one of the most nefarious sandbars in the Delta that time and again snagged paddle wheelers and put them out of commission— or at least delayed their voyages.

3. **River Mansion.** The 58-room Grand Island Mansion looks straight out of the antebellum South, but is located on Steamboat Slough. You can enjoy Sunday brunch there. It is also the site of many elegant weddings.

4. **Whale of a Monument.** People from all over the world followed the exploits of Humphrey the Humpback Whale during his 22-day visit to the Delta area in 1985. At the foot of Main Street in the river town of Rio Vista, you will find a monument erected in honor of the winsome whale.

5. **Travolta Sat Here.** Actor John Travolta likes the Delta and has filmed here. He came to Rio Vista one evening to take delivery of a vintage Ford T-Bird he had purchased and while in town dined at The Point Waterfront Restaurant. You can visit The Point and sit in the chair in which John Travolta sat. It is sort of enshrined in the restaurant's entryway.

have slalom and ski-jump facilities and stage competitive events. Owners of vessels over six feet in height will need to be aware of the bridges along their intended cruising routes (some open, some don't). You need to know the clearance of each bridge (this will vary with tide) and the hours of operation for drawbridges (this may vary with the season). Much of this information may be found on the Delta maps or charts, or in a free bridge booklet available from the U.S. Coast Guard in Alameda. The signal for

6. **Hilton Fireworks.** It started out with hotel magnate Barron Hilton shooting off a few fireworks for the amusement of his family some 40 years ago and grew into the largest boat-in event in the West. Today, some 3,000 boats are anchored out to watch the Hilton fireworks, shot from a barge anchored near Mandeville Tip Island. Sorry, landlubbers can't get to this big Independence Day celebration.

7. **A Ghost Town.** Back in the days when the Delta had a thriving commercial fishery, Collinsville was a lively little town of about 600 persons—almost all of them spoke Italian. The town's main street was an elevated boardwalk. When commercial fishing ended, so did Collinsville. Maybe a couple dozen people live there today.

8. **Al-the-Wop's.** If this irreverent name of one of the Delta's most popular restaurant bothers you, then you can call it Al's Place. You'll find it on Main Street in the Chinese hamlet of Locke. Dollar bills are thumbtacked to its high ceiling, the traditional jars of peanut butter and marmalade adorn every table, and its steak sandwiches and fried French bread are the best.

9. **Orwood Resort.** Some of the most amusing things that happen in the Delta occur at boat launching ramps. Orwood Resort in the South Delta, not far from Knightsen, erected bleachers near their two-lane launching ramp. Just purchase a can of your favorite beverage at the resort store and then sit out on the bleachers and watch the mere mortals try to launch and retrieve their boats.

10. **Vieira's Resort.** When the stripers, salmon, or sturgeon are biting, Vieira's Resort, located just south of the town of Isleton, is one of the busy places in the Delta for the weighing-in and picture-taking of fish. It is fun to hang around for a few hours just to watch it. Even as I write this, just a few days ago an angler brought in a 43.5-pound striper caught just a couple hundred feet from the marina launching ramp. But fish are fickle. They may decide not to bite the day you arrive.

asking a drawbridge to open is one long and one short toot of the boat horn. Most Delta drawbridges are also equipped with marine-band VHF radios and may be contacted on channel 9.

Most marinas and waterside resorts that offer public facilities have guest docks. With few exceptions, there is no charge to use the dock for a few hours during the day. Most marinas charge a fee for overnight moorings, which usually include connection to electrical power if it is available.

Sacramento River Delta near Walnut Grove

Reservations are not usually required, except for groups or especially large craft. Virtually all shoreside buildings, restaurants, and other structures at Delta resorts have handicap access. However, because of the considerable tidal action in the Delta, the angle of ramps at some guest docks and berthing areas may be steeper at times than is normally comfortable for easy handicap access.

History
You could spend days enjoying the unique quality of the Delta without ever getting your feet wet. The area's history is as varied—and vital—as any other part of the Gold Rush story. There are dozens of tiny towns, each with their own tales to tell, many popularized as "ghost towns" (although their current citizens might not think this is entirely accurate). Typical of Delta towns is Isleton, on the east side of the Sacramento River. Founded in 1874 by Josiah Pool, it was a regular stop for the paddle wheelers. The town has at least a half-dozen restaurants, and the old buildings in its Chinatown are slowly being renovated. New shops, such as antique stores, are locating here. Annual events include the Isleton Crawdad Festival on Father's Day weekend, the Isleton Rodeo in the spring, and the Chinese New Year Festival, which is usually in February.

Locke, also on the east bank of the Sacramento River a mile upstream from Walnut Grove, was built by and for the Chinese in 1915. The town is on the National Register of Historic Places, and the county has shown a keen interest in preserving it. Locke has two restaurants, a store, gift shops, a gambling museum, and the Boathouse Marina. The state has established a rustic park on the back side of Locke along what is informally called Railroad Cut or Locke Slough.

Getting there from Sacramento: The California Delta is immediately south of Sacramento. It covers an extensive area, but the most direct way to put yourself at its center within 30 minutes is to head down Freeport Boulevard (also labeled Highway 160). This road will more or less follow the course of the Sacramento River, touching on many of the Delta towns as it dodges from west bank to east bank and back again over colorful bascule drawbridges. Highway 12 runs east-west across the Delta, from Rio Vista on the west to Interstate 5, Highway 99, and Lodi on the east.

Day Trip: Whitewater Rafting Tours

Distance from Sacramento: 35 miles.

The American River between the Sierra Nevada and Folsom Lake is often cited as the second-most-popular rafting river in the entire nation, after the Colorado. It's actually three distinct rivers: the North, South, and Middle Forks. The South Fork is the most "doable" for the greatest variety of adventure seekers.

Rafting areas are rated for danger and difficulty, from Class I (your bathtub) to Class VI (apparently a euphemism for death). There is enormous fun to be had in the middle range. For comparison, the easy float down the river described in Sports and Recreation is a Class II, suitable for anyone over five years of age. There's quite a jump in excitement, however, from Class II to Class III, and the greater part of the South Fork is Class III. Teenagers who might complain of the lack of thrills in the river near the city will be kept plenty busy on the South Fork, as each group sets out in top-quality commercial paddle rafts in which all crew members participate, following their guide's instructions. The boats are modern, unsinkable, self-bailing 13-footers—ideal for the flow levels, drops, and whitewater rapids commonly encountered on the Forks. Commonly, rafting companies supply only U.S. Coast Guard–approved safety equipment.

There are a number of companies who supply all that amateur renters will need, and most of them are clustered around Coloma on Highway 49 below the Chili Bar Dam. A favorite is the **Chili Bar Outdoor Center** (CBOC), which typically provides a deli-style lunch on their trips. They also have a campground at the starting point for boaters who arrive the evening before a trip or for groups who want to camp away from crowded parks.

CBOC regards a Class III trip as having rapids that "we pay close attention to, but one that only rarely causes problems for competent guides," whereas a Class IV trip is very difficult, with a complicated route that requires a high level of maneuvering. A Class IV run can be found on other Forks, but not here. "When we rate a river trip as a Class III run, we are saying there are many Class III rapids, which are great for almost any group. Novices will have no problem and experienced boaters will have a blast."

You'll need to bring little more than the clothes on your back. Two suggestions to keep in mind: Whatever you bring, it'll get wet; don't bring it if you can't afford to lose it. Here is CBOC's shortlist of items:

- Shorts or swimsuit
- Light T-shirt (avoid heavy cotton)

- Shoes that won't slip off your feet (water shoes or old tennies)
- Sunglasses with a strap
- Hat with a strap
- Small tube of sunscreen
- Change of clothes for after rafting (to leave in your car)

That's all you need to have an hours-long thrill ride that beats the heck out of theme parks, taking you through historical Gold Country and unspoiled riparian habitat and bouncing you through granite boulders that make it obvious why water arrives in Sacramento still clear and clean. May and June might still be too cold to raft without a wet suit (which can be rented), and, if possible, you're better off avoiding major holiday weekends because hundreds of thousands of people take this trip every summer. That last bit may sound like bad news, but the upside of it is that no matter how timid you may feel about bouncing through boulder-strewn rapids, remember that millions—at all ages and levels of ability and fitness—have already done this and made out just fine. Kids should be old enough to actively participate, as each oar is needed to heed the guide's shouted instructions. (Generally this is about seven years old, or 12 years old when spring runoff from the mountains makes the water high. Call first, 800/356-2262 or 530/621-1236—you'll need to make reservations in any case.)

Another nice aspect of a rafting trip is that it can be tailored to suit a wide range of involvement. The season runs from March through September. The most popular way to go is a half-day trip, which in CBOC's case is the run from Chili Bar to Coloma, which they describe as "appropriate for beginners yet exciting enough to keep veteran boaters coming back year after year." They shuttle their clients to put in above Chili Bar, where they can practice paddling skills on some easy riffles before quickly moving on to the big water of Meatgrinder. "The pace then alternates from whitewater excitement to short, calm pools, passing through more than 10 major rapids until we reach

Trouble Maker Rapids on the American River

© Tom Myers 1999

Trouble Maker—the most dramatic drop on the river. [It's] a wonderful way to get acquainted with whitewater rafting, enjoy beautiful canyon scenery, and view historic Gold Rush sights along the way." This particular trip takes about four hours.

There are rougher sections downriver, where the rock walls narrow, the river picks up speed, and rafters encounter miles of back-to-back rapids with names like Satan's Cesspool, Haystack Canyon, Bouncing Rock, and Hospital Bar. Trips can last a half-day (as described above), all day, or even two days with overnight camping, where the company will supply the sleeping gear and fix gourmet meals for you. Another option is to raft all day, retreat to an area restaurant for dinner, stay in a bed-and-breakfast (such as the **American River Inn** in nearby Georgetown, 800/245-6566), and have at it the next morning for a second day of rolling down the river.

Getting there from Sacramento: Take U.S. 50 east out of Sacramento for about 30 miles. Take the Shingle Springs/Ponderosa exit, and at the top of the ramp go left to cross over the highway. On the far side of the highway, just past the off-ramp from the other direction, take a right and you'll be on North Shingle Road. Follow this about 4.5 miles to a fork and bear left on what is now Lotus Road. Take this to Highway 49, turn left, and cross over the South Fork. Immediately on the right is Ponderosa Park Campground, home of CBOC.

Day Trip: Tahoe

Distance from Sacramento: 100 miles.
The Tahoe area is only a Sacramento day trip by virtue of its nearness. It can't really be experienced in a day; in fact, it would take the better part of a day just to list everything available to do. The first required activity is simply

to gape. This is an alpine lake, its surface at over 6,000 feet in elevation, surrounded by perpetually snowcapped mountains. Though it is being "loved to death" by overuse and losing some of its legendary pristine quality, it's still a lake unmatched in beauty, clarity, and recreational offerings.

There are plenty of reasons to go year-round, but there are two primary seasons—summer at the lake and winter on the slopes. To several generations, Tahoe will always be identified with the **Squaw Valley** Olympics, and, in the years since that still-prime ski resort was the world focus of winter sports, the area has burgeoned with more than 20 ski areas. Among the better known are: **Heavenly** (877/243-0003), on the Nevada border at the south end of the lake, which has the highest elevation in the Tahoe Basin; **Homewood Mountain Resort** (530/525-2992), called the best tree-skiing resort in the United States by *Outside* magazine; and **Sugar Bowl** (530/426-9000), one of the first resorts you'll encounter coming from Sacramento on Interstate 80 and the beneficiary of the extra snow dumped at the top of Donner Summit. Each of these resorts (and many others) has courses for snowboarders, while cross-country and snowshoe trails are abundant in the area as well. The skiing by itself is world-class. Throw in the views of the lake as you stand atop a mountain peak and it's an unforgettable experience. As much as 500 inches of snow falls per year in what is the largest concentration of ski areas in North America, and the season generally lasts from November through April.

One of the area's tourist boards publishes a one-sheet brochure called "101 Fun Things to Do at Lake Tahoe," and it's no exaggerated boast or even an adequate total. It lists 36 beaches and picnic areas, 36 campgrounds, six horse stables, 14 golf courses, and 19 marinas and launching ramps. Of course there are many other things to do and see, too. The drive around the lake is locally touted as "the Most Beautiful Drive in America," and it's hard to dismiss this as hype. The highlights of the 72-mile tour only hint at the richness of experience available here.

If you start at South Shore, you can ride the **Heavenly Aerial Tram** up 2,000 feet above the lake for a stunning overview before setting out. West of here, U.S. 50 runs into Highway 89, which goes northward along the shore. At the **Tallac Historic Site** (530/542-2787) you'll find restored mansions and Tahoe's first casino. Next is **Emerald Bay**, one of nature's great photo ops. Below the curving road is **Vikingsholm**, a 38-room reproduction of a Scandinavian castle built in 1929 and open in summer for tours. North of this you'll find a beach and picnic spot at **D.L. Bliss State Park** and then **Sugar Pine State Park.**

Near the north end of the lake, Tahoe City sits along the **Truckee River,**

TRIVIA

Lake Tahoe contains more water than the 10 largest man-made reservoirs in the nation combined. If it were emptied out, the lake would cover the entire state of California with 14.5 inches of water.

Emerald Bay at Lake Tahoe

the lake's only outlet, where rafting and fishing are popular. Here, if you want, you can continue up Highway 89 to Squaw Valley, where, at any time of the year, you'll want to take their tram to **High Camp** (530/583-6955). The ride up the face of the mountain is gripping, and then you magically exit at a resort with an ice-skating rink, tennis courts, heated pool and spa, restaurants, hiking trails, and even bungee jumping. You can keep going north to Truckee and see the historical record of the tragic Donner Party at the **Donner Museum** (530/587-3841). You can also switch to Highway 28, continue around the edge of the lake, and see the **Ponderosa Ranch** (775/831-0691), home of the old *Bonanza* TV show; visit the white-sand beach at **Sand Harbor;** or hike between Spooner and Marlette Lakes. Mountain bikers will want to try **Flume Trail** from Marlette Lake. Going south, Highway 28 becomes U.S. 50 again and passes through solid stone at **Cave Rock.** At Zephyr Cove, the M.S. *Dixie II* paddle wheeler and the *Woodwind* trimaran offer lake tours (775/588-3508).

All this, and we haven't even touched yet on championship golf, sky diving, ballooning, cultural events, sailing, waterskiing, sports camps, and, of course, gambling at casinos with top-of-the-line entertainment and restaurants.

Getting there from Sacramento: Lake Tahoe can be reached from Sacramento either by taking Interstate 80 or U.S. 50 east. Interstate 80 is faster and arrives, after only 90 minutes, at Truckee, where you exit and head south on Highway 89 about eight miles toward Squaw Valley and six more to Tahoe City. U.S. 50 winds all the way into South Lake Tahoe and is a two-hour drive at best. Toward the end it's a twisting two-lane road, but with spectacular views. On either route, if you go at the peak hours for skiers coming or going, you're likely to get seriously bogged down in traffic. Chains are often required after heavy snowfall. Summertime has its own traffic congestion, with tourists clogging the surface streets in the urbanized areas of South Lake Tahoe or Tahoe City.

EMERGENCY PHONE NUMBERS

POLICE, FIRE, MEDICAL EMERGENCIES
911

POLICE
916/264-5471

FIRE
916/373-5840

SACRAMENTO COUNTY SHERIFF
916/874-5115

CALIFORNIA HIGHWAY PATROL
916/263-3550 (North of the American River; 916/681-2300 (South of the American River)

FEDERAL BUREAU OF INVESTIGATION (FBI)
916/481-9110

POISON CONTROL
800/876-4766, TDD 800/972-3323

CALIFORNIA YOUTH CRISIS LINE
800/843-5200

CRISIS LINE FOR THE HANDICAPPED
800/426-4263, TDD 800/421-4327

DIOGENES YOUTH SERVICES
800/339-7117

HEALTH AND HUMAN SERVICES
Child Abuse 916/875-5437
Elder and Adult Abuse 916/874-9377

PSYCHIATRIC CRISIS SERVICES, MENTAL HEALTH CRISIS LINE
916/732-3637

SUICIDE PREVENTION CRISIS LINE
916/368-3111

DOMESTIC VIOLENCE AND SEXUAL ASSAULT EMERGENCY RESPONSE SERVICES
916/920-2952

MAJOR HOSPITALS AND EMERGENCY MEDICAL CENTERS

KAISER PERMANENTE MEDICAL CENTER
2025 Morse Ave., Sacramento
  916/973-5000
6600 Bruceville Rd., Sacramento
  916/688-2000

MERCY GENERAL HOSPITAL
4001 J St., Sacramento
916/453-4545

METHODIST HOSPITAL
7500 Hospital Dr., Sacramento
916/423-3000

SUTTER GENERAL HOSPITAL
2801 L St., Sacramento
916/454-2222

SUTTER MEMORIAL HOSPITAL
5151 F St., Sacramento
916/454-3333

UC DAVIS MEDICAL CENTER
2315 Stockton Blvd., Sacramento
916/734-2011

SHRINERS HOSPITAL FOR CHILDREN
2425 Stockton Blvd., Sacramento
916/453-2000

RECORDED INFORMATION

ROAD CONDITIONS
916/445-7623

WEATHER
916/646-2000

VISITOR INFORMATION

VISITOR INFORMATION CENTER
1101 Second St. (near K St.), Old
Sacramento; 916/442-7644

**CALIFORNIA DIVISION
OF TOURISM**
800/862-2543, 916/322-2881
www.gocalif.ca.gov

**RIVER CITY SMALL BUSINESS
CONSORTIUM**
916/368-1422, 916/364-1725 (fax)
www.sactonet.org

**SACRAMENTO CONVENTION
AND VISITORS BUREAU**
916/264-7777, 916/264-7788 (fax)
www.sacramentocvb.org

**SACRAMENTO METROPOLITAN
CHAMBER OF COMMERCE**
916/552-6800
www.metrochamber.org

CITY TOURS

**CAL-EVENTS TOURS
AND SPECIAL EVENTS**
916/924-8661, 916/920-0448 (fax)

EXPLORE AMERICA TOURS, INC.
800/999-7567, 530/492-2384,
530/492-2388 (fax)

FRONTIER TOURS/GRAY LINE
800/356-9838, 916/927-2877

**TRAVEL WEST TOURS (GOLD
COUNTRY, YOSEMITE)**
209/962-0423
www.travelwesttours.com

**USA STUDENT TRAVEL—
USA EXECUTIVE SERVICES**
800/448-4444, 916/354-0167,
916/354-0170 (fax)

RESOURCES FOR
NEW RESIDENTS

**COMMUNITY SERVICES
PLANNING COUNCIL**
(Information book on county
services)
916/447-7063, ext. 7

**DEPARTMENT OF
MOTOR VEHICLES**
916/657-7669

**FOREIGN CURRENCY EXCHANGE,
AMERICAN EXPRESS**
916/441-1780

**MCCORMACK'S GUIDES,
*GREATER SACRAMENTO***
800/222-3602
www.mccormacks.com

SCHOOL TEST SCORES
http://star.cde.ca.gov

**TELEPHONE REFERENCE SER-
VICE, SACRAMENTO PUBLIC
LIBRARY**
916/264-2920

POSTAL SERVICE

MAIN POST OFFICE
2000 Royal Oaks Dr.
800/275-8777

CAR RENTAL

ALAMO
800/327-9633

AVIS
800/831-2847

BUDGET
800/527-0700

DOLLAR
800/800-4000

ENTERPRISE
800/736-8222

HERTZ
800/654-3131

NATIONAL
800/227-7368

THRIFTY
800/367-2277

DISABLED ACCESS INFORMATION

ACCESSIBLE TRAVEL
916/339-1557

NATIONAL FEDERATION OF THE BLIND OF CALIFORNIA
916/442-8080

SACRAMENTO COUNTY DEVELOPMENTAL DISABILITIES PLANNING & ADVISORY COUNCIL
916/452-0959

SACRAMENTO SOCIETY FOR THE BLIND, INC.
916/452-8271 (kids, ext. 324)

WINNERS ON WHEELS
916/791-5250

MULTICULTURAL RESOURCES

ASIAN COMMUNITY CENTER
916/393-9026

CALIFORNIA MULTICULTURAL MEDIA CONSORTIUM
916/421-2804

JAPANESE AMERICAN CITIZENS LEAGUE
916/447-0231

JEWISH COMMUNITY CENTER/JEWISH FEDERATION
916/486-0906

NATIONAL ASSOCIATION FOR THE ADVANCEMENT OF COLORED PEOPLE
916/733-0430

SACRAMENTO ASIAN-PACIFIC CHAMBER OF COMMERCE
916/446-7883, 916/446-7098 (fax)

SACRAMENTO BLACK CHAMBER OF COMMERCE
916/392-7222

SACRAMENTO HISPANIC CHAMBER OF COMMERCE
916/554-7420, 916/554-7429 (fax)
e-mail: sachispcc@aol.com
www.shccplaza.org

OTHER COMMUNITY ORGANIZATIONS

CALIFORNIA COMMUNITY SERVICES
916/445-8752

CAMELLIA CITY SENIOR CENTER
916/442-9014

COMMUNITY SERVICE GUIDES
916/442-2200

DEPARTMENT OF PARK AND COMMUNITY SERVICES
916/566-6581

PUBLIC LIBRARIES
916/264-2770

HOME-SCHOOLING CO-OP OF SACRAMENTO
916/455-1005

BABY-SITTING/CHILD CARE

CINDY'S SITTER SERVICE
916/857-0726

INFANT'S WORLD
916/361-2176

NANNY NETWORK REFERRAL AGENCY
916/961-7483

PANDA'S COMPLETE DOMESTIC AGENCY
800/559-6645, 916/686-6646

NEWSPAPERS

CHINESE COMMUNITY TRIBUNE
916/399-0123

MOM GUESS WHAT
Gay and Lesbian
916/441-6397

THE SACRAMENTO BEE
916/321-1000, 916/326-5578 (fax)

SACRAMENTO BUSINESS JOURNAL
Local business weekly
916/447-7661

SACRAMENTO NEWS AND REVIEW
Weekly arts, news, entertainment
916/498-1234, 916/498-7910 (fax)

SACRAMENTO OBSERVER
Weekly African American
entertainment, culture
916/452-4781

SING TAO DAILY
916/391-1188

VALLEY COMMUNITY NEWSPAPERS
Arden-Carmichael, East Sac, Land Park, and Pocket News editions
916/429-9901

MAGAZINES

CALIFORNIA COMPUTER NEWS
916/363-8191

OUTWORD
Gay and Lesbian
916/329-9280

SACRAMENTO
Monthly dining, entertainment, business, travel
916/452-6200, 916/452-6061 (fax)

SACRAMENTO PARENT
916/444-0110

BOOKSTORES

THE AVID READER
1003 L Street
916/433-7323

B DALTON BOOKSELLER
6137 Florin Road
916/428-4802

BARNES & NOBLE
1725 Arden Way
916/565-0644

BORDERS BOOKS MUSIC & CAFE
Fair Oaks Boulevard
916/564-0168

DOUBLEDAY BOOKSHOP
545 Downtown Plaza
916/442-7609

HORNET BOOKSTORE
6000 J Street
CSU Sacramento
916/278-6446

THE OPEN BOOK LIMITED
(specializing in gay/lesbian)
910 21st Street
916/498-1004

TOWER RECORDS VIDEO & BOOKS
2538 Watt Avenue
916/481-6600

UC DAVIS BOOKSTORE
Univ. of California Davis
Davis
530/752-9072

VILLAGE BOOKS
320 N. Mount Shasta Boulevard
Mt. Shasta
530/926-1678

RADIO/TV STATIONS

FM STATIONS
KXJZ 88.9	Jazz/news/NPR
KVMR 89.5	Full spectrum
KXHV 89.7	Alternative
KDVS 90.3	Alternativ/rock
KXPR 90.9	News/NPR
KYDS 91.5	Student radio
KZSA 92.1	Spanish
KGBY 92.5	Contemporary
KXOA 93.7	'70s and '80s
KSSJ 94.7	Smooth jazz
KYMX 96.1	Contemporary
KSEG 96.9	Classic rock
KRXQ 98.5	Album rock
KVMR 99.3	Full spectrum
KRCX 99.9	Spanish
KZZO 100.5	Alternative
KHYL 101.1	Oldies, 49ers
KRRE 101.9	Spanish
KSFM 102.5	Contemporary hits
KBMB 103.5	Contemporary hits
KHZZ 104.3	'70s and '80s R&B
KNCI 105.1	Country
KLNA 105.5	Dance
KCFA 106.1	Christian
KWOD 106.5	Modern rock
KDND 107.9	Top 40

AM STATIONS
KSTE 650	Talk
KFIA 710	Christian/talk
KNCO 830	News/talk
KAHI 950	Variety
KRCX 1110	Spanish
KHTK 1140	Sports (Kings)
KEBR 1210	Christian
KSQR 1240	Spanish
KCTC 1320	Nostalgia
KJAY 1430	Urban/religion
KRAK 1470	Gold country
KFBK 1530	News/talk
KCVR 1570	Spanish
KSMH 1620	Catholic

TELEVISION STATIONS
KCRA	Channel 3 (NBC)
KVIE	Channel 6 (PBS)
KXTV	Channel 10 (ABC)
KOVR	Channel 13 (CBS)
KUVS	Channel 19 (Univision)
KSPX	Channel 29 (PaxNet)
KMAX	Channel 31 (UPN)
KTXL	Channel 40 (FOX)
KTNC	Channel 42 (Ind.)
KQCA	Channel 58 (WB)

INDEX

AVALON
TRAVEL
publishing

BECAUSE TRAVEL MATTERS

AVALON TRAVEL PUBLISHING knows that travel is more than coming and going—travel is taking part in new experiences, new ideas, and a new outlook. Our goal is to bring you complete and up-to-date information to help you make informed travel decisions.

AVALON TRAVEL GUIDES feature a combination of practicality and spirit, offering a unique traveler-to-traveler perspective perfect for an afternoon hike, around-the-world journey, or anything in between.

WWW.TRAVELMATTERS.COM

Avalon Travel Publishing guides are
available at your favorite book or travel store.

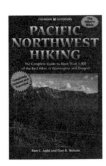

MOON HANDBOOKS provide comprehen-
ve coverage of a region's arts, history, land, people, and
ocial issues in addition to detailed practical listings for
:commodations, food, outdoor recreation, and entertain-
ent. Moon Handbooks allow complete immersion in a
gion's culture—ideal for travelers who want to combine
ghtseeing with insight for an extraordinary travel experi-
nce in destinations throughout North America, Hawaii,
tin America, the Caribbean, Asia, and the Pacific.

WWW.MOON.COM

Rick Steves shows you where to travel and how to trav-
—all while getting the most value for your dollar. His Back Door travel phi-
sophy is about making friends, having fun, and avoiding
urist rip-offs.

ick's been traveling to Europe for more than 25 years and
the author of 22 guidebooks, which have sold more than
million copies. He also hosts the award-winning public
evision series Travels in Europe with Rick Steves.

WWW.RICKSTEVES.COM

ROAD TRIP USA

tting there is half the fun, and Road Trip USA guides are
ur ticket to driving adventure. Taking you off the inter-
tes and onto less-traveled, two-lane highways, each guide
illed with fascinating trivia, historical information, pho-
graphs, facts about regional writers, and details on where
sleep and eat—all contributing to your exploration of the
erican road.

ooks so full of the pleasures of the American road,
u can smell the upholstery."
BC radio

WWW.ROADTRIPUSA.COM

TRAVEL ✦ SMART®

guidebooks are accessible, route-based driving guides focusing on regions throughout the United States and Canada. Special interest tours provide the most practical routes for family fun, outdoor activities, or regional history for a trip of anywhere from two to 22 days. Travel Smarts take the guesswork out of planning a trip by recommending only the most interesting places to eat, stay, and visit.

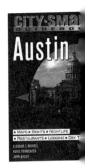

"One of the few travel series that rates sightseeing attractions. That's a handy feature. It helps to have some guidance so that every minute counts."
~San Diego Union-Tribune

Foghorn Outdoors

guides are for campers, hikers, boaters, anglers, bikers, and golfers of all levels of daring and skill. Each guide focuses on a specific U.S. region and contains site descriptions and ratings, driving directions, facilities and fees information, and easy-to-read maps that leave only the task of deciding where to go.

"Foghorn Outdoors has established an ecological conservation standard unmatched by any other publisher." ~Sierra Club

WWW.FOGHORN.COM

CiTY·SMaRT™

guides are written by local authors with hometown perspectives who have personally selected the best places to eat, shop, sightsee, and simply hang out. The honest, lively, and opinionated advice is perfect for business travelers looking to relax with the locals or for longtime residents looking for something new to do Saturday night.

There are City Smart guides for cities across the United States and Canada, and a portion of sales from each title benefits a non-profit literacy organization in its featured city.

www.travelmatters.com

User-friendly, informative, and fun:

Because travel *matters*.

Visit our newly launched web site and explore the variety of titles and travel information available online, featuring an interactive *Road Trip USA* exhibit.

also check out:

www.ricksteves.com

he Rick Steves web site is bursting
th information to boost your travel I.Q.
d liven up your European adventure.

www.foghorn.com

Visit the Foghorn Outdoors web site
for more information on the premier
source of U.S. outdoor recreation guides.

www.moon.com

e Moon Handbooks web site offers
eresting information and practical advice
at ensure an extraordinary travel experience.

K. J. Doyle

ABOUT THE AUTHOR

Pat Cosgrove is a novelist, screenwriter, and editor living in Sacramento with his wife Karen and sons Neal and Will.